O9-BTM-631

HQ 518 .F3423 1997

NEW ENGLAND INSTITUTE
OF TECHNOLOGY
LEARNING RESOURCES CENTER

THE FAMILY ON THE THRESHOLD OF THE 21ST CENTURY

Trends and Implications

THE FAMILY
ON THE THRESHOLD
OF THE 21ST CENTURY
Trends and Implications

Edited by

Solly Dreman
Ben Gurion University of the Negev

NEW ENGLAND INSTITUTE
OF TECHNOLOGY
LEARNING RESOURCES CENTER

LAWRENCE ERLBAUM ASSOCIATES, PUBLISHERS
1997   Mahwah, New Jersey   London

5/98   # 36458101

Copyright © 1997 by Lawrence Erlbaum Associates, Inc.
    All rights reserved. No part of the book may be reproduced in
    any form, by photostat, microform, retrieval system, or any other
    means, without the prior written permission of the publisher.

Lawrence Erlbaum Associates, Inc., Publishers
10 Industrial Avenue
Mahwah, New Jersey 07430

Cover design by Gail Silverman

Library of Congress Cataloging-in-Publication Data

The family on the threshold of the 21st century : trends and
    implications / edited by Solly Dreman.
        p.   cm.
    Includes bibliographical references and index.
    ISBN 0-8058-2217-8 (cloth : alk. paper).
    1. Family. 2. Family—Psychological aspects. I. Dreman, Solly.
HQ518.F3423 1997
    306.85—dc21   97-6089
                                                             CIP

Books published by Lawrence Erlbaum Associates are printed on acid-free paper,
and their bindings are chosen for strength and durability.

Printed in the United States of America
10 9 8 7 6 5 4 3 2 1

Solly Dreman is an associate professor of psychology in the department of Behavioral Sciences at Ben Gurion University of the Negev in Beer Sheva, Israel. He was one of the founding fathers of the Israeli Association for Marital and Family Therapy and has organized five national and international conferences dealing with family theory, research, and intervention. Dreman was the Director of the Center for Family Life Research and Counselling at Ben Gurion University from 1980 to 1995 and in this capacity, he and his staff dealt with over 400 families in crisis due to life stressors such as divorce, remarriage, immigration, and acts of war and terrorism. From 1991 to 1994 he served as the Director of the Graduate Clinical Program in Psychology in the Department of Behavioral Sciences. He has conducted several research projects dealing with the influence of stress and crisis on family coping and adjustment and has published extensively in this area. In 1994 he organized and served as chairperson for an international conference sponsored by the Ministry of Science and the Arts in Israel called "The Family on the Threshold of the 21st Century: Trends and Implications," which commemorated the UN Year of the family. A large interdisciplinary group of experts in family research and intervention were invited to this conference and also to contribute a chapter on current and evolving family trends. The present book represents the result of these efforts.

CONTENTS

PREFACE

Is there life for the family in the 21st century? Who will prevail—the optimists or the pessimists? The pessimists claim that family life in its present form is doomed. This gloomy forecast is attributable to increased demands from the workplace, rampant technological advancement, and the pursuit of personal achievement at the expense of interpersonal needs and values. The optimists claim the opposite, that is, that increasing alienation and emphasis on the occupational sphere necessitate a sense of family, community, and belonging as a haven from work-related stress. The present volume addresses these and related issues such as the interplay of personal versus interpersonal factors in family development, the role of the extended family, and the interface between work, community, and family.

A unique interdisciplinary rostrum of behavioral scientists in such diverse fields as psychology, sociology, anthropology, social work, industrial management, and demography discuss the latest theoretical formulations and empirical findings regarding family life around the world. A systems perspective is adopted—the family being examined at its interface with individual, community, society, and culture, with the interdependence of these different levels emphasized. In addition, an attempt is made to integrate the work of theoreticians, researchers, and practitioners in understanding the evolving family. Surprisingly, considerable agreement exists among the contributors to this volume regarding implications for future family study.

ACKNOWLEDGMENTS

I would like to thank the Ministry of Science and the Arts in Israel for its support and encouragement in organizing the conference, "The Family on the Threshold of the 21st Century: Trends and Implications," which took place in Jerusalem in the early summer of 1994. The Ministry sponsored the conference participation of the majority of the foreign contributors to this volume that emanated from this international gathering. I would also like to thank (in alphabetical order) Erica Frydenberg, Charles Greenbaum, Sherrill Hershberg, and Dan Hertz for their helpful comments on earlier versions of the book. Thanks are also extended to Judi Amsel, Kathy Dolan, and Sondra Guideman of Lawrence Erlbaum Associates, who contributed to its production. In addition, I thank all the contributors to this volume for their cooperation and willingness to accept suggestions, criticisms, and revisions regarding their chapters.

INTRODUCTION

1

ON THE THRESHOLD OF A NEW ERA: AN OVERVIEW

Solly Dreman
Ben Gurion University of the Negev

The concept of this book originated at an international conference celebrating the United Nations Year of the Family held in Jerusalem in the early summer of 1994. The major purpose of the conference was to contribute to the understanding and dissemination of information concerning past, present, and future trends in family life. An outstanding interdisciplinary roster of researchers and practitioners from all over the world presented their findings and drew implications about family life as the third millennium approaches. As conference chairperson, I requested the invited speakers to submit chapters prior to the conference dealing with the topic they would present. They were told that this volume would deal with contemporary family theory, research, and intervention and that their contribution would undergo editorial review to determine its suitability for the present volume. The contents of this book, therefore, are scholarly contributions representing the latest developments in research, theory, and practice in family studies.

On the threshold of the 21st century, profound changes are occurring in family life. The traditional two-parent nuclear family is viewed by many as a relic of the past. These changes are reflected demographically in major changes in divorce, marriage, fertility, and longevity rates, as well as increasing rates of female employment, accompanied by changes in family structures, lifestyles, and the family life cycle. Accelerating rates of stress and violence in the family may reflect strain between the work and the family arenas, evolving gender conflicts, ambiguity in parental roles of the biological versus the socializing parent in the case of the stepparent of divorce or from parenting roles resulting from high-tech reproduction techniques like surrogate parenting. In this era of rapid social, industrial, and technological change, family values of community, belonging, and family-related status are often usurped by individualism, autonomy, and the pursuit of career-related prestige. Indeed, the very essence of family life is being questioned, with the pessimists among us feeling that the traditional family is outmoded and no longer capable of coping with the realities of contemporary living.

This volume tests some of these attitudes and beliefs by providing a panel of renowned family researchers and practitioners who present theoretical formulations, empirical findings, and applied interventions regarding family life in different parts of the world. In assembling this group of contributors, the family is presented as a dynamic evolving system, with interaction occurring between its various interfaces: individual, nuclear family, extended family, community, society, and culture. We have also tried to consider the influence of changing situational contingencies such as economic recession, transnationalism, and geographic mobility on family life.

In considering family development, it is important to observe how the family affects individual development, as well as how the individual affects the family's development. Causation is viewed as being circular (Minuchin, 1985), with cause-and-effect relations changing over time. However, restricting ourselves to this context would be somewhat myopic and it is important to also consider the larger social context, or what Bronfenbrenner (1979) termed the *exosystem*. In this conceptual framework, relevant social support systems such as the workplace, community, and government have a profound influence on family life and may significantly influence such family-related phenomena as violence, aging, divorce, marriage, and parenting, just as these phenomena may influence social policy and planning.

By employing such a "systems perspective" (see Bowen, 1978; Minuchin & Fishman, 1981; Watzlawick, Weakland, & Fisch, 1974), we have tried to address these issues and discuss the interaction between these different "nested contexts" of individual, family, society, and culture (Bronfenbrenner, 1979) in their influence on the family. In accordance with this theoretical stance, individual and developmental issues, changing roles and structures within the family, extended family and alternate family forms, cultural and societal influences, as well as changing situational contingencies in their relation to family life, are discussed in Parts II through VI in this book. Part VII discusses family assessment and employs a systems perspective. Part VIII, the final section of the book, offers some thoughts and implications for the future based on the theoretical perspectives and empirical findings presented.

In Part II, "Individual and Developmental Influences and Family Life," Carolyn and Philip Cowan (chapter 2) examine the effects on children's development of two major family transitions: parenthood and the start of school. Spouses who begin their transition to parenthood in personal and marital distress develop more separate male–female roles and experience greater increases in marital disenchantment. Parents' marital quality also influences their parenting, including parent–child interaction, affecting children's development. Thus, poor adaptation to parenthood is reflected in children's academic, emotional, and social adjustment when they begin school. Nurturing and flexible spouse relationships help parents overcome some of the negative patterns that characterize their relationships with their children. Intervention techniques, such as group intervention for couples, in which mental health professionals work with parents on troublesome parenting and marital issues, lead to greater marital optimism and also contribute to children adjusting better in the school setting.

Yona Teichman (chapter 3) studies the effect of treating a spouse's depression within the marital context (i.e., interpersonally). She presents a reciprocal model of depression and an interpersonal treatment context that are based on an integration of systems theory and cognitive theories of depression. The main tenet of her approach is that depression affects the relationships of the depressed person with significant others and is in turn affected by them. Families with members who suffer from pathological or adjustment problems are caught up in repetitive cognitive, emotional, behavioral, and interactional reciprocities that maintain the problem. Overprotection, hostility or ambivalence, and complementarity of dysfunctional needs have been identified as three patterns of interpersonal reciprocities that maintain depression in the marital context. The primary aims of treatment were to increase the insight of the couple dyad regarding these reciprocities, namely, their respective part in maintaining depression and then to motivate search for alternative reciprocal behavior patterns. This cognitive marital therapy approach was compared with individual cognitive therapy, as well as with a traditional drug therapy regime and a control group. Cognitive marital therapy was found to be the most successful form of intervention, reducing global depression scores, as well as experienced and perceived hostility between spouses. Because pharmacotherapy was also effective in reducing hostility, the integration of the findings suggests that interweaving pharmacological treaments with marital treatment modalities bears potential for facilitating remission from depressive illness.

In Part III, "Changing Roles and Structures Within the Family," Frances K. Goldscheider (chapter 4) discusses the effects of the decline of fertility rates and the extension of the life cycle. Goldscheider particularly emphasizes the upper end of the developmental spectrum, as well as strengthening relationships *within* the family. Increased longevity has allowed for the possibility of family relationships of considerably longer duration. This development may necessitate parent–child and spousal roles that are qualitatively different from traditional perceptions of family life. Ongoing parental relationships with adult children may have to be less hierarchical and more reciprocal, than those with young children. There is also an extension of joint survival in couples, where a great part of one's married life is spent without children. This development may necessitate more attention to the nurturing of spousal roles that are capable of surviving the longer life span. A reduction of hierarchical gender-stereotyped marital roles may be necessary to ensure the continuation of longstanding marriages. Goldscheider also discusses the effects of life-cycle changes on contemporary issues such as the care of the elderly, young adults returning home, and the homeless, in line with the notion of strengthening the family from within. The family, for example, should not be criticized for taking care of its elderly or for providing lodging for its young adults. Community, family, and interdependence are not indicative of lack of individualism or pathological dependence but may provide a base for healthy coping and development in these populations.

Anna F. Steyn (chapter 5) examines traditional gender-based role structures within the contemporary South African family. Conventional wisdom holds that employment of married women and marital dissolution are causally related. Although this is a view supported by earlier research, recent studies have failed to support these earlier conclusions. Intervening variables, such as spousal support, may play a part in this causal chain, positively affecting both family and work adjustment of employed wives and their families. Rather than seeking out the negative effects of female employment on family life, Steyn examines family-related variables that may promote female employment. In addition, she investigates work-related variables that may positively affect family life. Among her findings was that spousal support is related positively to the work satisfaction of employed mothers and that work satisfaction was positively related to these mothers' sense of marital integration. These findings support notions of circular causality, with positive family variables affecting success in the work arena, while success in the work arena may positively affect family functioning. Other intervening family- and work-related variables such as the wife's commitment to growth in the marriage and career ambition were also found to be related to both family and work adjustment. Hence, this study suggests that the work and marriage may support each other, in contrast to popular notions of their antagonistic nature.

Considering the extended family and alternate family forms, Annette Weiner (chapter 6) suggests that extension of the family's interpersonal networks, *beyond* the traditional boundaries of the nuclear family, can strengthen the fabric of family life. At the turn of the century, capitalism perceived the nuclear family as a unit of domestic consumption, where purchasing power could compensate for the greater anomie and separation of these family units. Nation-states in the Western world once controlled family prerogatives and values, and families were encouraged to increase their purchasing power.

This occurred at the expense of extended family and community relations, which in the past were characterized by considerable economic cooperation that at that time were necessary for survival. However, increased consumption of foreign products and labor, female employment, and related developments, have eroded these traditional family foundations as reflected in decreased marriage and fertility rates, as well as increased divorce rates. Hence, the nuclear family that had created strong dependence on market forces that subsequently failed, also resulted in discouraged dependence on extended kin and neighbor ties, that throughout history have proven effective in time of need (in this regard, see Larissa Lomnitz, chapter 7). Weiner suggests that the increasing transnationalism, industrialization, and individualism of contemporary times increase, rather than diminish, the need for an interpersonal support base. However, such interpersonal support systems extend beyond the ideological and physical boundaries of the traditional nuclear family, whose values caused difficulties. No longer can traditional intergenerational and generational ties promote survival in a dynamic constantly changing society, where personal, interpersonal, and geographic boundaries are constantly being challenged. In this context, Weiner suggests that interpersonal support systems are important, however, family diversity and flexibility are a major challenge for the next century. Healthy families accept change and celebrate differences, with interpersonal bonds supporting autonomy and individualism, rather than conformity and dependence.

Larissa Adler Lomnitz (chapter 7), looking at the Latin American context, also emphasizes the importance of strong interpersonal networks for individuals in contemporary societies. However, whereas Weiner stresses the need for acceptance of a diversity of family forms, Lomnitz presents a strong case for the three-generational extended or "grand family" as a support base for the individual. Kindred networks provide a basic unit of solidarity within Mexican, and most Latin American rural and urban societies. This is expressed in economic and social solidarity, as well as in the ritual-ceremonial life of the family. The family is basic to the formation of social networks ensuring status maintenance among the privileged and physical survival among the poor. Like Weiner, Lomnitz notes that the economic crisis of the last decade has brought with it an economy based increasingly on free trade, private enterprise, and neo-liberal policies that have led to unemployment and a reduction in formal social security systems. This explains the increase in social and economic insecurity, which individuals resolve through social networks based on trust. In Latin America, this is evidenced by the growth of informal market mechanisms, characterized by small family enterprises and similar avenues of commercial enterprise. Lomnitz can be counted amongst the family optimists in her prediction that the 21st century will be characterized by a greater emphasis on the traditional extended family, as the economic crisis prevails in Latin America.

At the level of cultural and societal influences on contemporary family life, Beverly and Susan Birns (chapter 8) debunk the myth that violence is a personal problem and suggest that it must be resolved at the societal level. According to their thesis, even the term *family violence* is a misnomer, even though one in four women is assaulted by a partner or an ex-partner during her lifetime and 50% of abused children have mothers who are abused by the same man. If violence were a manifestation of family dynamics per se, then it would be expected that responsibility for this phenomenon would be found in the interpersonal domain and would be shared among family members. However, the evidence is overwhelming in showing that males are the major perpetrators of violence, which is more a reflection of societal attitudes than family dynamics. Thus, one must look beyond the boundaries of the family toward the larger social context to understand violence. In this context, they note that individual or couple interventions such as psychotherapy have been unsuccessful in preventing men's violence against women and children. Instead, they often support and justify these behaviors. In addition, the female victim is often blamed for her passivity and for not removing herself from the threatening situation. The latter hypothesis is based on myths such as women don't actively seek help or they usually have a place to seek refuge, but "choose" to stay. Such assumptions lead to dangerous interventions. The power structure of society lends itself to male entitlement and gender discrimination. "Gender neutrality" regarding violence is a myth, with the perpetrators more often being male. To correct such inequalities, women must be empowered and supported by social structures such as law, health care, and child protective services. These can ensure both women and children their rights to integrity, both as individuals and family members.

In discussing the "new links" workplace, Don Edgar (chapter 9) also relates to the interface between extrafamilial variables and family, namely how the workplace and community support systems can influence individual and family development. The quality of family life can also affect productivity in the workplace. Changes within the family such as evolving gender roles and increased longevity have profoundly affected the family, the workplace, and society at large, particularly the roles of women and the elderly. These changes require new links between the community, the workplace, and the family, because private lives are not only affected by, but also affect job performance including absenteeism, staff turnover, recruitment, and improved productivity. By dealing with the larger exosystem, not only will individual and family development be enhanced, but productivity will also be enhanced in the workplace and community at large. Edgar's model emphasizes *prevention*, building on strengths. This contrasts with traditional models of welfare and social policy that emphasize the *treatment* of weakness and deficiencies in the family. Neither the welfare state nor laissez-faire are productive solutions. Instead, the positive potential of families, the workplace, and community to benefit from new links that promote better functioning at all levels, is advocated. As contrasted to more pessimistic views of disintegrating family life in an increasingly industrialized, technological, and alienated society (see Toffler, 1971), Edgar advocates the positive and central role of family, supported at the interface of society, community, and the workplace. Several examples of this new links workplace in the Australian context are discussed.

Arlene Skolnick (chapter 10) also discusses the larger cultural, social, and historical trends affecting the U.S. family, analyzing the impact of large-scale shifts in the economy and society at large on family structure, the life course, gender, and intergenerational relations. The industrial revolution was one of the turning points in family life, with men working outside the home, which had previously been an economic unit. The home attained a "new domesticity," with women serving as a focal point in this domestic haven in the face of a "heartless world." At the turn of the 20th century, rapid economic, social, and cultural change destabilized the family. The concept of the *new woman*, including the women's suffrage movement and the sexual revolution, diminished the constraints placed on females and traditional notions of family and morality were challenged. Three major developments affected contemporary family life: the postindustrial economy, the decrease in mortality and fertility rates, and psychological transformation rooted in increasing levels of education. These were reflected, respectively, in increasing female employment with less emphasis on childrearing, more nurturing and less hierarchical family roles due to increased longevity, and more concern with individual needs than external roles and behaviors. These were also reflected in the work and governmental arenas, expressing themselves in more concern with employee need, as well as the recognition of the rights of disadvantaged groups such as women and children and the elderly. Skolnick notes, however, that these developments may also precipitate more uncertainty and anxiety because clear role directives may be lacking and interpersonal interdependence engendered. Skolnick places herself amongst the family optimists by noting that despite these profound social and economic transformations, the family prevails and is central to most people's lives. Public and private sector policies are required, however, which accommodate to these developments—the United States lags behind some other Western countries in this respect.

Adopting a sociological perspective, Wilfried Dumon (chapter 11) discusses major changes that have occurred in the western European family in the last three decades. Decreasing fertility and increasing longevity have changed the balance between the elderly and the young, profoundly influencing the family life cycle. Family formation has also changed radically. This is expressed in the increased independence and autonomy of youth, the dissociation of marriage from childbearing, as well as the dissociation of couplehood from parenting. Such developments are reflected in an increasing preponderance of unwed motherhood, cohabitation, and other alternate lifestyles like homosexual marriages. Family dissolution has also changed radically and since the 1950s, divorce, rather than death, has been the major cause of dissolution. Relatedly, changes in the nature of stepfamilies, resulting from divorce rather than death, express themselves in families where a stepparent often competes with a *living* biological parent in the child's upbringing. Since the late 1960s, divorce has changed from a fault to a no-fault procedure. This development has shifted the onus of responsibility from the family to society to correct family difficulties. This may be done through the provision of mental health facilities, child care, and appropriate legislation to promote adjustment in postdivorce families. Divorce, rather than involving *dissolution* of the family, creates the need for new family *reorganization*. Both family roles and social policy must accommodate to changes in family structure, such as the organization into a new binuclear family that spans two households. Although the contemporary family is more democratic and less coercive, recent changes in family structure and the family life cycle necessitate reallocation of power and the division of labor within the family. In this context, families must be empowered by society to enable them to function more effectively. Such provisions as child custody payments after divorce to ensure continued parenting, child-care services for the working parent, and incentives for family caretakers for the elderly are among the issues social policy must address. Dumon, in accordance with the systems approach and notions of circular causality, believes that just as the family in transition will affect current social policy, social policy will also affect the future of the family.

Antonio Golini and Angela Silvestrini (chapter 12) describe transitions occurring in family life in western Europe from a demographic perspective. They also discuss some of the broader social and psychological ramifications of these changes. In contrast to Goldscheider and Edgar who focus on the upper end of the developmental spectrum, these authors are concerned with the increasing neglect of the needs of the young due to changes in the family life cycle. They suggest that decreasing fertility rates and a longer average mortality rate have resulted in the "rarefaction of children" with shifting balances between the elderly and the young. There is a lower proportion of children, with a corresponding rise in the proportion of only children. These developments are causing a revolution in the psychological growth, development, and socialization of the child, which in turn affect interpersonal relationships with family and peers. In addition, increased rates of divorce and unwed motherhood, as well as decreasing marriage rates, have led to a diminished status of fathers. Fathers are often nonresidential parents with limited visiting rights, or in the extreme case with no rights of visitation or even knowledge of their children. The authors present some very interesting demographic information regarding different parts of Europe. Contrary to expectations, they report that northern European countries like Sweden have higher fertility rates than southern European countries like Italy. These phenomena and other provocative findings are discussed in terms of changing family values and the increasing pluralism of family types in contemporary European society.

In Part IV, "Situational Influences and Family Life," Shlomo Sharlin and Irina Elshanskaya (chapter 13) investigate the attitudes of immigrants from the former Soviet Union to various facets of life in the host country, Israel. Personal attitudes, such as satisfaction with life quality in Israel and the extent of Jewish identity, perceptions of interpersonal behaviors such as preparation for immigration in the country of origin and effectiveness of childrearing in Israel, as well as perceived situational contingencies such as the prevailing educational system are among the attitudes and perceptions studied in relation to their effects on parental stress and tension. The authors found that a wide spectrum of attitudes affect parental stress, whereas parental tension is affected mostly by attitudes related to childrearing and other family relations. They note that these attitudes could ultimately affect adjustment of both parents and children through the intervening variables of stress and tension experienced in the host culture. Although attitudes often reflect parental perceptions, which are subjective, they also may represent existing realities requiring social remedies. This is particularly true in the case of the educational system in Israel, which often falls well short of these immigrants' expectations for high standards of education, as well as for other child-related benefits in the host culture. Remedies are suggested for dealing with such situational deficits that could adversely affect child and ultimately family satisfaction and adjustment in Israel.

Solly Dreman and Eva Shinar (chapter 14) discuss a unique intervention attempt designed to assist in the integration of university students from the former Soviet Union to the host culture, Israel. Immigrant students, as well as native Israeli students, participate in a course called "Immigration as a Challenge," which has formal academic requirements, as well as components of an encounter group experience. This format is designed to increase understanding and interaction between the host culture and the immigrant group, not only by increasing cognitive understanding of the immigration process, but also by encouraging direct interaction and even confrontation between the hosts and the newcomers. This is done through formal lectures by the group leaders, as well as through various role-plays, simulations, and class projects. These strategies are designed to increase cognitive understanding and emotional integration of the immigration process, as well as promoting interaction between the hosts and the newcomers. In this context, immigration is viewed as a reciprocal process, with successful immigration not only involving accommodation of the immigrant to the host culture, but also an active attempt by the host culture to understand the new immigrants, their culture and the difficulties involved in the immigration process. Family processes that may affect adjustment of the new immigrant family are also discussed. In addition, the authors mention some of their recent interventive work with Black Jews from Ethiopia and their attempts to break down negative stereotypes bearing racial undertones.

Looking at family assessment in a systems context, David Olson (chapter 15) presents a multisystem perspective of family stress and coping. Olson views family adaptation (satisfaction) as occurring at a number of levels—personal, couple, family, and work. He proposes that it will be optimal when there are adequate coping resources to contend with the stressors or "hassles" that occur in the family's daily existence. For example, *personal* coping resources might include self-esteem and mastery, relational resources might involve *family* closeness and flexibility, *couple* resources often involve couple communication and problem solving, whereas coping with *work*-related stress might involve problem solving, and good communication. Stressors are also of a personal, couple, family, or work-related nature. The model is based on McCubbin and Patterson's (1983) double ABCX model of crisis adaptation. This model takes account of the pileup of stressors and strains (aA), ongoing coping resources (B) as well as perceptions of the crisis events (C), producing the crisis (X). This is a process model that perceives adaptation related to the *cumulative* stressors, coping resources, and perceptions of the situation occurring before, during, and after the crisis. It should be noted that Olson contends that coping with stress depends more on resources existing within the family than those existing outside of the family. However, other contributors to this volume such as Birns, Edgar, and Dumon have stressed the interface between these internal family resources and extrafamilial social, community, and work policies that actively consider the quality of family life.

In the final chapter of this book I summarize the prevalent themes presented by the contributors. I suggest that in an age of increasing technology and alienation the family may well provide the sense of community and belonging needed to reduce the existential anxiety precipitated by a changing and sometimes incomprehensible world. In conclusion, I review recent theoretical, research, and interventive findings and discuss trends and implications for families in millennia to come.

REFERENCES

Bowen, M. (1978). *Family therapy in clinical practice.* New York: Aronson.
Bronfenbrenner, U. (1979). *The ecology of human development.* Cambridge, MA: Harvard University Press.

McCubbin, H. I., & Patterson, J. M. (1983). The family stress process: The double ABCX model of adjustment and adaptation. In H. I. McCubbin, M. B. Sussman, & J. M. Patterson (Eds.), *Social stress and the family: Advances and developments in family stress theory and research* (pp. 7–37). New York: Haworth.

Minuchin, S. (1985). Families and individual development: Provocations from the field of family therapy. *Child Development, 56,* 289–302.

Minuchin, S., & Fishman, H. C. (1981). *Family therapy techniques.* Cambridge, MA: Harvard University Press.

Toffler, A. (1971). *Future shock.* New York: Random House.

Watzlawick, P., Weakland, J., & Fisch, R. (1974). *Change: Principles of problem formation and problem resolution.* New York: Norton.

INDIVIDUAL AND DEVELOPMENTAL INFLUENCES AND FAMILY LIFE

2

WORKING WITH COUPLES DURING STRESSFUL TRANSITIONS[1]

Carolyn Pape Cowan
Philip A. Cowan
University of California, Berkeley

This chapter describes two longitudinal intervention studies of the family during two early family transitions: first-time parenthood and the first child's entrance into school. We show that these major normative life transitions are accompanied by stress, which increases the risk of distress in parents and children, even in relatively well-functioning families who are not yet seeking psychological help. Our research is part of a new wave of studies that examine children's development from a family systems perspective. Although it seems obvious today that parents' styles of interacting with their children play a central role in their children's adjustment and behavior problems, only recently have results from family studies documented what clinicians have written about for years: When the relationship between the parents is troubled, children tend to have problems at home or at school. Observational studies show impressive correlations between prebirth marital quality and subsequent parenting behavior with infants (Cox, Owen, Lewis, & Henderson, 1989; Grossman, Eichler, & Winickoff, 1980; Heinicke, Diskin, Ramsay-Klee, & Oates, 1986). More harmonious marriages have been linked with greater developmental progress in infants and toddlers (Dickie, 1987; Goldberg & Easterbrooks, 1984), preschoolers (Kerig, Cowan, & Cowan, 1993; Miller, Cowan, Cowan, Hetherington, & Clingempeel, 1993), and young school-age children (Brody, Pellegrini, & Sigel, 1986; Cowan, Cowan, Schulz,

---

[1]Part of this chapter was presented at the International Conference, *The Family on the Threshold of the 21st Century: Trends and Implications*, Jerusalem, Israel, May, 1994.

& Heming, 1994; Katz & Gottman, 1994). Just as some studies show that good marriages promote children's competence and maturity, others show that prolonged marital conflict and marital dissolution tend to be associated with cognitive delay, school difficulties, and antisocial or withdrawn behavior in the early school years (Cummings & Davies, 1994; Fincham, Grych, & Osborne, 1994; Hetherington, Cox, & Cox, 1982).

We discuss the fallacy of assuming that nonclinical families experience little distress or dysfunction as they confront normative family transitions. The evidence shows that a significant proportion of contemporary parents with young children are at risk for depression, marital distress, and less-than-optimal relationships with their children, and that without intervention, problems in the family tend to grow worse rather than better over time. Because adaptation is relatively consistent and predictable across time even when life is in flux, it is possible to identify families at risk for posttransition distress and dysfunction from pretransition measures of their adaptation. We have, then, the basic prerequisites for the planning and evaluation of preventive interventions for families with young children.

We report the results of two preventive interventions. The first, a group intervention for couples in which mental health professionals worked with expectant and new parents on troubling marital, parenting, and three-generational issues, left both mothers and fathers more optimistic about their relationships as couples. Compared to their no-intervention counterparts who showed increased marital disenchantment and a 15% divorce rate, couples from the intervention groups reported stable marital satisfaction and intact marriages throughout the second year of parenthood.

In our second intervention study, we offered parents of preschoolers a similar group for couples before their first child entered elementary school. Preliminary analyses indicate that group participation leads to improved marital and parenting quality for the parents, and better school adjustment and fewer behavior problems for the children. Fathers from the couples groups were more effective with their children and fought with their wives less in front of their children during the kindergarten year. In turn, their children showed improved academic achievement and fewer behavior problems between the kindergarten and Grade 1 years. These results highlight the potential benefits of professionals reaching out to work with couples before their family problems require formal mental health services. Children benefit from their parents' participation in interventions that ultimately ease strain by improving the quality of their relationships as couples and as parents. As adaptation in family relationships is enhanced, the children's chances of making more optimal academic, emotional, and social adjustments to school increase.

Research on early family development and preventive intervention inevitably raises social policy issues. As we approach the year 2000, we examine the gap between what governments provide now in terms of prevention programs to support family stability and recent findings from intervention studies that highlight the potential benefits of providing more optimal family environments for children's academic and emotional development.

THE FIRST FAMILY TRANSITION: WHEN PARTNERS BECOME PARENTS

We begin with a description of what happens to couples becoming first-time parents and report the results of our attempt to facilitate parents' adaptation to parenthood by offering professionally led couples groups before, during, and after partners' transition to parenthood. In 1974, more than 10 years after we had become parents ourselves, we initiated an intervention study with couples about to become first-time parents. The conceptualization of the study and the design of the intervention was stimulated by our personal experience of marital strain in the early years of becoming a family (Cowan & Cowan, 1992).

The psychology and psychiatry research literature of the time revealed no studies of partners becoming parents—unless the women had suffered postpartum depression or psychosis (Cutrona, 1982; Hamilton, 1962) or the men had entered therapy (Wainwright, 1966; Zilboorg, 1931). The only studies of men, women, or couples who were not patients in the mental health system were conducted by family sociologists in retrospective studies asking parents after they had become parents how their lives as new parents compared with their "pre-baby" existence. A 1957 paper published by LeMasters described the results of interviews with a small number of couples who had become parents in the prior 1 to 5 years. Summarizing what he was hearing from the new parents themselves, LeMasters concluded that the transition to parenthood constituted a crisis for a marriage. Judging from the raft of published studies of new parent couples over the next two decades, sociologists must have found this conclusion quite startling. Most subsequent studies claimed that crisis was an overstatement of what happens to marriage when partners become parents. Hobbs (1965) bolstered his claim that crisis was an exaggeration by stating that "only" 20% of the new parents in his study had suffered moderate or extreme distress as a couple.

More recent longitudinal studies followed couples throughout the transition to parenthood (cf. Belsky & Kelly, 1994; Cowan & Cowan, 1992; Cox et al., 1989; Heinicke et al., 1986; Osofsky & Osofsky, 1984). The results show that at least 50% of partners becoming parents experience stressful changes, particularly in terms of increasing marital disenchantment. Despite the apparent consensus from intensive longitudinal studies, new parents themselves appear to be unprepared for the serious disruptions they experience in their relationships as couples, as indicated by their increasing marital disenchantment and a divorce rate of 15% to 20% in the first 2 years of parenthood (Cowan & Cowan, 1992; Eiduson, 1981; Morgan, Lye, & Condran, 1988).

Although many studies of the transition to parenthood in the 1970s minimized the stress of the transition, Rapoport, Rapoport, and Strelitz (1977) and Caplan (1970) suggested during this period that the expectable stresses of life transitions constituted ideal environments for providing interventions, to keep stress from leading to more serious mental health problems, and to promote growth by fostering the development of new coping skills to deal with the disequilibrium of shifting lives. A search of the research literature of the early 1970s revealed no evidence of interventions for couples expecting babies or parenting young children. Long after we had launched our first intervention study, we discovered reports of two systematically evaluated interventions for expectant parents: Shereshefsky and Yarrow's (1973) study, which offered a counseling intervention to expectant mothers in Bethesda, Maryland during their last trimester of pregnancy, and a once-a-month group offered to expectant mothers and fathers by Clulow's (1982) *First Baby Project*, in which marital experts from the Tavistock Institute of Marital Studies teamed up with Health Visitors from the British Health Service in London, England to help both partners explore changes in their relationships as couples. Despite some promising indications that the interventions had helped some parents adapt to the early months of parenthood, both projects ended soon after the babies were born. Looking back now, it is clear that these ambitious endeavors reflected remarkably similar ideas about (a) capitalizing on the vulnerability of the transition to parenthood by providing interventions to bolster one or both parents' mental health, and (b) strengthening the marital relationship to foster the development of healthier relationships between parents and babies. Despite these and our own encouraging results of preventive interventions for new parents (Cowan & Cowan, 1992), these ideas have not resulted in the creation of programs to buffer children from the risk of their parents' strain, depression, or marital distress (Cowan & Cowan, 1995).

Based on our concern about the impact of becoming a family on both the couple's relationship and the parents' relationships with their children, we began to evaluate systematically a preventive intervention in which mental health professionals with expertise in family relationships offered expectant couples a setting in which they could work on impasses in their relationships as partners so that they could cope more successfully with the strains and challenges of the family-making period. One of our major goals was to help keep the unexpected stress of this major transition from spilling over into other relationships in the family. Furthermore, given the tendency for destructive relationship patterns to be repeated from one generation to another, we hoped to reduce the generational transmission of dysfunctional patterns by helping relatively well-functioning couples learn more about the legacies from their families of origin and strengthen their resources as partners—while they were becoming parents and before their stress affected their relationships with their children.

THE *BECOMING A FAMILY PROJECT*

We invited expectant couples into our *Becoming a Family Project* as they approached their seventh month of pregnancy, and followed them regularly with visits, in-depth interviews, and questionnaires at five points until their children had completed kindergarten at approximately 6 years of age. Because one of our central questions was "What happens to marriage when partners become parents?" we also included a comparable set of couples who had not yet decided whether to become parents, which allowed us to compare shifts over time in couple relationships with and without children.

The Couples

We recruited couples through clinic and private obstetric/gynecology practices and public service announcements in local newspapers and on the radio. These efforts attracted 96 couples who lived in 28 cities and towns in northern California; 72 of the couples were expecting a first baby and 24 had not decided whether to become parents. The expectant parents ranged in age from their early 20s to their early 40s on entering the study: The average age of the expectant mothers was 29 years, of the fathers, 30 years. The childless partners were, on the average, 1 year younger, the women 28 and the men 29 years. The expectant couples had been together for an average of 4 years, some as few as 8 months, and several as many as 10 or 12 years. Most of the couples were married, and all were living together and considered themselves to be in a long-term relationship when they entered the study. Fifteen percent of the participants were African American, Asian American, or Hispanic, and 85% were Caucasian. All of the men and women had completed 13 years of school, and a number had gone on to complete additional vocational training or college degrees. Their family incomes spanned a range from working class to upper middle class.

We offered a randomly chosen one third of the expectant couples an opportunity to work with us in one of our couples groups for 6 months during their transition to parenthood and they filled out "pre" and "post" measures; another one third completed pre- and postbirth interviews and questionnaires, which the final one third did only after their babies were born. The childless couples completed interviews and questionnaires at comparable intervals.

Conceptualization and Assessment of Family Members' Distress or Well-Being

What would we need to know in order to understand more about whether adults and children are doing well or having difficulty? Our ideas about indicators of adults' and children's adaptation led us to gather information about five key aspects of family life that would give us a sense of how the parents and children were managing.

- At regular intervals, we asked about each family member's sense of self as an individual. We asked about parents' and later children's views of themselves, their feelings of vulnerability, and their symptoms of distress, and we assessed their self-esteem.
- We asked about many aspects of the parents' relationship as a couple, to capture both his and her experience of the tone of their relationship: how they show caring and experience intimacy, their division of family labor, the issues that lead to conflict or disagreement, their style of solving the problems that confront them, and their satisfaction and disappointments with their overall relationship as a couple.
- In detailed interviews, we asked both partners about the relationships between them and their parents, to get a sense of the legacies that each new parent brings from the past generation to the present one.
- We observed the relationship between each parent and his or her child during visits to our project playroom: how warm, responsive, strict, or permissive each parent was, how often he or she set limits for the child, how much anger or humor the parent used when working and playing with the child, and so on. Parents also described their perceptions of their child and their ideas about parenting.
- Because we know that having jobs outside the family and relationships with extended family, friends, and coworkers can provide extra support or added stress for both men and women, we calculated the balance between stress and support—using each parent's description of stressful life events and the availability of people to provide support.

We evaluated these five aspects of family life systematically at five periods: in pregnancy, 6 and 18 months after the baby was born, and again when the children were 3½ and 5½ years old. All of our interviews, questionnaires, observations, and discussions in the couples groups focused on these aspects of the family, on how they become intertwined, and on how they affect each family member.

The Decision to Become Parents

We found that couples' decision-making style about whether to become parents had long-term ramifications for their marriages (Cowan & Cowan, 1992). From their responses to the question of how they "came to be having a baby at this time," we described four general styles of making a decision about becoming a family. Whereas approximately half the couples were quite deliberate in becoming pregnant, the other half were distributed among three groups characterized by less planning or no planning at all.

1. About 50% of the couples were *Planners*. Over time, they talked about their feelings, ultimately came to the decision that they felt ready, and initiated a pregnancy that both partners welcomed.
2. Even in this age of commonly understood birth control technology, a significant number of couples either failed to discuss the issue or stopped using birth control, as if they were leaving the decision about having a child to fate. We characterize this 15% of the couples as *Accepting Fate* because they described that they became pregnant "accidentally" but willingly accepted what fate had determined for them.
3. We characterize another 17% of the couples as *Ambivalent*—not just at the beginning of their decision-making process as most partners are for a time, but still going back and forth about what they wanted to do near the end of the pregnancy.
4. A final 17% of the couples had serious disagreements about going ahead once the pregnancy was confirmed. One partner was very enthusiastic or determined to have the baby, whereas the other did not feel ready but was giving in to maintain the relationship. Of nine couples in this *Yes–No* category, seven husbands were saying "No" while their wives were saying "Yes."

The *Planners* managed the transition very well, with relatively stable marital adjustment throughout the first 2 years of parenthood. By contrast, the marital satisfaction of the *Yes–No* couples plummeted from late pregnancy to 18 months after the birth of their babies. More dramatic outcomes emerged when we had followed all of the couples through their first children's entrance to elementary school: All seven couples in which the husbands were initially resistant to parenthood had separated or divorced by the time their first child was 5 years old. This is a graphic example of how qualities of the partners' relationship as a couple before they become parents foreshadows their later adaptation once they become parents.

Changes in the Lives of Partners Becoming Parents

It seems as if everyone "knows" that when partners become parents their lives change dramatically, but our intensive investigation of the family formation period makes it clear that knowing and being able to tolerate significant personal shifts are quite different matters. The couples who stayed together but remained childless showed remarkable stability over the 7 years of the study in all five aspects of life that we assessed. By contrast, the couples who became parents described significant and often unexpected or disturbing shifts in every domain.

A Shifting Sense of Self

We examined change in partners' sense of self by having them complete an exercise we call *The Pie* before and after having a baby. On a circle 5 inches in diameter, partners included "pieces" that represented important aspects of themselves, such as son, daughter, parent, lover, worker, electrician, teacher, salesperson, friend, and so on. We asked them to decide on the size of each piece based on how large each of these aspects of life feels, not on how much time is spent "being it."

Differences between men's and women's experience of continuity and change in their sense of self were vivid. For example, from pregnancy to 18 months after birth, the size of the *worker* or *student* piece increased for new fathers but decreased for new mothers. The *parent* piece increased significantly for both—twice as much for women as for men. Which aspects of the self get squeezed as the parent piece expands? For both men and women, the *partner* or *lover* aspect of their self-descriptions declined, disappearing altogether in a few cases during the first 2 years of parenthood. As we see here, these differences between partners are central contributors to both men's and women's satisfaction with their overall relationship as a couple.

Parent and Child: A New, Intense Primary Relationship

As they gave birth, each parent began to report astonishment at the intensity of feelings—about the baby and about what was happening to their relationship as a couple. Many parents reported that the powerful feelings they were experiencing about their baby were unlike any other emotions they had felt. Their wonder at the baby's ability to elicit powerful feelings of love and protectiveness was matched by their confusion at discovering that newborns come without "owner's manuals" (Lamott, 1993). Each time they thought they had figured out the general principles of what would soothe or stimulate their infants, the babies changed in ways that sent the parents "back to the drawing board." Virtually all of the parents described this new, intense relationship as one of the most exciting, fulfilling, and complex they had experienced, but they were exhausted from the ongoing state of excitement, fatigue, and disequilibration of struggling to master the requirements of new parenthood while attempting to carry on with their pre-baby roles and responsibilities.

Shifting Relationships Between the Generations

Almost all of the couples who gave birth described shifting relationships with their parents and in-laws. For some, the baby's birth stimulated sadness if their parents were estranged or no longer alive. For the existing generations, there was a sense of a new closeness but this could be a mixed blessing for the couple. Typically, the woman wanted her parents to come as soon as the baby was born. More often than not, the man wanted the three of them to have a private period "with just the three of us." Most grandparents who visited came intending to be helpful, but the new parents experienced their parents as needing looking after too. Sometimes blatant, more often subtle, tensions tended to catch new parents and grandparents off guard, leaving everyone depleted at the end of the visits.

Disappointments With Friends and Coworkers

All of the new mothers took some time off work, and 51% stayed home full time for the first year or 2 of their child's life. This shift altered women's identities as workers and limited their opportunities for daily contact with coworkers and friends. Friendship networks began to shift for both men and women. Close friends who were not parents seemed to be drifting away, partly because they did not know how to respond to the new parents' preoccupation with their baby, and partly because the new parents balked at their invitations for get-togethers or outings where babies were not entirely welcome.

Men began to work longer hours, to establish themselves as the major breadwinner given the increase in family expenses and to make up for the income their wives had given up to stay home with the baby. New fathers often felt that there was nothing substantial they could do for babies that nursed and slept most of the time. Some new mothers felt abandoned during this period, which confused their husbands, who thought of their increased work outside the family as making a major contribution to the security of the growing family.

Shifts in Marriage

Given all the changes we described, it should not be surprising that men and women experienced significant shifts in their relationships as couples in the early years of becoming a family. Here we focus on two central and interrelated, changes: The division of "who does what?" and parents' overall feelings about the quality of their marriage.

Who Does What? Before the birth of the baby, expectant parents describe their current division of household tasks and decision making on our *Who Does What?* questionnaire (Cowan & Cowan, 1990). We asked them to predict how they would share a number of tasks related to the daily care of their baby, such as feeding, diapering, putting the baby to bed, and arranging for babysitters. Despite studies of families in industrialized societies that show that mothers still take most of the responsibility for child care and housework, even when both partners work outside the home, we found that many modern couples are convinced that a new egalitarian family exists in which men join women in active caretaking roles with babies and young children. We found that the division of household and family tasks became much more salient and traditional after the baby was born; the women did significantly more, and men significantly less, of the housework and baby care than either partner had predicted they would.

Given the pervasive belief that egalitarian families are now the norm, this reality was both unexpected and disturbing to men and women. Couples told us that arguments about "who does what" topped the list of issues they tended to fight about. In fact, the greater the discrepancy between their pregnancy predictions of how they would care for the baby and the husband's actual involvement in baby care later, the more symptoms of depression wives reported when the baby was 18 months old. Furthermore, the less husbands were involved in household and child-care tasks, the more unhappy their wives were with their overall relationship as a couple. Of course, this story can be told the other way around: When husbands are more involved in the day-to-day family tasks in this family-making period, their wives are less depressed and significantly happier with the overall state of their marriage. These results are consistent with studies of family work across the family years.

Marital Disenchantment. In the changes we have described so far, partners with a new baby are shifting as individuals, as couples, as parents, and in their relationships with the older generation. The women are becoming isolated from work and friends. Partners' mutual role arrangements at home are becoming more traditional, the partner–lover aspect of self is getting squeezed, and relationships with parents and in-laws are undergoing complex rearrangements. Not surprisingly, 9 of 10 couples reported more conflict and disagreement between them. At first glance, it does not seem difficult to explain why we and many other researchers find that satisfaction with marriage goes down during the couple's transition to parenthood.

Yet, the explanation for why some couples change more and some less is not quite so straightforward. We find that change alone does not predict decline in marital quality over this period. Compared with couples who remain childless over the same period of time, partners having babies become more different from one another, not only in their views of themselves but also in their roles, their ideas about childrearing, and their perceptions of what is occurring in their family. Men's and women's different family and work shifts propel them into separate worlds. When we measure these differences *between the spouses*, we see that it is couples whose differences became more pronounced and whose fighting increased that became more disenchanted and less satisfied with their marriage during this early family transition.

Who Does Well During the Transition to Parenthood?

The picture we have been painting about strain on new parents' marriages focuses on group trends or averages, but there is significant variation in how couples fare during the transition to parenthood. Overall, the couples who make the best adjustments in terms of fewer symptoms, less stress, and more satisfaction after having a baby are those who were doing best before the baby was born. In other words, children do not come along to disrupt idyllic marriages, but, as we see in the case of the *Yes–No* partners who disagreed about whether to have a baby, children do not bring warring couples together. These conclusions about continuity over time are supported by results of studies from other research teams: Belsky's in Pennsylvania (Belsky & Kelly, 1994), Cox and Lewis' in Texas and North Carolina (Cox et al., 1989), Grossman's in Massachusetts (Grossman et al., 1980), Osofsky and Osofsky's in Kansas (Osofsky & Osofsky, 1984), and Heinicke's in southern California (Heinicke et al., 1986).

RISKS ASSOCIATED WITH THE TRANSITION TO PARENTHOOD

Although on the face of it, the couples entering our study appeared to be starting as fairly low-risk families, we continue to be concerned about the level of stress and distress we found in these well-educated, two-parent, above-the-poverty-line families during the early years of parenthood. Our results leave us convinced that the difficulties encountered by ordinary couples with young children tend to get lost in the attention paid to "families at risk," usually described as those with the least financial, social, and psychological resources. Researchers and clinicians who focus on problems of poverty, alcoholism, and emotional disorders like depression, antisocial behavior, and schizophrenia, tend not to come in contact with normative family distress and its sequelae. As a result, they do not discover that a substantial proportion of "normal" families are at risk for developing mental health problems.

Postpartum Depression. Although the research literature would lead us to expect only 1 or 2 women in 1,000 to suffer from clinical postpartum depression, 1 of 100 women *and 1 of 100 men* in our studies suffered an episode of clinical depression that required hospitalization and medication after their babies were born. In both families, despite earnest attempts to recuperate from the strain of the early parenthood period, both couples had separated by the time their first child entered elementary school and divorced by the time the child was 8 years old. Although many factors play a role in the emergence of postpartum depression, its occurrence puts a severe strain on both parents and their marriage.

Depression. We asked men and women to complete a short list of symptoms of depression on the Center for Epidemiological Studies of Depression Scale (Radloff, 1977). From the time their babies were 1½ to 5½ years old, between 25% and 33% of the new mothers and fathers reported enough symptoms of depression to place their scores in the clinical cutoff range, which suggests that they may have needed professional help. Although depression in a parent of a young child does not guarantee a strained relationship between the parents or with the child, our data suggest that parents' depression is often accompanied by marital conflict. The combination of depression and marital conflict places their children at greater risk for compromised academic achievement and behavior problems in the early years of school (Cowan, Cowan, Schulz, & Heming, 1994).

Risks That Span Generations. In talking to us about their growing-up years, 20% of the new mothers and fathers spontaneously described themselves as adult children of alcoholics. Although none of the parents in our study appeared to be abusing alcohol or drugs themselves, those whose parents had suffered from serious alcohol problems described their 3½-year-olds as doing less well developmentally than parents with no alcohol problems in their backgrounds. This is troubling because our research staff's observations of all of the study children revealed no significant developmental differences between those two groups during the preschool period. Two years later, when all the children were 5 to 5½ years old and in kindergarten, the grandchildren of alcoholics were described by their kindergarten teachers as more withdrawn or shy or as having more aggressive behavior problems than the other children in our study (Cowan, Cowan, & Heming, 1988). This is a clear example of the type of family problem that cycles through several generations unless it is better understood and attended to.

Marital Distress. When we looked at parents' descriptions of their over-all marriage on a questionnaire to assess marital adjustment and satisfaction (Locke & Wallace, 1959), we found that between 9% and 35% of the fathers and mothers had scores in the clinical distress range at different points between pregnancy and 6 years later. If we count the maritally distressed and the divorced couples 6 years into the study—20% by then—more than half of the husbands and wives had indicated significant marital disenchant-ment or distress by the time their first child made the transition to elemen-tary school.

Academic, Emotional, and Behavior Problems in the Children. When the children completed kindergarten, at age 6 to 6½, approximately 10% of them were showing serious enough academic or emotional problems that their parents had sought professional help to assess or treat learning or behavior problems like attention deficit disorder or aggression with peers or siblings, or emotional problems like seriously low self-esteem or depres-sion. Not surprisingly, these problems often went along with children's dif-ficulty in concentration, which was also associated with lower achievement scores and difficulties in relationships with peers (Cowan et al., 1994).

The research findings from our studies and investigations by colleagues in the United States (e.g., Belsky & Pensky, 1988), England (Fonagy, Steele, Moran, & Steele, 1993; Paar, 1995), and Germany (Engfer, 1988; Schneewind, 1983) support three conclusions. First, couples who are in distress when they begin their transitions to parenthood continue to be so after the baby arrives. Second, the transition to parenthood tends to amplify preexisting distress in the early years of family life. Third, the relative consistency between pre- and posttransition adaptation means that it is possible to identify families who are particularly at risk for early family distress during pregnancy. All of these findings point to the need for preventive interven-tions to help couples avoid or reduce what appears to be an expectable increase in individual and relationship dissatisfaction during the transition to parenthood.

A COUPLES GROUP INTERVENTION

Because many contemporary men and women in the United States start their families far from kin and isolated from other couples going through this major transition, we made couples groups the context for preventive work. Each group, with four couples expecting a baby about the same time and one staff couple as co-leaders, met every week for 6 months throughout the last 3 months of pregnancy and the first 3 months of parenthood. Our group discussions focused on central aspects of family life that family researchers and mental health professionals have shown are key ingredients in happy or unhappy marriages and in the development of young children's competence or early emotional and behavior problems.

There were three staff couples in our Becoming a Family Project: Philip Cowan and Carolyn Pape Cowan, Ellen Garrett and William Coysh, and Harriet Curtis Boles and Abner Boles. The staff couples met twice weekly, once with the participating couples and once in staff training meetings in which we monitored and tried to be systematic about our work with the expectant couples. All couples participating in the study had personal interviews with their staff couple and completed questionnaires before the groups began, which encouraged them to focus on each of the aspects of life we have been describing: how they see themselves as individuals and as couples; their division of family labor; how they work out differences between them and how successfully they resolve their problems; the parenting they experienced in their families of origin, and their ideas about parenting their children.

As the babies were born, they became part of the groups. Now the discussions mirrored the couples' lives at home. It was difficult to complete a thought or sentence, so preoccupied were we with the babies' cries, movements, and new developments. We tried to capitalize on the moderate levels of confusion, anxiety, or distress that many men and women experience as they embark on this often joyous but stressful transition. The group leaders encouraged couples to explore their ideas, their dreams, and the impasses in their relationship with one another or their babies—before they felt overwhelmed and discouraged by unexpected shifts in their lives as couples, before their discouragement spilled over into the tone of their relationships with their children, and before they developed unrewarding patterns that would require longer term help in the mental health system.

The discussions in the couples groups were semistructured in the sense that our staff couples provided part of the "agenda" for each evening and the participants supplied the rest with questions or problems for the group to consider. Over the months of meetings, we talked with the couples about their reactions to the questionnaires they had already completed and about their experiences of being parents of newborns. We worked with them on the kinds of challenging marital, parenting, and three-generational issues that most of us confront at some time in our development as partners and parents.

The problems couples brought to the groups ranged from manageable to overwhelming. An expectant mother tearfully pleaded with her husband to tell his mother that it was the couple's role to name their baby. Her husband argued that telling his mother that would put distance between them when he had just reconnected with her around the news of the pregnancy. When his baby was 2 months old, another new father became disturbed about the prospect of their daughter sleeping between them "for years." His wife became emotionally distraught at the idea of giving up the closeness she had developed with their daughter. Another mother began to consider returning to her job outside the family, which troubled her husband because he felt that their baby needed her at home.

We worked to help couples experiment with more satisfying ways of balancing their own and their children's needs. We shared our conviction that having differences is not a sign of a problematic relationship; the challenge is to find ways of working out these differences so that both partners feel as if their needs have been appreciated and addressed in an adequate fashion. We encouraged partners to keep their disagreements from pulling them apart. We explored the origin of the issues that each felt passionate about. Some parents were determined never to let their baby feel anxious or frightened. Others were equally impassioned about having their partner respond in a manner that respected their feelings. Many partners needed help hearing each other out or knowing when to postpone a problem discussion because one or both of them were too angry to feel safe working together. Spouses who received a sympathetic hearing in the groups learned that they were not the only ones with unresolved problems and that other couples, too, had embarrassingly ineffective ways of arguing. Learning more about the human condition seemed to be reassuring or consoling and allowed some spouses to move beyond their arguments toward more productive solutions.

The Impact of the Couples Group Intervention

When we analyzed the information men and women had provided from pregnancy into the second year of parenthood, almost 2 years after the couples groups had ended, we found different patterns in couples who did and did not participate in a couples group (Cowan & Cowan, 1992). The fathers who had participated in a group described themselves as more psychologically involved with their babies than fathers with no intervention; their "father" pieces of the "pie" were significantly larger in the second year of parenthood than those of fathers with no group. The mothers from the groups felt more satisfied with the "who does what" of their lives. Although their husbands were not significantly more involved than other new fathers in the study, wives who had been in a couples group during the transition to parenthood appeared to feel as if their husbands were collaborating with them on important family issues, even if their roles in the hands-on work of caring for their babies were not equal. Intervention participants also reported fewer negative changes in their sexual relationships after having a baby, possibly because the groups had provided a safe setting in which to discover that most partners experienced shifts in their sexual relationship that required patience and some adjustment.

Between pregnancy and 6 months after giving birth, group couples reported less marital disenchantment, and their level of marital satisfaction remained stable into the second year of parenthood, whereas parents with no group experience showed an even steeper drop in marital satisfaction in the second year of the study than they had in the first.

What occurred in the groups to produce these effects? One of the most consistent findings is that couples discovered that their own experiences were reflected by others in the group. This allowed them to see their own and their partner's unexpected shifts in a more sympathetic perspective. In fact, the views of spouses who participated in a group diverged less from one another's—about themselves, their marriage, and their family. It is as if working with us in the groups kept both husbands and wives from slipping into more separate and traditional ways of thinking and being, and staved off the marital disenchantment reported in almost every study of modern parents. The groups gave both men and women a chance to hear others' experiences and views, which enriched their perception of relationship issues in "normal" families.

Our separation and divorce data are consistent with the finding of more stable satisfaction in the intervention couples for the first 3 years of parenthood. By the time their children were 3 years old, 15% of the parents with no intervention had separated or divorced, whereas all of the parents from the couples groups were still in intact marriages.

Although we would like to report that the intervention effects lasted until the children started school, the reality was that the positive effects of the intervention on the parents' feelings about their marriages begin to wane at the end of the preschool period, as we might expect with a time-limited intervention. By the time all of the children in the study entered kindergarten at about 5 years of age, the separation and divorce rate had climbed to 20% in couples with and without the intervention. At first glance, this sounds discouraging, but the marital status of the couples who remained childless helps put this figure in perspective: Compared to the 20% divorce rate for the new parents, the rate for couples who remained childless over the same 7 years is 50%. That is, despite the stressful changes and disappointments of new parenthood, having a baby helps keep many couples together, at least for a time. Our early intervention results about parents' optimism for the first 3 years of parenthood suggests that "booster shots"—additional groups that meet periodically during the early childrearing years—might avert the negative effects of the pileup of additional stresses such as second and third children, illness, financial stress, and job loss, stressors that accumulate over time and wear down the resilience of even the most resourceful couples.

THE TRANSITION TO ELEMENTARY SCHOOL

Data from our original study showed that parents' well-being or distress as individuals, couples, and parents was linked with their children's adaptation to the first year of elementary school. Our intervention, ending when the babies were only 3 months old, was designed to assist parents in helping their children cope with the demands of elementary school. Because studies of both low-risk (Alexander & Entwisle, 1988) and high-risk student populations (Kellam, Simon, & Ensminger, 1982) show that problems that are evident in kindergarten and Grade 1 are the best predictors of later educational, social, and mental health problems during adolescence, we designed a second intervention study to focus on this important period. Karl Alexander and Doris Entwisle (1988), who studied the role of the family in children's transition to school, suggested a metaphor to illustrate why it can be helpful to learn more about families in the process of making a major life transition. They liken families approaching the challenges of a transition to bicycle racers approaching a steep hill: Some begin to have difficulty as the skills that served them well on flat terrain prove inadequate to meet the challenge posed by steep grades. These obstacles tend to spread the cyclists apart, differentiating those who have the skill or stamina to reach their destination from those who do not. By studying families as members are approaching the challenges of major transitions, we are in the best position to explore what makes it possible for some to overcome the obstacles and make the necessary adjustments while others begin to falter and fall farther behind.

THE *SCHOOLCHILDREN AND THEIR FAMILIES PROJECT*

In our *Schoolchildren and Their Families Project*, we focus on how families manage the first child's transition to elementary school in order to isolate the family factors in children's adaptation and difficulty as they set out on the trajectories of their school careers. With a new sample of 120 families with a 4-year-old, we assessed the same five aspects of family life that we investigated earlier in the *Becoming a Family Project* at three points in time: before the children entered kindergarten, at the end of kindergarten, and at the end of Grade 1, by which time the children were approximately 7 years old.

We adapted our couples group intervention to work with parents at this early point in their children's learning careers, based on our earlier finding that parents with more satisfying and effective marriages and parent–child relationships would provide more supportive environments for their children's adaptation to the academic, emotional, and behavioral challenges of school. Once again, we are trying to help parents modify unsatisfying or dysfunctional patterns in these key family relationships before their children begin to develop debilitating or intractable academic and social problems. To a randomly chosen two thirds of the couples expressing interest in this study, we offered an opportunity to work with one of our staff couples in a group that meets weekly for 4 months before the children enter kindergarten. To the other one third of the couples entering the study, we offered a brief consultation intervention, in which parents were invited to consult their staff couple once a year if they wished about any family problems or dilemmas that arose during their 3 years in the study. Then we followed each family with personal interviews, family visits to our project playroom, questionnaires to the parents, and home visits to each child in each of the 3 years.

When we invited families to our project playroom, parents were usually in their early to mid-30s and their children were preschoolers. During a 2-hour visit, we invited them to work on a number of challenging tasks. First, the child met alone with two members of our staff to work on tasks that assess children's developmental level and problem-solving styles. This was followed by a session in which the mother and then the father worked and played separately with the child. The final segment of the visit involved the whole family, including younger siblings, working or playing at tasks that were both challenging and fun.

Of course, there is no way that we can come to know a family intimately in one 2-hour period, but we designed a range of situations to give us an idea of how each family gets along and works together. Throughout the visits, some parents were warm and supportive, others were warm and demanding, and some were controlling and critical. The videotapes support our vivid impression that families reacted to these visits in many and varied ways.

In our observation and coding of the videotaped visits, we focused on various aspects of the parent–child relationship in the separate visits, and on how the parents behaved toward each other when the whole family was together. In the parent–child sessions we were particularly interested in two dimensions of behavior: (a) whether the parents tended to be warm and responsive or cold and critical; and (b) whether the parents tended to set limits and structure the situation to assist the child or were distanced and disengaged. Diana Baumrind (1979, 1991), a researcher at the University of California at Berkeley who followed children longitudinally from age 3 to young adulthood, showed that children develop best when parents are warm and responsive *and* set age-appropriate limits. Baumrind calls this style *authoritative* parenting. The children of authoritative parents developed more adaptive intellectual and social skills than children whose parents were *authoritarian* (cold and limit-setting), *permissive* (warm and responsive without setting limits), or *disengaged* (neither warm nor limit-setting).

From videotapes of the whole-family session, we also coded the parents' co-parenting style—the level of warmth and cooperation or anger and competition that parents showed toward one another as they attempted to help their child manage challenging tasks.

Finally, 1 and 2 years later, when the children completed kindergarten and Grade 1, we gave each one an individual academic achievement test during a home visit. Even though the children were scattered in many classrooms in many school districts, we enlisted their teachers' help by asking them to fill out a 106-item checklist to describe every child in the class. Teachers agreed to do this without knowing which child from our study is enrolled in the class. This allowed us to see how the child in our study fared in a number of different aspects of classroom life, compared to all the other students in that class. We were particularly interested in whether teachers saw the child as academically curious and competent, socially accepted, shy and withdrawn, or expressing their difficulties in hostile and aggressive behaviors or in tension, anxiety, or depression.

THE ROLE OF THE MARRIAGE
IN PARENT–CHILD RELATIONSHIPS

When we analyzed the family information at three different points in the transition to school, we were looking for information about the role of the parents' marital quality in their relationships with their children and in their children's adaptation to school. We discovered four patterns that describe the role of the parents' marriage in family life: a simple and more complex spillover effect from the parents' marital quality to the parent–child relationships, one pattern in which the marriage acts as an amplifier of negative things and another in which it provides a buffer to protect children from stressors in other parts of life.

Simple Spillover

When parents are hostile and angry at each other as they work and play with their child in the family visit, they are less warm, less responsive, less limit-setting, and less structuring in the separate parent–child sessions. It is as if the anger generated between the parents overflows its container and spills over into at least one of the relationships between parent and child.

Complex Spillover

A study with Patricia Kerig (Kerig et al., 1993) showed that the spillover scenario is quite complex if we take the gender of the child into account. In general, mothers and fathers appeared to treat sons more positively than daughters. Comparing fathers' and mothers' visits in families with sons or with daughters, we found that both parents, especially fathers, were more authoritative (warm, responsive, structuring) and less authoritarian (cold, angry, not responsive, disengaged) with sons.

On closer inspection, we found that it was not the case that parents were treating sons more positively, but rather that they were treating daughters more negatively. But, this pattern occurred only in families in which the parents were distressed about their marriage. Mothers who were dissatisfied with their marriage tended to respond negatively to their preschool girls when the daughters asserted themselves. Fathers who were maritally dissatisfied treated their daughters negatively, regardless of what the girls were doing. It looked as if maritally unhappy fathers were reacting to their daughters as they did to their wives. The negative spillover from marital distress to tensions in the parent–child relationships was most pronounced between fathers and daughters.

Marriage as an Amplifier of Negative Effects

We have been talking as if problems for the child originate in the parents' marital quality, but the marriage can also be "in the middle," where it functions as an amplifier of difficulties in other aspects of family life. For example, in our study of preschoolers' families, mothers' and fathers' symptoms of depression were not directly related to their 3½-year-olds' level of aggressive behavior (Miller et al., 1993). Nevertheless, mothers and fathers who endorsed more symptoms of depression on a questionnaire were more likely to be in a distressing marital relationship. When parents were depressed *and* in a troubled marriage, their parenting was less effective, and the children showed more aggressive behavior. This pattern was mirrored in Hetherington and Clingempeel's sample of families of preadolescents. In families of 3½- to 4½-year-olds, and also in families of 9- to 11-year-olds, then, conflict and competition between the parents *amplifies* the impact of parents' depression, which is linked with both less effective parenting styles and children's aggressive behavior.

Marriage as a Buffer

Lest we convey that parents' marital quality has only negative effects on their parenting, let us focus on the potential for a satisfying relationship between the parents to keep a parent's depression from spreading to other aspects of family life. Investigators of child development and family relationships have shown a growing interest in the ways that maladaptive behavior is repeated in subsequent generations. An intriguing new body of research has emerged in which adults are asked to recall memories of their early relationships with *their* parents, using the Adult Attachment Interview, developed by George, Kaplan, and Main (1984) at the University of California at Berkeley. Coders analyze the content (descriptions of childhood) and formal aspects of the interview (especially the coherence of the narrative) to create categories that represent adults' "working models" or conscious and unconscious mental and emotional pictures of their early attachments. Men and women who describe relatively happy childhoods in a vivid, convincing, and coherent fashion are described as having a *secure* state of mind with reference to early attachment relationships. Even more to the point, adults who describe relatively unhappy childhoods in a vivid, convincing, and coherent manner are also described as having a secure state of mind concerning attachment relationships.

Insecure states of mind were found in approximately one third of most nonclinical samples. Adults are placed in this category when they assert that their early relationships were happy but that they cannot remember much about them or when they continue to be preoccupied, angry, and incoherent as they talk about past or current relationships with their parents. Of course, we do not know what actually occurred in those relationships, but this method assumes that state of mind about key family relationships influences one's current attitudes and behavior in intimate relationships.

Indeed, in a study with Deborah Cohn and Jane Pearson (Cohn, Cowan, Cowan, & Pearson, 1992), we found that parents' insecure states of mind about their early attachments, as coded from their personal interviews, are correlated with our observations of their behavior with their children in the family visits. In cases in which both parents were classified as having secure states of mind, their parenting style in individual visits with their child was warm and included appropriate limit setting. In cases in which both parents were classified as having insecure working models, there was little warmth or limit-setting in their individual parenting styles. The unique finding from these studies is that when mothers classified as insecure were married to fathers classified as secure, the mothers' parenting quality was as effective as that of mothers classified as securely attached.[2] Furthermore, the quality of their marital interaction was more positive and less negative than that of couples in which both wife and husband were classified as insecure. These results are consistent with the hypothesis that a satisfying marital relationship can buffer the negative impact of one partner's impoverished early experiences and provide a more nurturant family context in which more responsive, effective parenting can emerge in the next generation. What we are suggesting is that a good marriage can provide an opportunity for a parent who is still affected by his or her early negative family experiences to develop a new, more optimistic and positive state of mind about what can be expected in intimate

---

[2]We had only two couples in which husbands with insecure states of mind were married to wives with secure states of mind, so we could not examine the outcome of this marital pairing.

relationships; this, in turn, can allow the development of a more positive relationship between that parent and his or her child.

THE ROLE OF MARRIAGE AND PARENTING IN CHILDREN'S ADAPTATION TO SCHOOL

We offer two schematic diagrams (see Figs. 2.1 and 2.2) to summarize the central role of marriage in children's adaptation to school. The information in Fig. 2.1 comes from a collaborative paper (Cowan et al., 1994) in which we analyzed information from the families in our first study from pregnancy through that child's completion of kindergarten.

As we move from left to right in the figure, we follow couples as they begin the transition to parenthood, cope with the first 6 months of becoming a family, settle into the issues raised by toddlerhood, and show us how they work and play with their 3½-year-olds, separately and then together as a family. Before we discuss school achievement in kindergarten, note that the parents' descriptions of their family environment are linked with what we observe when they are working and playing with their preschoolers in our project playroom. We focus here on the paths to family difficulty, but the same findings could be used to follow the paths to family strengths.

We find two "pathways" leading to strained relationships between parents and their preschoolers. First, parents who reported more conflict and dissatisfaction in their marriage during the late stages of pregnancy tended to be more unhappy with their marriage almost 2 years later. When their children were 3½, those unhappily married parents were observed by our staff as more angry, cold, and competitive and less warm, responsive, and cooperative with each other. These couples in observably conflictful marital relationships tended to be less authoritative—less warm, responsive, and

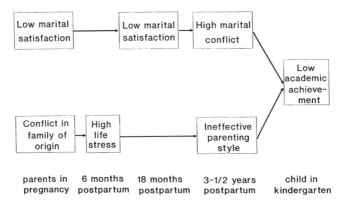

FIG. 2.1. Early family factors predicting children's academic achievement in kindergarten.

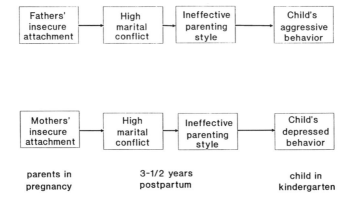

FIG. 2.2. Early family factors predicting children's behavior problems in kindergarten.

structuring—during the parent-child visits than parents whose marriages were more harmonious.

A second pathway to children's difficulty begins with parents who recall more conflict in *their* families of origin. Those parents reported more stressful life events and symptoms of depression during their pregnancy-to-afterbirth transition, and, 2 years later, they showed more conflict as a couple and less effective parenting with their preschoolers.

Family Contributions to the Child's Academic Achievement

How well does this information during family formation explain the variation in children's scholastic achievement in kindergarten? Although it may sound low, the ability to predict 20% of the variation in studies such as ours is considered quite satisfactory. We were able to predict 52% of the variation in children's scores on academic achievement tests at the end of kindergarten using the family information parents gave us. That is, if we take into account parents' general perceptions of conflict in their families of origin, their stress during their transition to parenthood, their marital quality before and after the birth of their baby, and the level of warmth and structure they provide when the child is a preschooler, we can explain a great deal, though not everything, about how the child is faring academically at the end of the first year of formal schooling.

Family Contributions to Children's Relationships With Their Peers

The same family variables that explain half of the variation in children's academic competence predict only 20% to 25% of the variance in how well they manage their relationships with other students, depending on which aspect of relationships with peers we examine. However, in a new study in collaboration with Deborah Cohn and Jane Pearson (Cowan, Cohn, Cowan, & Pearson, 1996) we were able to add the detailed information from the Adult Attachment Interview about each mother's and father's growing-up years and about the quality of their current relationships with their parents. With these richer data about parents' early experiences with *their* parents, we can explain children's social adaptation with their peers at school with more precision.

Here we see that mothers' and fathers' attachment histories are associated with different outcomes in their children. When fathers' narratives about their growing-up years were not coherent, either because they talked of idyllic relationships with no supporting examples to illustrate, or because they seemed angry or preoccupied with their parents' lack of loving behavior, they tended to be in high-conflict marriages. As we described earlier, marital conflict seems to color the parent–child relationship. Our observations show that these fathers classified as insecure with regard to attachment relationships have harsher, less responsive reactions to their children during the preschool period. Two years later, the kindergarten teachers saw these sons and daughters as significantly more aggressive toward their peers than children whose parents had less conflict. This set of family relationship predictors accounts for 69% of the variation in the teachers' ratings of the children's aggression at school.

Mothers who described their growing-up years as harsh or rejecting or without some coherent integration of their narrative tended to be in marriages that were high in conflict. These women were more angry and less structuring with their children during the preschool visits, and, 2 years later, their children tended to be more depressed, shy, and socially rejected at school. These predictors account for 60% of the variation in the teachers' descriptions of the children. Although we cannot jump to very general conclusions from one study, the results lead us to speculate that even though both fathers and mothers who are insecurely attached tended to be in more conflictful marital relationships, the spillover from insecure working models of attachment for fathers and mothers may lead to different kinds of problems in the children's adjustment.

We have known for some time that when parents' marital conflict leads to divorce, their children have more academic problems and difficulties with peers at school. Our study suggests that when *married* parents fail to regulate their conflicts successfully as a couple, their children are also at risk for social and academic problems early in their school careers. Let us clarify what these result signify and what they do not. The fact that we can predict a substantial proportion of children's academic and social competence from family assessments at the preschool stage in part reflects the fact that parents and children share a set of partially overlapping genes. Even if all the predictive power comes from the quality of family relationships, we need to remember that we cannot predict children's competence perfectly. Some children do much better and some do much worse than we would expect from what we know about the family environment. Nevertheless, if our goal is to help foster more nurturant environments for the developing child, it will be necessary to pay attention to the quality of the parents' marriage because of its power to color the child's everyday life in the family and at school.

INTERVENTION EFFECTS

Because all of the results we have described are based on correlations, we do not know from these studies whether there is any *causal* relationship between the quality of the marriage and the parent–child relationships. Furthermore, if there is a causal relationship, we cannot tell from these data how it works. The *Schoolchildren and their Families Project* was designed to test these ideas about the marriage–parenting connection more directly. Making sure that each subsample was equivalent on preintervention marital adjustment and symptoms of depression scores, we randomly offered couples one of three interventions:

A Couples Group With a Focus on Marriage. Couples in this intervention participate in a group that meets weekly for 16 weeks prior to their children's entrance to kindergarten. In addition to helping them discuss a variety of family topics specified in our theoretical model, leaders engage the couples in discussions about their marital issues and problems. Sometimes one or both partners directly ask for help in communicating more effectively with one another. More often the discussions begin with a description of tensions or disagreements about childrearing or about dealing with parents and in-laws. The group leaders help partners explore the implications of these tensions for their relationship as a couple.

A Couples Group With a Focus on Coparenting. Couples in this intervention participate in a couples group that meets weekly for 16 weeks prior to their children's entrance to kindergarten. In addition to helping participants discuss family topics specified in our theoretical model, leaders engage the participants in examining how strains in various aspects of family life affect how mothers and fathers work together to parent their children. A husband complained that he is always depleted when he comes home from work, but his wife made extraordinary demands on him to look after the children from the moment he steps through the door. In contrast with the leaders of the marital groups, who try to help partners resolve their marital conflict, the leaders of groups with a coparenting focus help parents explore more satisfying ways of cooperating in looking after the children during the stressful work-to-home transition times.

Short-Term Consultation on Family Problems. Couples in this intervention are offered an opportunity to consult with a staff couple once in each year of the study in order to discuss any troubling family issues or problems. The issues raised by the couples who used the consultation were often similar to those raised by the group participants, but they had much less time with our staff to resolve them, and they did not have the opportunity of listening to other couples struggle with similar problems in their own ways.

The couples groups in this intervention study resemble those for couples making the transition to parenthood in the Becoming a Family Project. All were semistructured, and focused on many of the individual and relationship issues in the five domains of family life we have described in our model. A male–female staff team of mental health professionals worked with couples to modify some of their negative attributions of one another, to regulate their strong emotional reactions more effectively, and to find more adaptive and satisfying problem-solving strategies as partners and parents. The groups met weekly for four months before the children entered kindergarten.

Here we report preliminary results obtained in analyses of the first two of three waves of study participants. In comparison with parents in the Consultation intervention, mothers and fathers in both marital *and* coparenting groups reported fewer symptoms of depression after the intervention groups, especially between the kindergarten and Grade 1 follow-ups. On the average, couples who participated in the maritally focused groups showed less conflict in front of their child after the intervention.

Couples who had participated in the coparenting groups showed even more positive results. Like our earlier transition to parenthood intervention, the coparenting groups benefited fathers in their relationships with their children. Fathers who participated in a group focused on coparenting worked and played more effectively with their children in the year after the intervention. Fathers *and* mothers from the coparenting groups reported an increase in satisfaction with their marriage. Although we could not find effects on the children's early adaptation in our earlier transition to parenthood study, there were intervention effects on children's adaptation to school in the transition to school study: When parents participated in a coparenting group, their children showed significant improvement from kindergarten to Grade 1 in their Reading and Spelling Achievement scores, they described themselves as more accepted and less socially rejected by their peers, and their teachers reported that they showed fewer shy or withdrawn, depressed behaviors than other children in the study.

Although we have been emphasizing the importance of the parents' marriage for the relationships between each of the parents and the child, the maritally focused group had some but not the most comprehensive benefits. Further analysis suggests that when couples entered a group with a Marital focus and were already experiencing fairly high marital conflict, their conflict tended to *increase* over time. By contrast, high-conflict couples entering the coparenting groups tended to show less conflict the next year—at least in front of their children in our playroom. When their marriage was in difficulty, parents in these couples groups seemed able to use our help to work together on issues about rearing their children. This had positive effects on their parenting *and* on the level of marital conflict. These results suggest that even parents with a fairly high amount of conflict can learn in a group that focuses more on their child that they can settle their differences about dealing with their child in ways that ultimately reduces their irritability and tension with one another, at least when their child is present.

The unique aspect of these coparenting groups is that they included fathers as well as mothers. An intervention that puts the spotlight on marital difficulties during a complex transition for their child may create more than ideal disequilibrium for already warring couples. By contrast, a couples group in which mental health professionals help both parents work together on what is important to each of them as parents during this major transition has the potential for increasing their satisfaction as a couple and reducing their conflict in their child's presence. It makes sense that both of these things would facilitate their child's early academic and social adaptation.

IMPLICATIONS FOR FAMILY POLICY

We recognize that current economic concerns about the provision of health care and other social programs make recommendations for additional family services risky. Nevertheless, the results of longitudinal studies of low to moderate risk families, along with data from interventions with parents all along the continuum of risk (Cowan & Cowan, 1995), suggest that without intervention, the problems and vulnerabilities of new parents will spill over into other relationships in the family, leaving the children at risk for compromised development.

We are concerned that with little support from business or government, men and women who are parents of young children are virtually on their own to address the competing needs of marriage, children, and families. We believe that as long as it is up to each man and woman to find a satisfying balance of gender role and work–family issues during the family formation years, the relationships between them—and between them and their children—will be vulnerable to strain. In our view, a serious concern about the preservation of strong family relationships argues for the allocation of increased resources for programs to strengthen families all along the risk continuum.

CONCLUSIONS

We have argued that when normal families face normative life transitions, they tend to experience a great deal of disequilibrium and some distress. The data showing that we can predict children's academic, emotional, and social adaptation to school from family information obtained during the early years of childrearing means that we know enough to identify which parents and children are at risk for difficulty before that difficulty comes to the attention of teachers and mental health professionals.

Our correlational and intervention studies have shown that the quality of the couple's relationship is central in the dynamics of family life. If the relationship feels positive to the partners, it increases the probability that they will relate warmly and effectively to their children; in turn, the children tend to have fewer difficulties relating to teachers and peers and more success at meeting early academic challenges. If the tone of the parents' marriage is negative and full of unresolved conflict, there are risks for the child unless the parents do something to alter the tone and process of their interactions.

Despite the fact that we have been focusing exclusively on two-parent families at the lower risk end of the spectrum, our work shows that low risk does not necessarily mean no distress or low distress. Some of the children who will be identified as having academic and behavior problems in their early years of schooling come from relatively well-off middle class families. It is becoming clearer that poverty, single parenthood, and divorce are not the only risks for children's developmental course. When parents cannot regulate their exchanges of hostile or negative feelings, or work together successfully to solve the problems that disturb them, their children are at risk for academic and behavior problems as they embark on their school careers. Unless something interrupts these negative patterns, children are likely to follow a trajectory that ends in negative outcomes in early adolescence and adulthood.

What about single-parent families, which in research terms usually means single mothers? We know that despite added stress, fewer financial resources, and only one parent to juggle the tasks of making a living and rearing a family, many children from single-parent families are doing well. When they have difficulties, the reasons appear to be similar to the ones we have described in studies of two-parent families. We know that poverty and other stresses in life tend to affect children by disrupting the quality of parent–child relationships (Conger et al., 1992; McLoyd, 1990). We also know that the transmission of positive and negative relationships across the generations affects the current relationship between parent and child. Many single mothers are in intimate relationships with partners; when those relationships are satisfying and productive, we expect their children to be advancing academically, emotionally, and socially. We will examine these links more closely in a new study of single mothers whose children are making the transition to school. We expect that many of the aspects of family life that we have been assessing apply to the success or difficulty of children in single-parent families as well.

The focus of parent educators and mental health professionals who are concerned about children's well-being tends to be on improving the quality of parenting they receive. While we are enthusiastic about programs to help parents establish more satisfying relationships with their children, we have learned that in order for parents to be nurturant and responsive to their children, they need adult relationships in which they feel responded to, nurtured, and valued. Particularly in these days of an increasingly demanding economy and hurried family lives, in which parents must work and juggle the needs of their children, it is not uncommon for their intimate relationships to be put "on the back burner" for the first few years of parenthood. Our results suggest that it is possible to identify nonclinical families who are at risk for distress in th early family years, and to create opportunities for parents to make their lives as partners and parents less stressful and more satisfying. Both children and their parents will be the winners if these strategies are successful. As we approach the year 2000, we have the knowledge and the tools to enhance early family life for parents and their children. The question is whether we have the will to translate this knowledge into action.

ACKNOWLEDGMENT

The research described in this chapter has been supported by Grant MH-31109 from the National Institute of Mental Health.

REFERENCES

Alexander, K. L., & Entwisle, D. (1988). Achievement in the first 2 years of school: Patterns and processes. *Monographs of the Society for Research in Child Development, 53*(2, Serial No. 218).

Baumrind, D. (1991). The development of instrumental competence through socialization. In A. D. Pick (Ed.), *Minnesota symposia on child psychology* (Vol. 7). Minneapolis: University of Minnesota Press.

Baumrind, D. (1991). Effective parenting during the early adolescent transition. In P. A. Cowan & M. E. Hetherington (Eds.), *Family transitions: Advances in family research* (Vol. 2, pp. 111–164). Hillsdale, NJ: Lawrence Erlbaum Associates.

Belsky, J., & Kelly, J. (1994). *Transition to parenthood.* New York: Delacorte Press.

Belsky, J., & Pensky, E. (1988). Marital change across the transition to parenthood. *Marriage and Family Review, 12,* 133–156.

Brody, G. H., Pellegrini, A. D., & Sigel, I. (1986). Marital quality and mother-child and father-child interactions with school-aged children. *Developmental Psychology, 22,* 291–296.

Caplan, G. (1970). *The theory and practice of mental health consultation.* New York: Basic Books.

Clulow, C. F. (1982). *To have and to hold: Marriage, the first baby and preparing couples for parenthood.* Aberdeen, Scotland: Aberdeen University Press.

Cohn, D. A., Cowan, P. A., Cowan, C. P., & Pearson, J. (1992). Mothers' and fathers' working models of childhood attachment relationships, parenting styles, and child behavior. *Development and Psychopathology, 4,* 417–431.

Conger, R., Conger, K. J., Elder, G., Lorenz, F., Simmons, R., & Whitbeck, L. (1992). A family process model of economic hardship and adjustment of early adolescent boys. *Child Development, 63,* 526–541.

Cowan, C. P., & Cowan, P. A. (1990). Who does what? In J. Touliatos, B. F. Perlmutter, & M. A. Straus (Eds.), *Handbook of family measurement techniques* (pp. 447–448). Newbury Park, CA: Sage.

Cowan, C. P., & Cowan, P. A. (1992). *When partners become parents: The big life change for couples.* New York: Basic Books.

Cowan, C. P., & Cowan, P. A. (1995). Interventions to ease the transition to parenthood: Why they are needed and what they can do. *Family Relations, 44,* 412–423.

Cowan, C. P., Cowan, P. A., & Heming, G. (1988, November). *Adult children of alcoholics: What happens when they form new families?* Paper presented to the National Council on Family Relations, Philadelphia, PA.

Cowan, P. A., Cohn, D. A., Cowan, C. P., & Pearson, J. (1996). Parents' attachment histories and children's externalizing and internalizing behavior: Exploring family systems models of linkage. *Journal of Clinical and Consulting Psychology, 64,* 53–63.

Cowan, P. A., Cowan, C. P., Schulz, M., & Heming, G. (1994). Prebirth to preschool family factors predicting children's adaptation to kindergarten. In R. Parke & S. Kellam (Eds.), *Exploring family relationships with other social contexts: Advances in family research* (Vol. 4, pp. 75–114). Hillsdale, NJ: Lawrence Erlbaum Associates.

Cox, M. J., Owen, M. T., Lewis, J. M., & Henderson, V. K. (1989). Marriage, adult adjustment, and early parenting. *Child Development, 60,* 1015–1024.

Cummings, E. M., & Davies, P. T. (1994). *Children and marital conflict: The impact of family dispute and resolution.* New York: Guilford.

Cutrona, C. (1982). Nonpsychotic postpartum depression: A review of recent research. *Clinical Psychology Review, 2,* 487–503.

Dickie, J. (1987). Interrelationships within the mother-father-infant triad. In P. Berman & F. Pedersen (Eds.), *Men's transitions to parenthood: Longitudinal studies of early family experience* (pp. 113–144). Hillsdale, NJ: Lawrence Erlbaum Associates.

Eiduson, B. (1981, April). *Parent–child relationships in alternative families and socio-emotional development of children at three years of age.* Paper presented at the biennial meetings of the Society for Research in Child Development, Boston, MA.

Engfer, A. (1988). The interrelatedness of marriage and the mother-child relationship. In R. A. Hinde & J. Stevenson-Hinde (Eds.), *Relationships within families: Mutual influences* (pp. 104–118). Cambridge, England: Cambridge University Press.

Fincham, F. D., Grych, J. H., & Osborne, L. N. (1994). Does marital conflict cause child maladjustment? Directions and challenges for longitudinal research. *Journal of Family Psychology, 8,* 128–140.

Fonagy, P., Steele, M., Moran, G., & Steele, H. (1993). Measuring the ghost in the nursery: An empirical study of the relation between parents' mental representations of childhood experiences and their infants' security of attachment. *Journal of the American Psychoanalytic Association, 41,* 957–989.

George, C., Kaplan, N., & Main, M. (1984). *Attachment interview for adults.* Unpublished manuscript. University of California, Berkeley.

Goldberg, W. A., & Easterbrooks, M. A. (1984). Role of marital quality in toddler development. *Developmental Psychology, 20,* 504–514.

Grossman, F., Eichler, L., & Winickoff, S. (1980). *Pregnancy, birth, and parenthood*. San Francisco: Jossey-Bass.

Hamilton, J. A. (1962). *Postpartum psychiatric problems*. St. Louis, MO: Mosby.

Heinicke, C. M., Diskin, S. D., Ramsay-Klee, D. M., & Oates, D. S. (1986). Pre- and postbirth antecedents of 2-year-old attention, capacity for relationships and verbal expressiveness. *Developmental Psychology, 22*, 777–787.

Hetherington, E. M., Cox, M. J., & Cox, R. (1982). Effects of divorce on parents and children. In M. E. Lamb (Ed.), *Nontraditional families* (pp. 233–288). Hillsdale, NJ: Lawrence Erlbaum Associates.

Hobbs, D. F., Jr. (1965). Parenthood as crisis: A third study. *Journal of Marriage and the Family, 27*, 367–372.

Katz, L. F., & Gottman, J. M. (1994). Patterns of marital interaction and children's emotional development. In R. Parke & S. Kellam (Eds.), *Exploring family relationships with other social contexts: Advances in family research* (Vol. 4, pp. 49–74). Hillsdale, NJ: Lawrence Erlbaum Associates.

Kellam, S. G., Simon, M. B., & Ensminger, M. E. (1982). Antecedents in first grade of teenage drug use and psychological well-being: A ten-year community-wide prospective study. In D. Ricks & B. Dohrenwend (Eds.), *Origins of psychopathology: Research and public policy* (pp. 17–42). Cambridge: Cambridge University Press.

Kerig, P. K., Cowan, P. A., & Cowan, C. P. (1993). Marital quality and gender differences in parent-child interaction. *Developmental Psychology, 29*, 931–939.

Lamott, A. (1993). *Operating instructions: A journal of my son's first year*. New York: Pantheon Books.

LeMasters, E. E. (1957). Parenthood as crisis. *Marriage and Family Living, 19*, 352–355.

Locke, H., & Wallace, K. (1959). Short marital adjustment and prediction tests: Their reliability and validity. *Marriage and Family Living, 21*, 251–255.

McLoyd, V. C. (1990). The impact of economic hardship on Black families and children: Psychological distress, parenting, and socioemotional development. *Child Development, 61*, 311–346.

Miller, N. B., Cowan, P. A., Cowan, C. P., Hetherington, E. M., & Clingempeel, G. (1993). Externalizing in preschoolers and early adolescents: A cross-study replication of a family model. *Developmental Psychology, 29*, 3–18.

Morgan, S. P., Lye, D. N., & Condran, G. A. (1988). Sons, daughters, and the risk of marital disruption. *American Journal of Sociology, 94*, 110–129.

Osofsky, J. D., & Osofsky, H. J. (1984). Psychological and developmental perspectives on expectant and new parenthood. In R. D. Parke (Ed.), *Review of child development research, 7: The family* (pp. 372–397). Chicago: University of Chicago Press.

Radloff, L. (1977). Sex differences in depression: The effects of occupation and marital status. *Sex Roles, 1*, 249–265.

Rapoport, R., Rapoport, R., & Streilitz, Z. (1977). *Mothers, fathers, & society: Towards new alliances*. New York: Basic Books.

Schneewind, K. A. (1983). Konsequenzen der Erstelternschaft [Consequences of the transition to parenthood: An overview]. *Psychologie in Erziehung und Unterricht, 30*, 161–172.

Shereshefsky, P., & Yarrow, L. J. (Eds.). (1973). *Psychological aspects of a first pregnancy and early postnatal adaptation*. New York: Raven Press.

Wainwright, W. H. (1966). Fatherhood as a precipitant of mental illness. *American Journal of Psychiatry, 123*, 40–44.

Zilboorg, G. (1931). Depressive reactions related to parenthood. *American Journal of Psychiatry, 87*, 927–962.

3

DEPRESSION IN A MARITAL CONTEXT

Yona Teichman
Tel-Aviv University

For quite a while there were suggestions about how to understand and treat depression interpersonally. The underlying assumption of these views is that depression affects the relationships between the depressed person and her or his significant others and is affected by them in return. Interpersonal models of depression focus on the relationships between depressed patients and their significant others and attempt to explain etiological and maintaining factors of depression as context-related. Most of the models also outline suggestions for treatment. Interpersonal treatments of depression may be classified as focusing on general issues in the marital relationship (Friedman, 1975; Glick et al., 1985), expansions of individual treatments like Klerman, Weissman, Rounsaville, and Chevron's (1984) individual interpersonal therapy (IPT), or Beck, Rush, Shaw, and Emery's (1979) traditional cognitive therapy, to a couple approach (Foley, Rounsaville, Weissman, Sholomskas, & Chevron, 1989; Rush, Shaw, & Khatami, 1980). However, most of the interpersonal treatments offered to depressed patients and their spouses may be identified as behaviorally oriented (Beach, Sandeen, & O'Leary, 1990; Jacobson & Margolin, 1979; McLean, Ogston, & Grauer, 1973; O'Leary & Beach, 1990) or systems theory oriented (Coyne, 1988; Gotlib & Colby, 1987; Teichman & Teichman, 1990). Each of the two last orientations has a variation which offers a combination or integration with cognitive therapy (Dobson, Jacobson, & Victor, 1988; Feldman, 1976; Jacobson, Dobson, Fruzzeti, Schmaling, & Salusky, 1991; Teichman & Teichman, 1990). It is interesting to examine the interpersonal treatments more closely and to look at studies that evaluated their efficacy.

EFFICACY OF MARITAL THERAPY
WITH DEPRESSED PATIENTS

The slowly accumulating body of studies which examined the efficacy of marital therapies with depressed patients indicates that this intervention yields promising results. Apparently, this mode of therapy addresses meaningful issues and processes in the lives of depressed patients and their spouses. Friedman (1975) found that, in the long run, a combination of drug and marital therapy was superior to drug therapy alone in reducing depressive symptoms and improving family adjustment. Glick et al. (1985) and Haas et al. (1988) tested the efficacy of family therapy treating hospitalized, affective disorder, and schizophrenic inpatients. Although the first study did not produce significant results, the second study demonstrated that depressed female patients benefited from marital therapy more than did male patients. This effect was maintained in two follow-ups. Female patients with schizophrenia also reacted better to marital therapy than did their male counterparts. Foley et al. (1989) evaluated the efficacy of a couple version of interpersonal therapy (IPT), comparing it with traditional individual IPT (Klerman et al., 1984). They reported that marital therapy was especially effective with patients who reported pretreatment marital problems.

The behavioral treatments emphasize the quality of the marital relationship of depressed patients. Based on findings regarding marital problems reported by depressed patients before the depressive episode, during it, or even following it (Collins, Kreitman, Nelson, & Troop, 1971; Crowther, 1985; Hautzinger, Linden, & Hoffman, 1982; Hinchliffe, Hooper, & Roberts, 1978; Merikangas, Prusoff, Kupfer, & Frank, 1982; Weissman & Paykel, 1974), these approaches view marital discord as an etiological or maintaining factor in depression. Accordingly, their therapeutic aim is to help couples improve their marital relationships. This aim directed attention to stresses encountered by couples, to problems related to intimacy and cohesion, to the need to improve communication and negotiation skills, to problem-solving skills, and to attempts to increase awareness regarding reasons for marital discord. The integration or combination of this approach with cognitive principles recognizes the relevance of cognitive process to depression and expands the focus of therapy to issues like problem definitions, expectations for self and spouse, beliefs about change, and attributional patterns.

Studies that evaluated behavioral marital therapies (BMT) demonstrate the importance of the marital context for treatment results with depressed patients. McLean et al. (1973) reported that BMT with emphasis on verbal communication between spouses was more effective in reducing depression, and improving interpersonal behaviors and verbal communication, than medication, group therapy, individual therapy, or combinations of these treatments. Paying attention to the relationship between changes in depression and quality of pretreatment marital relationship, Beach and O'Leary (1986) and Beach et al. (1990) compared couples in marital therapy, in individual cognitive therapy and in a waiting-list control group. They reported that both therapies were effective in reducing depressive symptoms, but marital therapy was more effective in reducing depression to recovery criterion and more effective in increasing marital satisfaction. Similar results were reported by Jacobson et al. (1991). It is interesting to note that the last group of researchers also included in their comparison a group of patients who were exposed to a combination of behavioral and cognitive therapy. The combined treatment focused primarily on behavior therapy techniques, and only secondarily included cognitive interventions. Contrary to the prediction, the combination was not the most effective treatment. The investigators attributed this finding to the way in which the combination of the two treatments was structured: division of the total number of sessions between the two treatment modalities with a predetermined minimum for each, and conducting part of the sessions on an individual basis and part on a marital one. An alternative explanation may suggest that this therapy did not produce the expected results because it did not provide an adequate opportunity for generating change for any of the applied techniques. On the other hand, an *integration* of cognitive and marital therapy that includes elements of both treatment orientations may prove to be more effective.

Marital therapies based on a systems orientation aim at more than improving couple relationship or functioning. In addition, they focus on reciprocal processes in the marital relationship which are related to depression, and maintain it. They claim that the goal of treatment of depressed patients and their spouses is to reveal the dysfunctional reciprocities in their relationship, to bring them to the couple's awareness, and substitute these reciprocities with adaptive patterns. As observed by Dobson et al. (1988) and by Gotlib and Hammen (1992), the efficacy of treatments based on systemic principles was rarely evaluated. Integrations between systemic and cognitive principles are also rare (Dobson et al., 1988; Teichman & Teichman, 1990). The purpose of this chapter is to present a reciprocal model of depression that is based on an integration of a systems approach and a cognitive approach, to describe the therapy that stems from it, and to review studies that evaluated its efficacy and specific influences.

In summarizing the studies that investigated the efficacy of different types of marital therapy with depressed patients, it is evident that the results are encouraging and point out the potential embedded in this intervention for treating depression. Additionally, it appears that marital therapy is particularly effective in reducing depression of maritally distressed patients, and in increasing marital satisfaction. However, it is important to note that even without differentiating patients according to whether they display evidence of marital distress, favorable results for marital treatment of depression are obtained as well (Friedman, 1975; Haas et al., 1988; Teichman, Bar-El, Shor, Sirota, & Elizur, 1995). The positive results encourage finer theoretical and practical elaborations of these techniques.

THE RECIPROCAL VIEW OF DEPRESSION AND IMPLICATIONS FOR TREATMENT

The reciprocal model of depression proposed by Teichman and Teichman (1990) is based on integration of systems theory (Bertalanffy, 1964), central concepts of cognitive therapy (Beck et al., 1979), and Bandura's (1978) concept of *reciprocal determinism*. The basic assumption of systems theory is that a living organism is a configuration of component parts that are in constant mutual interaction. The *wholeness* of the interdependent parts creates an entity in and of itself that is different from their accumulative sum. This means that looking at isolated parts or summing their characteristics in order to understand the whole would provide only partial information about it. A better way for understanding a system is to examine it as a whole and to understand the transactional processes that take place among its components. In applying these ideas to families Minuchin (1974) wrote, "a family is more than the individual biopsychodynamics of its members. Family members relate according to certain arrangements, which govern their transactions. These arrangements though not explicitly stated or even recognized form a whole—the structure of the family. The reality of the structure is of a different order from the reality of the individual members" (p. 89).

Living systems have *boundaries* that differentiate them from their environment. The openness or closeness of the boundaries determine the level of the ongoing exchange that systems have with their physical environment, and in case of animals and humans, with their social environment as well. A family unit represents a system that is composed of several individuals, each being a differentiated system in her or his own right, a part of one or more subsystems in the family, and of the family as a whole. Each family system organizes its individuals and subsystems in a *structure* that is functional for achieving its goals. The organization may be based on universal dimensions such as gender or age, or idiosyncratic dimensions like specific preferences or interests (Minuchin, 1974).

All events produced by any system are considered to be *communication* and provide a positive or negative *feedback* to others. Positive feedbacks enhance the system's goal-oriented activities whereas negative feedbacks diminish or call for correction of these activities. Negative feedbacks may be as important as positive ones, but this depends on their intensity and frequency. One of the most frequently mentioned issues regarding depressed people is the scarcity of their involvement in positive exchanges with their significant environment (Coyne, 1976a, 1976b; Hops et al., 1987; Lewinsohn, 1974; Lewinsohn, Hoberman, Teri, & Hautzinger, 1985).

An important assumption that is related to the notion of feedback is the assumption regarding *circular causality*, which is preferred by systems theorists over linear causality. Whereas linear causality assumes that *A* causes *B* (psychopathology is caused by childhood experiences or environmental influences), circular causality states that any event affects the system as a whole, and all the elements in the system, including the one that initiated the event. The circular process is continuous and never stops. This means that in a family, each member has a constant influence on other family members, and at the same time, is influenced by them. The reciprocal patterns in systems tend toward stability—*homeostasis*. In family terms, the purpose is to maintain a certain mode of relationships and prevent their change. At the same time, because of being open, at least to some extent, to outside input, systems have a potential for change—*morphogenises*. The compromise between the tendency for stability and change creates a *dynamic homeostasis,* which tolerates small and gradual changes and resists great and sudden changes. This means that as in any other system, families resent change and differ in the way they define small or great change. Systems-theory-oriented therapists try to overcome the resistance and introduce change which affects the repetitive reciprocal patterns, which constitute the reality of the family.

In introducing cognitive therapy, Beck et al. (1979) based their thinking on the idea of feedback. They describe a process in which negative ideation leads to a negative emotion, which is labeled as a sign of inadequacy, helplessness, and hopelessness. This sequence paralyzes the will and ability to act. The depressed person's passivity further strengthens the negative cognitions and dysphoric mood and thereby perpetuates the cycle. Beck and his associates (1979) dealt with feedback and reciprocity, but they viewed the individual as a closed system, and the depression reinforcing process is described in intrapersonal concepts. They see their model as an autonomous cognitive model "that is divorced from the current environmental situation" (p. 22). According to them, "the autonomous cognitive model might be more suitable for developing hypotheses and devising relevant experiments for studying the psychologically disturbed person" (p. 22). Thus, priority was assigned to the individual thinker who was conceived as detached from meaningful context. Accordingly, a basic tenet of cognitive theory of depression is that maladaptive cognitive operations are the primary link in the chain of events that lead to depression. Based on this tenet, in cognitive therapy of depression, the cognitions of the depressed patient are the main target of treatment, and it is assumed that changes in cognitions will initiate changes in depression.

Thus, despite the fact that Beck et al.'s (1979) cognitive model of depression is a reciprocal model that highlights important intrapersonal reciprocities, it excludes the context in which these reciprocities occur, their influence on it and its influence on them. These missing aspects may be supplemented by integrating Beck et al.'s (1979) thinking and Bandura's (1978) concept of reciprocal determinisms. Using what may be called *systemic thinking*, Bandura maintained that internal events, behaviors, and environmental influences operate as elements interlocking with one another, that is, they maintain a continuous reciprocal interaction. These two paradigms complement one another. Whereas Beck et al. (1979) focused on the intrapersonal sphere and neglected the interpersonal aspects, Bandura (1978) minimized intrapersonal processes, with the affective component not receiving any representation in his model. The integration of these two models creates a model which includes four elements: cognitions, affects, behaviors, and environment. Following systems theory, it is suggested that any experience involves a dynamic reciprocal interrelationship among the above elements which constantly influence each other. The outcome of these reciprocities is reflected in all of them and initiates endless cycles of mutual influences on the intrapsychic and interpersonal levels. In every family, the network of the reciprocal patterns forms a unique wholeness which characterizes this family. The basic unit of the reciprocal model applied to an interaction between two individuals that is two spouses, is presented in Fig. 3.1.

According to the model, in each individual cognitions, affects, behaviors, and environmental feedbacks are in constant reciprocal interaction among themselves. The environmental feedback includes the partner's perceived behaviors, affects and the thoughts ascribed to him or her. The cognitions, behaviors, and affects of each partner are determined by his or her own internal reciprocities and at the same time by the interpretations of the cognitions, behaviors, and affects of the other partner. From this perspective, symptoms are created as a result of distorted interpretations that

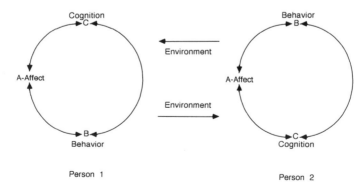

FIG. 3.1. The reciprocal model.

produce dysfunctional reciprocities and relationships. In the case of long-lasting pathology, the distortions are reflected in cognitions, feelings, and behaviors of all the individuals who are involved in a significant relationship and in the transactions among them. Families with members who suffer from pathology or adjustment problems are caught in repetitive cognitive, emotional, behavioral, and interactional reciprocities that maintain the problem. These ideas lead us to consider the patient and his or her interpersonal context in order to search for problem-specific reciprocities and appropriate therapeutic interventions in this context. Although, thus far, biological components have not been mentioned, it goes without saying that biological mechanisms are involved in all the outlined reciprocities, influence them, and are influenced in return. However, the focus of interest of models that underline psychotherapeutic interventions is the conceptual organization of intrapsychic and interpersonal reciprocities.

A therapist who views cognitions, emotions, behaviors, and interactions as interrelated will be interested to discover the reciprocities that maintain the dysfunctionality and to intervene in such a way that the relevant reciprocities will change. The reciprocal model provides a conceptual paradigm for tracing the intrapersonal and interpersonal components involved in maintaining dysfunctionality. This paradigm may serve as a frame of reference for evaluating, defining, and demonstrating to the patients and their family members the underlying reciprocities that guide their personal and interpersonal functioning and elucidate the consequences of these reciprocities. Broadening the insight of each participant regarding their part in maintaining the dysfunctionality may be used to encourage and motivate reevaluations and a search for alternative patterns of interpersonal relationships.

Because the model emphasizes reciprocity, it is possible to assume that change occurring in any of its components will cause change in all of the other components. Indeed, unlike the original cognitive model, this model does not advocate any preferred target for intervention or sequence of change. For each relationship it is the therapist's task to evaluate the full reciprocal pattern, which includes cognitions, emotions, behaviors, and feedback loops, and to lead the patients and their significant others to recognize them and explore alternatives that will lead to better adjustment. It may be suggested that significant therapeutic results will be achieved when the intrapsychic and interpersonal reciprocities change.

The primary assumption of this model of depression is that the interpersonal context of the depressed person is affected by his or her depression and affects it in return. The effect of depression can be observed on the cognitive, affective, and behavioral levels of each of the individuals involved as well as in their reciprocal transactions. Thus, the therapeutic process ought to take place within significant interpersonal contexts, the most significant of which is the marital relationship, and should aim to change the dysfunctional reciprocities that maintain depression. Based on the literature referring to depression (Coyne, 1976a, 1976b; Feldman, 1976; Lewinsohn, 1974; Lewinsohn et al., 1985), and their own experience, Teichman and Teichman (1990) identified three patterns of dysfunctional reciprocities and referred to them as *context-related interpersonal mechanisms* that maintain depression. These mechanisms are: overprotection, hostility or ambivalence in the couple's relationship, and complementarity of dysfunctional needs, such as self-enhancement, mutual dependency, or irrational role assignment. In each of these mechanisms, specific intra- and interpersonal reciprocities of cognitions, affects, and behaviors may be identified. These concepts are used to define and trace with the patients and their spouses the underlying reciprocities in which they are involved and to elucidate the consequences of these reciprocities. The primary aim is to increase the insight of the spouses regarding their respective part in maintaining the depression, and then to motivate search for alternative reciprocal patterns. The approach is structured, limited to 15 sessions, and provides specific guidelines for choosing priorities, that is, for focusing on the cognitive, affective, behavioral, and interactive aspects of the depression-maintaining mechanisms already discussed. The implication is that change in the depressed patient is insufficient and it must be accompanied by changes in significant others with whom the patient is involved and in their reciprocities. The depression-maintaining mechanisms are described in more detail in the following discussion.

In dyads in which depression elicits *overprotection* toward the depressed patient, a reciprocal pattern emerges that creates or validates for the depressed patients self-deprecating cognitions and perceptions of others as resourceful and competent. A husband of a depressed woman who said "she was born as a premature baby, and remained one all through her life," expressed a view of his wife as being utterly incapable of dealing with life problems or stress. He became so involved in "protecting" and "helping" her that, in order to spare her, he assumed all responsibilities at home, to the extent of preventing her from answering the phone. The wife identified her husband's cognitions about her, perceived his concern and behaviors, and interpreted them as validating her own low expectations from herself. She became more depressed, passive, and dependent. Her passivity elicited more activity from him and this continued to stabilize the depression-reinforcing cycle.

The clinical observations described here were empirically validated in studies that performed controlled observations in the homes of depressed patients. Biglan et al. (1985) and Hops et al. (1987) reported that depressed women's dysphoric affect lowered the probability that their husbands and children would express aggressive affect toward them, and that men whose wives were depressed displayed higher rates of *care* toward their children than men whose wives were not depressed. Similar findings were reported by Zaslow, Pedersen, Cain, Suwalsky, and Kramer (1985), who studied behaviors of mothers toward infants when the father was depressed. These findings represent situations in which due to the depression of one parent the other assumes a more active role, possibly further damaging the competence, image, and feelings of both partners and contributing to exacerbating the depression.

When depression elicits *hostility* or criticism toward the depressed patient a similar pattern can be detected. Accusations such as, "if you wanted you could cooperate," "you always spoil the best plans," and "because of you we never do things" convey disappointment and rejection, which reinforce the depressed patient's negative self-image and maintain the discrepancy between self-perception and significant others' images. This causes negative feelings in both spouses, most likely reinforces depression in the depressed patient and further negative or ambivalent feelings in the spouse, as well as withdrawal from one another. Both partners' interpretations of their own and each other's intrapersonal sequences produce a "more of the same" pattern, and strengthen the depression. Coyne (1984) described this interactional sequence between the depressed person and his or her spouse as follows:

> Depressed persons elicit displays of support, reduce demands and inhibit hostility from others by conveying their distress. Significant others for their part, temporarily reduce the aversiveness of depressed persons by seemingly providing what is being asked, even while their growing impatience, hostility and withdrawal leak to the depressed person. The subtle and overt hostility and rejection that the depressed person thus receives elicits further expression of distress, strengthening the pattern. (pp. 53–54)

When we deal with *complementarity of dysfunctional* needs such as self-enhancement needs, mutual dependency, and irrational role assignment, we encounter the same reciprocal patterns, but they stem from more general personal predispositions rather than from the depression of one of the spouses. Feldman (1976) referred to this situation as related to "unconscious needs." In these cases depression reinforces the personal predispositions and is reinforced by them. For example a depressed patient and spouse both may suffer from very low self-esteem and construe themselves as failures. In order to enhance their self-esteem they may create a reciprocal interaction that involves both overprotection and criticism. The overprotected depressed person enhances his or her self-esteem by eliciting care and concern from the nondepressed spouse while the protecting spouse enhances his or her worth by providing care. Often other family members and friends reinforce this pattern by expressing respect toward the faithfulness and loyalty of the care provider. All of these elements contribute to enhance the self-esteem of both spouses. The "protector" receives direct social recognition, whereas the "protected" feels more valuable by being cared for by a partner who gains social respect. In this sequence of events there eventually comes a point in which the depressed patient's image is restored to the point that his or her mood becomes more positive, and he or she becomes more active and self-sufficient. At this point the nondepressed spouse feels threatened and becomes critical and hostile. This initiates the previously described hostility-related reciprocities. Depression reoccurs and triggers a new overprotection or caring cycle, which is substituted by a hostility cycle, and so on. When this type of reciprocity between spouses is detected it is logical to assume that short-term intervention will not be able to change patterns that are nourished by deeply rooted intrapersonal problems. In these cases, marital therapy has to be more dynamically oriented and, most probably, longer.

The interpersonal depression-maintaining mechanisms were described as separate mechanisms. However, it has to be pointed out that they should not be viewed as mutually exclusive. In some families only one of them may be identified, in others more may coexist. Coyne (1984) mentioned the possibility of displaying both hostility and positive affects toward depressed people and termed it *ambivalence* toward the depressed patient. Indeed, the most common combination we have observed is hostility and overprotection. This combination may be attributed to guilt feelings which develop as a result of displaying hostility toward a weak and suffering depressed member of the family.

In treating patients and spouses and enlightening them regarding their intra- and interpersonal reciprocities, we work toward achieving change in thinking about self and other, in ideas about the relationship, in emotional and behavioral reactions, and in expanding awareness toward the interpretations of feedbacks stemming from different levels. Because this approach integrates cognitive and systemic principles, we refer to it as cognitive marital therapy (CMT). Believing that in working with couples, it is impossible to impose rigid structure, we did not develop a session-by-session treatment manual, but the treatment protocol was clearly outlined. The therapists are trained to identify the mechanism, or mechanisms which operate in each couple to recognize the specific personal and interpersonal reciprocities of cognitions, affects and behaviors which are involved, to expand the spouses' awareness of their unique intra- and interpersonal reciprocities, and to help them substitute them with more functional reciprocities. Both spouses participate together in all sessions.

The first attempt to evaluate the efficacy of this therapeutic procedure was performed by comparing it with individual cognitive therapy (CT) and no intervention (Teichman et al., 1995). Results indicated that CMT produced quicker reduction of depression than individual CT, and was more effective in reducing depression to recovery criterion. At 6-month follow-up there was no difference between the two psychotherapy groups. After treatment, spouses of depressed patients reported reduction in depression only in the CMT group. Surprisingly, the depression level of spouses of patients in the traditional cognitive therapy group elevated significantly at the after-treatment evaluation. At follow-up spouses of patients reported similar levels of depression in all the investigated groups. These results indicate that both patients and spouses react differently to different treatments. Assuming that the relationship between patient and spouse plays a role in the patient's depression or recovery from it, the reactions of spouses to different types of therapy become important as well.

Following the previously described results, an additional comparison was performed, a comparison with traditional drug therapy involving tricyclic antidepressants, mainly Amitriptyline. This evaluation is important because it enables us to compare the effectiveness of the new approach with a reference treatment that previously demonstrated efficacy with depressed patients. In the following section, the comparison of the two psychotherapy groups (CMT and CT), with a pharmacotherapy (PT) group, and no treatment group (NT) is described. Additionally, in an attempt to assess the effect of the compared treatments on changes in variables related to one of the outlined depression-maintaining mechanisms, changes in patients' and spouses' *hostility* were evaluated. We consider hostility ascribed by patient and spouse to self and other before treatment, after treatment, and at follow-up.

CHANGES IN PATIENTS' AND SPOUSES' DEPRESSION

Patients' and spouses' reactions to the different treatments were evaluated by comparing depression levels as reflected in the Beck Depression Inventory (BDI; Beck, Ward, Mendelson, Mock, & Erbaugh, 1961), before treatment, after treatment, and at 6-month follow-up.

The final sample we studied included 60 patients and their spouses. They were recruited from an outpatient clinic in a large mental health hospital in Israel, serving mainly middle and lower middle class communities. Patients who met *DSM-III-R* (American Psychiatric Association, 1987) criteria for major depression (MD) or dysthymia (D) and who scored 16 or above on the BDI were included in the study. The final sample included 36 patients diagnosed as suffering from MD and 24 as suffering from D. The spouses of all patients had to agree to participate in evaluations, and when invited, in therapy as well. Thirty-one of the patients were females, and 29 were males. The male–female ratio in the groups was comparable (chi-square not significant). Patients ranged in age from 28 to 65 ($M = 46.6$). Spouses ranged in age from 24 to 65 ($M = 44.5$). Marriage length ranged from 3 to 38 years ($M = 16.1$). One-way analyses of variance (ANOVAs) on means of patients' and spouses' age and length of marriage did not reach significance in the different groups.

Patients were assigned to three treatment groups, CT, CMT, and PT. A no treatment (NT) waiting list group was added when conditions in the clinic did not allow additional assignment of patients to the previous groups. Assignment to treatment groups was determined by therapist availability. The groups were matched on diagnosis and number of patients who received medications.

A total of 24 therapists participated in the study: 9 psychiatrists, 5 psychologists, and 10 psychiatric social workers. Pharmacotherapy was provided by 5 psychiatrists. The other 4 psychiatrists, the psychologists, and social workers were almost equally represented in the two other treatment groups. Nineteen of the therapists were women, and 5 were men with a mean age of 38.1. The mean clinical experience of therapists was 8.57 years.

Therapists were assigned to treatments on the basis of personal preference and treated patients only in one treatment modality. Each therapist treated 1 to 3 patients. Therapists who chose to deliver one of the psychological treatments committed themselves to participate in an introductory seminar (6–8 hours) that presented the theory and techniques of the treatment they delivered, to practice these techniques, to record or videotape therapy sessions, and to participate in group supervision sessions on a weekly basis. The meetings were used to expand learning, increase treatment efficacy, and assure treatment adherence. Supervision was based on verbal reports of therapists, and audio or video tapes.

Psychotherapy treatments were planned to last for 15 weeks, but in several cases were terminated after a shorter time. The average number of sessions was 12.95. Therapy was provided on a weekly basis, but toward termination, therapists had the option to schedule sessions every second week. Pharmacotherapy, on the other hand, was planned to last 12 weeks. The average number of sessions was 10.6.

The rationale, goals, and techniques of CMT were described earlier. Individual CT was conducted according to the guidelines described by Beck et al. (1979). The supervisor of this group was trained in the Center for Cognitive Therapy in Philadelphia, and is strongly identified with the technique. The medications prescribed to patients in the PT group were tricyclic antidepressants, mainly Amitriptyline. The dosage of medications were within the accepted therapeutic range and were prescribed for 8 to 12 weeks. The psychiatrists who prescribed the medications and supervised their effects met with the patients once a week and did not engage in therapeutic interventions aside from expressing general interest, support, and, when needed, advice. The meetings lasted about 20 minutes. The NT group was actually a waiting list group. It was composed of patients who, due to lack of therapist availability, had to wait for treatment for approximately 3 months. These patients were evaluated during their first visit to the clinic, provided with routine guidance or, if needed, with medications, and were reevaluated before the onset of their therapy. After the second evaluation these patients were excluded from the research. As such, only evaluations conducted before and after waiting were used in examining the NT group.

Outcome: Patients

Figure 3.2 presents the means of BDI scores of patients and spouses in the four compared groups in the three evaluations for the therapy groups and the two evaluations for the NT group. Although the initial level of patients' and spouses' depression in the different groups did not differ significantly, the scores obtained in the after-treatment and follow-up evaluations were compared by analysis of covariance (ANCOVA). The initial levels of depression were the covariates. The before-treatment scores represent raw means while the after-treatment and follow-up means are adjusted means derived from the analysis of covariance procedure.

The after-treatment ANCOVA on patients' mean BDI scores yielded a significant result, $F(3, 56) = 4.22$, $p = .009$. Contrast comparisons among pairs of groups indicated that the CMT group reported a close-to-significant ($p < .10$) and lower level of depression than the other three groups. The differences between CT and PT groups and between them and the NT group were not significant. At follow-up, the ANCOVA result was also significant, $F(2, 31) = 7.82$, $p = .002$. Contrast comparisons indicated that the CMT and CT groups reported a significantly lower level of depression than the PT group, $p < .01$ and $p < .05$, respectively. At this stage the comparison CMT–CT groups did not reach significance.

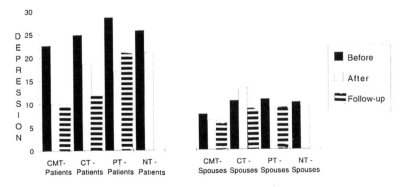

FIG. 3.2. Patients' and spouses' depression scores.

It should be noted that in order to protect against Type I error, in all the post hoc comparisons of pairs of treatments, the Bonferroni correction was applied (p value was divided by the number of the performed comparisons). This means that for the after-treatment comparisons we report as approaching significance comparisons which reached at least $p = .01$, and for the follow-up, comparisons that reached at least $p = .03$. Using this stringent significance criterion allows the consideration of close-to-significant results.

After looking at group differences in patients after treatment and at follow-up, it was important to establish whether the decreases in depression reached a level that may be defined as a recovery level. Comparable to previous studies, the recovery criterion was defined as obtaining a post-therapy BDI score of 10 or less. Due to small numbers of recovered patients according to this criterion, in most of the groups, our analysis was performed on numbers of unrecovered patients in each group. Table 3.1 presents the proportion of unrecovered patients in the different groups in the two evaluations, and the respective chi-square values. As can be seen in Table 3.1, in both evaluations, the highest recovery proportion occurred in the CMT group; the next highest recovery was in the CT group. In the two other groups recovery was minimal and did not last.

The findings of the comparative analysis in the patients' sample indicate that although all treatments were effective in reducing depression, especially in the long term, CMT was more effective than the other interventions. After treatment, the level of depression was lower than in the two other treatment groups. It was also the only group that proved to be superior to the control group. When the recovery criterion was applied, the efficacy of CMT became even more evident, having succeeded in reducing depression to recovery level in a significantly greater proportion of patients than the other groups.

TABLE 3.1
Unrecovered Patients by Evaluative Group

CMT	CT	PT	NT	df	χ^2
		After Treatment			
5 (15) 33.0%	13 (15) 86.6%	14 (15) 93.3%	14 (15) 93.3%	3	21.24[b]
		At Follow-Up			
5 (12) 41.6%	6 (11) 54.5%	12(12) 100.0%		2	9.95[a]

Note. [a]$p < .05$, [b]$p < .001$.

In the long term, CMT proved the most efficient intervention modality both in reducing depression level and increasing recovery proportion. In this stage, however, patients in this group reported a significantly lower level of depression only when compared with patients in the PT group. Additionally, meaningful differentiations emerged between CT and PT. Patients who received CT manifested a reduction in depression level, reaching a significantly lower level of depression than that reported by patients in the PT group and almost the same recovery rates as the CMT group. In this stage, patients in the PT group still reported a significantly lower level of depression than in their initial evaluation, but the trend started to change and an elevation in depression (though not significant) was observed.

The relatively slow effect demonstrated by CT in this study does not correspond to findings reported in previous studies. This difference may plausibly be attributed to the fact that the sample in this study was composed of relatively older subjects (average age in the CT group 43.5). As indicated in a metaanalysis study (Dobson, 1989), in 22 studies which evaluated outcome of CT and reported subjects' age, a significant negative correlation was obtained between age and clients' improvement in CT. It is important to mention, however, that despite the slower manifestation of improvement, the effects of treatment in this group were long lasting.

Looking at the changes in patients' depression in the three treatment groups, in the three evaluations, it is interesting to note that the trend of a lower depression level, that was manifested after treatment in the two groups which received psychological treatments, continued through the follow-up stage. On the other hand, the PT group demonstrated an opposite trend. Apparently, while the psychological treatments had an effect which continued to reduce depression after treatment's termination, pharmacotherapy reduced patients' depression only as long as it lasted. This replicates Friedman's (1975) findings following a comparison of marital therapy and pharmacotherapy applied to depressed patients, and Hollon, Shelton, and Loosen's (1991) contention that, in treating depression, pharmacotherapy has a lower preventative potential than psychotherapy.

Outcome: Spouses

Spouses' BDI scores in all the groups, in all evaluations, were within the normal range, and much lower than patients' scores. Looking at data obtained from spouses (Fig. 3.2) it is interesting to note that our results differ from previously reported findings (Coyne, Kessler, Tal, Turnbull, & Wortman, 1987; Krantz & Moos, 1987; Mitchell, Cronkite, & Moos, 1983). Although it was not confirmed that living with a depressed person elevates spouses' depression beyond normal range, there are enough findings in the literature that indicate that spouses of depressed patients experience distress. This distress may be expressed in physical or psychological symptoms, other than depression.

The group effect obtained from the ANCOVA performed on after-treatment mean BDI scores was significant, $F(3, 56) = 9.70$, $p < .000$; the follow-up comparison did not reach significance. When the actual changes, in the after treatment evaluation, are examined it appears that changes occurred in the CT and CMT groups, although in opposite directions. While after-treatment, spouses in the CT group reported a close to significance elevation in depression, $t(14) = 1.86$, $p = .08$, spouses in the CMT group reported a close to significance decrease in depression, $t(14) = 2.01$, $p = .06$. These opposite trends, created a significant difference between these groups. Indeed, contrasts comparisons among pairs of groups indicated that, in this stage, spouses who participated in CMT reported a significantly lower ($p < .05$) level of depression than spouses in the CT group. Also, spouses in the CT group reported a significantly higher depression level than spouses in all the other groups. Because the ANCOVA results in the follow-up of the spouses sample did not reach significance level, multiple comparisons between pairs of groups were not performed.

The two findings obtained regarding spouses' low level of depression and low variability in depression may be related. That is, the relative stability in depression might be attributed to its initially low level, or to a "floor effect." With this in mind, it is interesting to examine what caused the changes in spouses' depression in the CMT and CT groups. The change demonstrated by spouses in the CMT group was in accordance with our expectation: Spouses who actively participated in therapy received tools to understand and affect their own and their spouse's moods. It is plausible to assume that they observed the changes in their initially depressed spouses and could perceive themselves as contributing to this change. This may have encouraged them and reduced their depression. It is more difficult, however, to explain the opposite trend manifested by spouses in the CT group. A plausible explanation may be found in the process which occurred in the patients in this group. It was noted previously that, in the CT group, the significant change in patients' depression and patients' reaching recovery criterion occurred only in the follow-up stage. Thus, spouses, who after treatment did not experience a clear change in their partners and who themselves did not participate in the treatment, might have felt discouraged about the prospect of the treatment's outcome. This discouragement might have caused an elevation in their depression. Only in the long term, when patients in this group manifested a positive change in their depression level, and many of them reached recovery, the spouses reacted in a similar fashion.

Spouses in the PT and NT groups reacted positively, though not at statistically significant levels to the fact that their partners either received medications or established contact with a clinic. Spouses in the PT group actually observed a quick change in the depression level of their partners.

Spouses in the NT group did not have any grounds to expect change. Apparently, the mere prospect of intervention helped their feelings. This suggests that the significant influence on spouses' depression has to be attributed mainly to their active participation in the treatment. Observing or hoping for change helps, but is less effective.

A comprehensive look at the trends in patients' and spouses' changes in depression in the research groups suggests that mutual influences of spouses on each other's mood occur. This supports a systems perspective and demonstrates the importance of including both spouses in therapy as well as viewing both of them as agents of change. Thus, involvement of a spouse may be considered as a specific contributing factor to outcome.

HOSTILITY: PATIENTS AND SPOUSES

Influences of the different treatments on self-ascribed hostility by patients and spouses and the hostility they ascribed to each other were evaluated by three subscales of the Buss and Durkee Hostility–Guilt Inventory (1957). Subscales that represent expression of hostility (Indirect Hostility, Irritability, Verbal Hostility), were used. Figures 3.3 and 3.4 present the mean hostility scores obtained from the three subscales. Figure 3.3 presents self-ascribed hostility by patients and spouses, and Fig. 3.4 presents the hostility they ascribed to each other. In the initial, pretreatment evaluations no significant differences were detected among groups on level of patients' and spouses' self-ascribed hostility or on perceived level of patients' hostility by spouses. However, patients in the PT group perceived their partners as more hostile than patients in the other groups, $F(3, 56) = 2.76$, $p < .05$. Using ANCOVA, the initial difference among groups on this variable, were accounted for.

Looking at the different aspects of hostility, different trends emerge for patients and spouses, and for short-term and long-term comparisons. Pa-

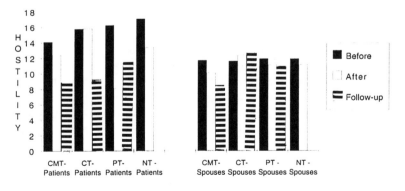

FIG. 3.3. Patients' and spouses' hostility scores.

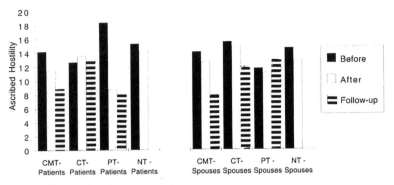

FIG. 3.4. Ascribed hostility by patients and spouses to each other.

tients manifest more significant results than spouses, and different treatments seem to affect hostility differently at different times. After treatment, the level of hostility of patients in the compared groups differed significantly, $F(3, 56) = 4.63$, $p < .001$. Contrasts comparisons of pairs of groups, indicated that patients who received medications had significantly lower level of hostility than patients in the CT and NT groups. However the difference between them and patients in the CMT group did not reach significance. In the follow-up evaluation the differences among groups did not reach significance. The second measure obtained from patients—the hostility they attributed to their spouses, after treatment—showed the same trend: Differences among groups were significant, $F(3, 56) = 5.60$, $p < .001$. Specific groups comparison indicated that patients who received medications ascribed significantly lower level of hostility to spouse than patients in the CMT, CT, and NT groups. In the follow-up, the comparisons among groups were still significant, $F(2, 31) = 5.08$, $p = < .01$ but the PT group reported significantly lower perceived hostility of spouse only in comparison with the CT group. Additionally the CMT group reported significantly lower spouse hostility than the CT group.

Considering spouses, it appears that differences in their hostility became significant only in the follow-up comparison, $F(2, 31) = 3.95$, $p < .05$. The significant difference between groups was obtained only in the comparison of the psychotherapy groups, namely, the hostility level of spouses in the CMT group was lower than in the CT group. Perceived spouse hostility by spouses of patients did not differ significantly in the after-treatment comparison, but in follow-up the differences among groups were significant, $F(2, 31) = 4.98$, $p < .01$. In this comparison, spouses of patients in the CMT group reported that they ascribed a significantly lower level of hostility to the patients than spouses in the PT group.

Summarizing the results regarding the different aspects of hostility that were evaluated in this study, it can be stated that the two treatments that reduced significantly self- and spouse-ascribed hostility were PT and CMT. The first had only a direct effect on patients, and it was manifested mainly in the short-term evaluation while the second affected both patients and spouses, and its effects appeared only in the long term. These findings suggest that in producing changes on the biochemical level, PT influences not only moods (depression), but also different aspects of hostility. However, the fact that the changes lasted only as long as medications were provided, supports the finding that drug treatments have a short-term influence (Friedman, 1975; and Hollon et al.'s review, 1991). On the other hand, the marital intervention which was utilized in this study, was capable of initiating in both patients and spouses new ways of experiencing and dealing with their own and their spouses' hostility. The fact that CMT reduced both self- and spouse-ascribed hostility, and that these changes became evident after treatment was discontinued suggests that the therapeutic intervention initiated a process which gradually established new hostility-related reciprocities. Integrating these findings with findings which indicate that marital discord precipitates the onset of depressive symptoms (Beach et al., 1990), and that relapse of depressed patients is related to critical attitude of their spouses and to patients' view of their spouses as critical (Hooley & Teasdale, 1989), points out the relevance of identifying expressed and perceived hostility in the marital system of depressed patients as a depression-maintaining mechanism, and directing therapeutic interventions at the different dimensions of hostility.

Finally, on the theoretical level it may be mentioned that two theoretical models deal with the role of hostility in depression. The psychoanalytic school suggests that depression is caused due to introjection and inhibition of aggression. An alternative hypothesis was formulated by theorists who represent the systems approach to depression. These theorists view hostility as a maintaining mechanism of depression rather than its cause. According to this view, one of the main depression-maintaining mechanisms is continuous experiences related to self- and other-attributed hostility by depressed patients and their spouses. Thus the problem is not internally directed aggression, but experienced hostility by both spouses within the marital system. The reported findings, offer support to the second view. The group which demonstrated long-term changes in self- and other-ascribed hostility, was the group which, at termination and follow-up, reported lowest depression scores, and highest recovery rates. On the other hand, the short-term influence of drugs on depressed mood and different aspects of hostility, brings to attention the fact that pharmacotherapy has the same potential. As already suggested by Hollon et al. (1991), a continuation of medications following remission, may help prolong the effects of this treatment. This in turn may provide a longer opportunity for controlling hostility related experiences, establishing different reciprocities with significant others, and preventing relapse or recurrence of a depressive episode.

CONCLUSIONS

From a theoretical point of view this study supports the interpersonal view of depression which highlights the importance of patient–significant other reciprocities in maintaining or reducing depression. It demonstrates that an interpersonal intervention approach which focuses on interpersonal depression maintaining mechanisms has noticeable potential for reducing patients' depression to recovery level, for influencing positively spouses' level of depression, and for changing hostility patterns in marital dyads. Moreover, the study demonstrates that rather than adopting an either–or orientation regarding the interpersonal and cognitive views of depression (Coyne et al., 1987), a theoretical integration between these views may be achieved and might serve as a basis for a new interpersonal treatment modality. Our findings also suggest that interweaving pharmacological interventions with interpersonal treatments also has a potential for facilitating a remission from or cure of depression.

REFERENCES

American Psychiatric Association. (1987). *Diagnostic and Statistical Manual of Mental Disorders-III-R*. Washington, DC: Author.

Bandura, A. (1978). The self system in reciprocal determinism. *American Psychologist, 33*, 344–358.

Beck, A. T., Rush, A. J., Shaw, B. L., & Emery, G. (1979). *Cognitive therapy of depression*. New York: Guilford Press.

Beck, A. T., Ward, C., Mendelson, M., Mock, J., & Erbaugh, J. (1961). An inventory for measurement depression. *Archives of General Psychiatry, 4*, 561–571.

Beach, S. R. H., & O'Leary, K. D. (1986). The treatment of depression occurring in the context of marital discord. *Behavior Therapy, 17*, 43–49.

Beach, S. R. H., Sandeen, E. E., & O'Leary, K. D. (1990). *Depression in marriage*. New York: Guilford.

Bertalanffy, L. A. (1968). *General systems theory: Foundation, developments, applications*. New York: Braziller.

Biglan, A., Hops, H., Sherman, L., Friedman, L. S., Arthur, J., & Osteen, V. (1985). Problem solving interactions of depressed women and their husbands. *Behavior Therapy, 16*, 431–451.

Buss, A. H., & Durkee, A. (1957). An inventory for assessing different kinds of hostility. *Journal of Consulting Psychology, 21*, 343–349.

Collins, J., Kreitman, N., Nelson, B., & Troop, J. (1971). Neurosis and marital interaction III. Family roles and functions. *British Journal of Psychiatry, 119*, 233–242.

Coyne, J. C. (1976a). Depression and the reponse of others. *Journal of Abnormal Psychology, 85*, 186–193.

Coyne, J. C. (1976b). Toward an interactional description of depression. *Psychiatry, 39*, 28–40.

Coyne, J. C. (1984). Strategic therapy with depressed married persons: Initial agenda, themes and interventions. *Journal of Marital & Family Therapy, 10*, 53–62.

Coyne, J. C. (1988). Strategic therapy. In J. F. Clarkin, G. L. Haas, & I. D. Glick (Eds.), *Affective disorders and the family, assessment and treatment* (pp. 89–113). New York: Guilford.

Coyne, J. C., Kessler, R. C., Tal, M., Turnbull, J., & Wortman, C. B. (1987). Living with a depressed person. *Journal of Consulting & Clinical Psychology, 55*, 347–352.

Crowther, J. H. (1985). The relationship between depression and marital maladjustment. A descriptive study. *The Journal of Nervous and Mental Diseases, 173,* 227–231.

Dobson, K. S. (1989). A meta-analysis of the efficacy of cognitive therapy for depression. *Journal of Consulting & Clinical Psychology, 57,* 414–419.

Dobson, K. S., Jacobson, N. S., & Victor, J. (1988). Integration of cognitive therapy and behavioral marital therapy. In J. F. Clarkin, G. L. Haas, & I. D. Glick (Eds.), *Affective disorders and the family, assessment and treatment* (pp. 53–88). New York: Guilford.

Feldman, L. B. (1976). Depression and marital interaction. *Family Process, 15,* 389–395.

Foley, S. H., Rounsaville, B. J., Weissman, M. M., Sholomskas, D., & Chevron, E. (1989). Individual versus conjoint interpersonal psychotherapy for depressed patients with marital disputes. *International Journal of Family Psychiatry, 10,* 29–42.

Friedman, A. S. (1975). Interaction of drug therapy and marital therapy in depressive patients. *Archives of General Psychiatry, 32,* 619–637.

Glick, I. D., Clarkin, J. F., Spencer, J. H., Haas, G. L., Lewis, A. B., Peyser, J., DeMane, N., Good-Ellis, M., Harris, E., & Lestelle, V. (1985). A controlled evaluation of inpatient family intervention: I. Preliminary results of the six-month follow-up. *Archives of General Psychiatry, 42,* 882–886.

Gotlib, I. H., & Colby, C. A. (1987). *Treatment of depression: An interpersonal systems approach.* New York: Pergamon.

Gotlib, I. H., & Hammen, C. L. (1992). *Psychological aspects of depression: Towards a cognitive–interpersonal integration.* Chichester: Wiley.

Haas, G. L., Glick, I. D., Clarkin, J. F., Spencer, J. H., Lewis, A. B., Peyser, J., DeMane, N., Good-Ellis, M., Harris, E., & Lestelle, V. (1988). Inpatient family intervention: A randomized clinical trial. II. Results at hospital discharge. *Archives of General Psychiatry, 45,* 217–224.

Hautzinger, M., Linden, M., & Hoffman, N. (1982). Distressed couples with and without a depressed partner: An analysis of their verbal interaction. *Journal Behavior Therapy & Experimental Psychiatry, 13,* 307–314.

Hinchliffe, M. K., Hooper, D., & Roberts, F. J. (1978). *The melancholy marriage: Depression in marriage and psychosocial approaches to therapy.* New York: Wiley.

Hollon, S. D., Shelton, R. C., & Loosen, P. T. (1991). Cognitive therapy and pharmacotherapy for depression. *Journal of Consulting & Clinical Psychology, 59,* 88–99.

Hops, H., Biglan, A., Sherman, L., Arthur, J., Friedman, L. S., & Osteen, V. (1987). Home observations of family interactions of depressed women. *Journal of Consulting & Clinical Psychology, 55,* 341–346.

Hooley, J. M., & Teasdale, J. D. (1989). Predictors of relapse in unipolar depressives: Expressed emotion, marital distress, and perceived criticism. *Journal of Abnormal Psychology, 98,* 229–237.

Jacobson, N. S., Dobson, K., Fruzzetti, A. E., Schmaling, K. B., & Salusky, S. (1991). Marital therapy as a treatment of depression. *Journal of Consulting & Clinical Psychology, 59,* 547–557.

Jacobson, N. S., & Margolin, G. (1979). *Marital therapy, Strategies based on social learning and behavior exchange principles.* New York: Brunner/Mazel.

Klerman, G. L., Weissman, M. M., Rounsaville, B. J., & Chevron, E. S. (1984). *Interpersonal psychotherapy of depression.* New York: Basic Books.

Krantz, S. E., & Moos, R. H. (1987). Functioning and life context among spouses of remitted and nonremitted depressed patients. *Journal of Consulting & Clinical Psychology, 55,* 353–360.

Lewinsohn, P. M. (1974). A behavioral approach to depression. In R. J. Friedman & M. M. Katz (Eds.), *The psychology of depression: Contemporary theory and research* (pp. 157–185). New York: Wiley.

Lewinsohn, P. M., Hoberman, H., Teri, L., & Hautzinger, M. (1985). An integrative theory of depression. In S. Reiss & R. Bootzin (Eds.), *Theoretical issues in behavior therapy* (pp. 331–359). New York: Academic Press.

McLean, P. D., Ogston, L., & Grauer, L. (1973). Behavioral approach to the treatment of depression. *Journal of Behavioral Therapy and Experimental Psychiatry, 4,* 323–330.

Merikangas, K. R., Prusoff, B. A., Kupfer, D. J., & Frank, E. (1985). Marital adjustment in major depression. *Journal of Affective Disorder, 9*, 5–11.

Minuchin, S. (1974). *Families and family therapy.* Cambridge, MA: Harvard University Press.

Mitchell, R. E., Cronkite, R. C., & Moos, R. H. (1983). Stress coping and depression among married couples. *Journal of Abnormal Psychology, 92*, 433–448.

O'Leary, K. D., & Beach, S. R. H. (1990). Marital therapy: A viable treatment for depression and marital discord. *American Journal of Psychiatry, 147*, 183–186.

Rush, A. J., Shaw, B., & Khatami, M. (1980). Cognitive therapy of depression: Utilizing the couples system. *Cognitive Therapy & Research, 4*, 103–113.

Teichman, Y., Bar-El, Z., Shor, H., Sirota, P., & Elitzur, A. (1995). A comparison of two modalities of cognitive therapy (individual and marital), in treating depression. *Psychiatry, 58*, 136–148.

Teichman, Y., & Teichman, M. (1990). Interpersonal view of depression: Review and integration. *Journal of Family Psychology, 3*, 349–367.

Weissman, M. M., & Paykel, E. S. (1974). *The depressed woman: A study of social relationships.* Chicago, IL: University of Chicago Press.

Zaslow, M. J., Pedersen, F. A., Cain, R. L., Suwalsky, J. T. D., & Kramer, E. L. (1985). Depressed mood in new fathers: Associations with parent–infant interactions. *Genetic, Social, and General Psychology Monographs, 111*, 133–150.

CHANGING ROLES AND STRUCTURES IN THE FAMILY

4

FAMILY RELATIONSHIPS AND LIFE COURSE STRATEGIES FOR THE 21ST CENTURY

Frances K. Goldscheider
Brown University

The purpose of this chapter is to consider how demographic change is shaping the family of the 21st century. However, to understand the context in which to view families at the end of the 20th century, it is necessary to consider the following: A popular psychology magazine in the United States presented some frequently found research results showing that death rates are lower for married people than single people, and that this difference is greater for men than for women (Horn, 1977). The piece was headed with a cartoon, showing the comedian and film director, Woody Allen, sitting at a bar with Sigmund Freud. Allen is asking Freud: "Is it true that married men live longer?" Freud replies, "No, it just feels longer." This cartoon is an antifamily denial of the profamily research results. It is a male-centered antifamily denial of the particularly strong profamily results for men. The analysis of demographic change serves to elaborate this point.

This chapter discusses how demographic changes affect the family and will continue to multiply their impact over the next several generations. I review the effects of the decline in fertility and the extension of the life course to demonstrate that massive changes are coming but that change is necessarily uneven, with some changes occurring very rapidly and others taking several generations. The primary focus of the presentation emphasizes three aspects: (a) the increased potential length of family relationships; (b) the need for extreme transformations in these relationships if they are to achieve their potential increased length; and (c) the reduced focus on parenting roles and on hierarchical relationships between men and women and between parents and their children.

As Arlene Skolnick (chapter 10, this volume) wrote in clear, nondemographic images, the decline in mortality and fertility rates known as the *demographic transition* has a dramatic effect on the age structure of a population, transforming it from a pyramid, with many young people and few older ones, to a rectangle with similar proportions of people in each age group. It is this transformation that underlies the changes presented here, and they mean that we cannot go back—to the family of 18th century Poland with its many children and segregated gender roles, or even to the family of the United States in the 1950s. If we want to maintain low mortality rates, if we do not want a population explosion, we must accept low fertility. As a result, caring for the young can no longer be a full-time career for one half of the adult population.

THE EXTENSION OF JOINT SURVIVORSHIP

The challenge resulting from these demographic processes is the refashioning of family relationships to take into account the enormous growth in their duration. Demographers commonly focus research on length of life on the increase in life expectancy for individuals, which has more than doubled in the last century. It is also not difficult to calculate measures of joint survivorship—how long after marriage both a husband and wife will live (and assuming no divorce, will live together); or how long parents and children will survive together—although this is much less commonly done.

The few calculations that have been made are normally used to illustrate arguments about growth in old age dependency and burden. To take one example, on average, women can now expect their mothers to live 55 years after their own birth. This has been interpreted as meaning that daughters now live many years with an elderly mother and that women will spend more time caring for a parent over age 65 than for a child under 18 (Mencken, 1985). Similarly, one third of couples who marry before age 25 can expect to reach their golden wedding anniversary. But will they still be able to relate to each other? For these added years to involve continuous, strong, family relationships, considerable transformation will be necessary in both male–female and parent–child relationships.

Parent–Child Relationships

I first consider the easier case—parent–adult child relationships. Nearly two thirds of the joint years women survive with their mothers are spent when they are each adults.[1] As a result, people live not only long enough to see their

---

[1]The same phenomenon characterizes males, although not so dramatically, because children are born later in their father's lives than their mother's, and men have lower life expectancy than women.

children grow up but are also often present and in good health when their grandchildren marry. Rather than interpreting these new facts by extending our metaphors of hierarchy and dependency, these changes should tell us that the lengthening of the potential duration of familial relationships will require a change in their character, increasing their flexibility and reducing their hierarchical nature, if they are to continue to provide the satisfactions that enduring family ties can contribute to human life.

The working out of this new reality of joint parent–child survivorship is exemplified in the slowing of generational succession. To assume hereditary responsibilities, a child may need to wait to age 50 or 60 or beyond. Many parents who hope to pass on a family firm or farm (or kingdom) to their children have learned that to keep the younger generation involved in their activities, they must bring their children in as near equal partners, or lose them to some other line of work and incorporate "outsiders"–nonkin–as a result.

Parent–child relationships thus have to undergo transformation over the life course, since at one stage, they involve adults and growing children, and at another, only adults. The ideal parent–child relationship is authoritative, with two components: warmth and affection and clear rules and supervision that vary with the age of the child and wane as the child matures (Dornbusch, Ritter, Leiderman, Roberts, & Fraleigh, 1987). If one of these two ingredients is missing, there will be problems. If there is discipline but no warmth or affection, the relationship is authoritarian–based on hierarchy and power. Such relationships necessarily end after adolescence, unless power is maintained over resources into the child's adulthood. If there is only warmth but little discipline, the relationship is permissive and one in which children do not develop respect for their parents and others or, eventually, for themselves. However, between adults, warmth and a respect for boundaries on both sides is all that is necessary or appropriate. It is this, together with the many years of shared history as the child developed in safety and the rules fell away, that give family bonds their unique power to sustain and enrich. Between adults, hierarchy gets in the way.

So even when there is no family enterprise to take into account, the same dynamics apply. The kind of parent–child relationship that makes sense while children are very young has to change to remain effective when the parent–child relationship is between two mature adults. Hence, the extension of joint survivorship requires a transition in the structure of parent–child relationships to retain the benefits of this historic and powerful tie.

As yet, few parents who now have grown children had models for such a transition in their relationships with their own parents. Some women are beginning to reach for a more "sisterly" relationship with their daughters, but there is little evidence that men are learning to become "partners" with their sons, and we still have a considerable way to go before this transition becomes normal and comfortable, in part because few define it as anything other than a personal issue. Many adult children would say that it is impossible for them to have adult relationships with their parents. Yet it is a genuine social problem as well, because, as parents and as adults with parents, most of us are struggling with this revolution in one way or another, sometimes exercising too little authority over our small children and sometimes feeling rebellious when our aging parents try to exercise too much authority. All change is difficult, but in this case, I doubt that we will want to reverse course, which would require a mortality regime in which few parents survived into their children's adult years. What would be better is to learn how to provide social support to help people negotiate this transition in parent–child relationships.

Male–Female Relationships

Family relationships among those of the same generation are also under pressure from the extension of joint survivorship. We know very little about forces maintaining or undermining sibling relationships during adulthood, but from a few qualitative studies of sisters (cf. Norris & Tindale, 1994, chapter 7), it is clear that a major relaxation of the importance of sibling order occurs. Parallel studies have not yet been carried out on brothers to see whether men can achieve the family closeness possible when competition is not the expected basis for interaction.

However, the central family relationship among those of the same generation in a nuclear family system is the marital bond, and here the challenge is clear. Married couples can now expect their marriages to last a long time. The "golden wedding anniversary" is becoming nearly normative, so that what had once been a rarely achieved and very much admired goal is now widely available. We have some interesting theories about what this change can mean for male–female relationships. For example, the increase in divorce can be viewed as in some sense the direct result of the increase in expectation of married life, because under the new mortality regime, the gains of divorce can be realized for a much longer period (Skolnick, chapter 10, this volume).

The central implication of the extension of married life is *transformation*. I demonstrated that parent–child relationships ideally should undergo transformation, which may be disruptive and difficult. However, our current gender arrangements mean that long-lasting husband–wife relationships have to transform repeatedly, and we have been reaping the disruptive consequences of such transformations in rising divorce rates.

The male–female relationship, which is between two adults, has become fraught throughout the life span with transitions of a nearly gymnastic quality as a result of the extension of joint survivorship. The same calculations that allow us to see that the parent–child relationship will normally survive long into the child's adult years demonstrate that the connection between *marital* and *parental* roles must also loosen. Men and women who marry in their twenties or early thirties and have an average of two children can expect their marital relationship to survive until long after the children are grown and are actively involved in their own parental and even grand-parental roles. The "empty nest" stage, which once was achieved only rarely is now the rule in marriages that survive divorce (Glick & Parke, 1965).

Thus, parenthood can no longer be the major focus of adults' family lives, but the unfolding of this reality has led to some amazing contortions. As demographic and technological changes made the lives of men and women increasingly similar by reducing the need for men's greater physical strength and women's frequent childbearing, 20th-century Western societies reacted *against* this trend with a broad range of responses. In the United States, the response that was the most prominent was to maximize the remaining differentiation in men's and women's roles by assigning nearly all parenting responsibilities to women.

Whereas in the 17th and 18th centuries men were primarily responsible for the practical and moral education of their children, this began to erode in the 19th century as the movement of men out of the home to more distant work sites gave women the leverage and the incentive to take over, leaving men with little more than the responsibility to provide and perhaps to spank. Much as obstetricians in the face of a shrinking market for baby delivering were able to drive out midwives by professionalizing (Kobrin, 1966), many women actively resisted the decline in their parenting roles by monopolizing parenthood and pursuing domesticity. This insured that the opportunities to earn cash in the emerging urban-industrial economy were disproportionately developed to replace men's subsistence contributions. It also meant that women were participating in a process that I feel has reconfigured the industrial, Western family in such a way that a fault line runs through it, with men on one side and women and children on the other. And it is currently a fault with earthquake potential.

Women's increased specialization in parenting also created a life course trajectory for them that had several distinct segments and hence a marriage trajectory for both men and women marked by built-in radical transforma-tions. If we were to describe the "ideal" life course stages of a traditional marriage today, they would include, sequentially: (a) both partners childless and employed, a transition for both from full-time student; (b) parenthood, with women redefining themselves as childraisers and drastically increased male financial responsibility; (c) the empty nest, as women "retired" from daily parenthood, and to a less productive role, if they had not already disrupted their family lives by returning to work; and finally (d) the hus-band's retirement. If one renegotiation is difficult for parent–child relationships, think what all these do to the quality and strength of the marital tie. But this growing fault line in marriage was not recognized in time, because with the decline in the production value of women's work in the home, men's incomes had become increasingly necessary to them. So women were expected to be social gymnasts in the ideal separate-spheres marriage.

Think what this means: If women are primarily involved with childrearing and provide little financial contribution to the family economy, there is a greater need for men to work long hours away from the home to provide support for the children and for their wives while they are raising them. The closeness and warmth developed during courtship and nurtured in the early years of marriage are often allowed to wither as their separate roles separate their lives and their primary relationships as women and men increasingly focus on the disparate responsibilities linked with being the mothers of children and the breadwinners of families.

That basis for their relationship dwindles as their children mature, so that even as they have more time for each other and perhaps fewer financial pressures, the old closeness must be recaptured, which is often difficult after an interval of so many years. If it is not recaptured or a new bond forged in middle age, the woman may feel that her role in the relationship has dwindled to that of unpaid housekeeper and servant. And the man may feel that his only connection to his wife and home is the financial responsibility he bears to maintain them.

Further, when it comes time for him to retire, they are likely to have a major crisis to challenge them, since his work life is over but her home tasks are not. There are four possibilities for this situation: (a) husbands often successfully invade their wives' "turf," expecting increased domestic services and supervising their wives' activities more directly now that they have greater opportunity and access to do so, which often leads to anger and resentment among their wives. In other families, wives successfully defend their separate sphere, either (b) letting their husbands in on the wives' terms—as her bumbling assistant—or (c) keeping them "out of the kitchen" altogether. In both of these cases, the *husbands* are likely to suffer, because just when they are experiencing separation from their full-time employment, they feel like outcasts—or servants—in their own homes.

A few families find their way to a fourth possibility, and become more egalitarian after the children leave home, and particularly as husbands have fewer work hours to justify their noninvolvement in the home and its tasks (Waite & Goldscheider, 1989). But the extent of this change is rarely large, implying that the long years under a different, separate regime are difficult to undo, since it is a transformation at least as great as that between parents and their adult children. Only families that have been used to sharing both tasks and leisure in the home will be able to negotiate changes smoothly as the balance of work and leisure shifts.

Thus, the extension of joint survivorship puts pressure on the internal dynamics of family relationships, both between parents and children and between husbands and wives. The extension of family roles into new life course territories based on increased joint survivorship, then, requires a restructuring of these roles: for parents and children, who spend more of their joint years as adults, and for husbands and wives, who spend fewer and fewer of their joint years as the parents of dependent children. This will be a great challenge, since such change requires rewriting old social scripts and writing new ones.

THE AGE PYRAMID AND THE LIFE COURSE

The need to restructure family roles will be increasingly clear to everyone, since we are confronted in our daily lives with the children, parents, and spouses with whom the old relationships no longer "fit." However, these demographic changes—lower mortality and fertility rates—also lead to change in population structure—the fundamental insight of the population pyramid— and in the relative proportions of older and younger people. The dramatic shift in the age pyramid of a population that occurs with population aging is also a shift in the relationships between the young and the old—generations. Under high fertility, the middle, "productive" generation had many young dependents and few old dependents. With low fertility, at least after the passage of a few generations, the sizes of older and young cohorts become more similar. This shift has major implications for the organization of the life course—the work and family careers of men and women. How to adjust to these changes is likely to be even more difficult than the changes required by the extension of joint survivorship.

Occupational Careers

First consider men and their occupational careers. Some scholars have pointed to the impact of this age-pyramid shift on the structure of employment and on career progress. Firms are normally pyramidal in shape, with many low-level workers, fewer supervisors, and even fewer senior officers. This structure is consistent with a high fertility age pyramid, because the large numbers of young people relative to older ones "fit" the firm's structure. Young workers are numerous, with low wages reflecting not only their inexperience but also the effects of their numbers and the competition with each other that results. With the entrance of even larger numbers of younger workers, the workers who survive into their middle productive years can expect rapid promotion. This demographic structure reinforces the normal increase in productivity with experience to maximize the likelihood that the most responsible and highly paid members of the labor force would be old and vice versa.

However, with low fertility and hence an older age pyramid, younger workers, who have less competition from others of their age, can expect better starting wages than under high fertility regimes, weakening the relationship between age and salary differentials. Further, age becomes a less secure basis for promotion, as others of their age survive to compete for supervisory positions, and the numbers of new, younger workers to supervise do not increase (Myrdal, 1940; Keyfitz, 1973). This further weakens the relationship between age and position in the firm's hierarchy and forces firms to begin to consider productivity directly in promotion decisions, rather than assuming its link to age.

As these processes unfold, younger people increasingly supervise older people. If past wages have been based at least partially on age, this can lead to older people being discharged as firms seek to lower costs and retain younger workers whose salaries are lower but who are not much less productive. The traditional relationship between age and occupational career, then, comes apart under a low fertility age pyramid, altering the relationships between older and younger workers who must compete more nearly as equals. Careers become "disorderly" for more people, who may in turn become frustrated in one line of work when their advancement is slow and try again in some other occupation. The challenge of constructing satisfactory career lines, so that work advancement and age can be planned together, becomes increasingly difficult. This, obviously, is particularly a problem for men.

Caregiving Careers

Changes in the population pyramid also disorder age patterns of caregiving. Under high fertility, the greatest share of the dependent population is young; proportionally few are old. One of the most dramatic consequences of an aging population pyramid is the great increase in the number of elderly men and women relative to those in the middle generation.

This can be shown by calculating changes in the relative numbers of older women and their daughters over time and by projecting them into the future. For example, in the United States, the ratio of women in the central caregiving ages (aged 35–44) to older widowed and divorced women (aged 55+) remained stable, at about 2.8 "daughters" per unmarried older "mother," between 1890 and 1930, years in which rapid fertility decline was underway, but had only influenced aging at the base of the population pyramid. However, over the next 50 years, this ratio dropped by more than half, to 1.2 "daughters" per "mother" (Kobrin, 1976). Similarly, the ratio of women aged 30 to 35 to those aged 55 to 60 in the population of the former

Federal Republic of Germany is projected to decrease from 1.8 to 0.6 "daughters" per "mother" during the 70 years between 1950 and 2020 (Heilig, Lutz, & Wolf, 1987).

Although we argued earlier that the elderly are not dependent for most of these years, it is nevertheless clear that the structure of caregiving has been altered drastically by these shifts in the population age pyramid. A recent suggestion from family traditionalists, particularly in Asia, is that women's increased free time from childraising should move to caring for the elderly. This is not unreasonable when first considered, because when demographers first began looking at the relationship of changes in the age pyramid to changes in dependency, many noted that the increase in the dependent elderly was balanced by a decrease in the dependent young. Indeed, under many combinations of fertility and mortality, the decrease in dependency at younger ages was greater than the increase in dependency at older ages. This pattern suggested that as women reduced their burden of care for children, they became increasingly freed to provide the care of the elderly that in the past was fit in around their childcare responsibilities.

However, this way of thinking about responding to population change does not take into account the structure of the life course. To understand whether it is likely that women will be able to reorder their lives to substitute eldercare for childcare, it is necessary to see how this shift in the structure of caregiving fits into women's lives—their family career tracks—and increasingly, into their occupational career tracks.

The decline in fertility and the changes in economic opportunities linked with industrialization have led women around the world to a series of life course strategies to combine work inside and outside the home. Commonly, the first response has been for women to go out to work in firms or factories in the interval between the end of schooling and marriage. But this strategy rarely lasts long—it soon becomes clear that the needs of a healthy, employed husband are not enough to preclude a young wife's continuing to work outside the home, particularly if they still need her income to save for a home. The division between unmarried and married women as workers falls, and women remain in the paid labor force until their children are born, before retiring to become full-time housewives and child-minders. However, with only a few children and with increased health and survivorship, the continued growth in opportunities for women in the labor market, and perhaps increased financial needs to support children longer, particularly in school, the time soon comes when women begin to "return to work."

Thereafter, the period out of the labor force begins to shrink, with many women returning to work in only a few weeks.[2] With the ability to time their

---

[2]This often occurs far earlier than their own physical needs or the emotional needs of their child would dictate in countries without adequate family leave policies, such as the United States.

childbearing offered by modern contraceptives, abortion, and sterilization, women organize their family lives around the rhythms of their work lives and press for help in combining the two from whomever they can: from governments, from employers, from their husbands (and sometimes from their children). However, women's work and family strategies rest securely on being able to *time* their caregiving responsibilities: to begin having children when it makes the most sense, that is, when enough education has been achieved and adequate career momentum established, and to space children carefully, either to minimize the period of interruption via short spacing or to minimize the caregiving burden at a given time via long spacing.

Of course, even in this modern contraceptive society, "accidents" happen, but this is rare among those with the most education and, hence, the most investment in developing an orderly career. And it is these women, by and large, who are most adamant about retaining control over reproduction in the face of an unwanted pregnancy (Luker, 1984). But caregiving for the elderly is not so easy to time. Bypass operations perhaps can be timed like caesarean sections, but a stroke, or the descent into Alzheimer's disease, are less adjustable to the schedules of those who the traditional approach assumes will provide their care.

As the dependency challenge shifts from children to the elderly, it becomes increasingly clear that we know almost nothing about the transition to caregiving. Most studies that provide information about the caregivers for the elderly are based on samples of impaired persons, who are either asked about their caregivers, or, in some cases, their caregivers are interviewed directly. These studies suggest that nonspousal caregivers are very likely to be women, to be unmarried, to be currently unemployed, and to be living with or near the person needing their care.

However, how the selection process operates is not known, and how potential caregivers trade off in terms of their own careers, marriage and family plans, and migration patterns, are all areas that need detailed research. What *is* clear is that keeping an army of nonemployed women in reserve to care (if necessary) for elderly parents and husbands is not an efficient use of labor power, any more than was keeping married women home before their children were born and after they were in school turned out to be. It is likely that to maintain the *family* as the locus of care, the logic of demographic change requires that we have to begin to involve men in this activity as well. After all, women's increased participation in the paid work force results in a decline in familism and family care only to the extent that there is no compensating increase in the reinvolvement of men in family roles (Goldscheider & Waite, 1991). Furthermore, many men will have more time for caregiving. The emerging structure of male employment facilitates this new role. As a result, many men will be able to take time off for caregiving, and this trend will increase.

IMPLICATIONS

But will men and women respond to these new challenges, and maintain the family as the major caregiving institution in which men and women, parents and children, work together to care for each other, so that our specialized institutions do not become the caregivers of the 21st century?

It is possible; families have undergone major changes throughout history, and despite these changes, have continued to provide the long-term, committed, sharing relationships we have depended upon them for. But new, antifamily processes have been accelerating, which make it possible that this time family centrality will dangerously erode.

The most important of these processes is the growth in nonfamily living. This is a key issue that is missed by nearly everyone who studies families—that increasingly, fewer and fewer people are living in them. In the United States in 1980, 23% of households contained only one person. In Sweden, this was the case for one third of households by 1980; in Israel, the proportion increased greatly, reaching nearly one fifth in 1983 (United Nations, 1989). Another small handful of adults live with roommates who share very little of their lives. This creates an important option to any but the most perfect marriage.

Another important trend is the growth in ideological commitment to autonomy and independence, which sometimes translates in the family realm as a rejection of financial dependency and coresidence. Most want to maintain the unmarried elderly independent and autonomous and living alone, since they see the only alternative as a dependent burden. Similarly, most are concerned to see a 23-year-old unmarried person living in his or her parental home, because this alternative we see as childish dependency. If an unmarried old or young person is living with family, we do not see community and interdependence; we see dependence. Hence, family living has a bad image. For the unmarried, we see only the loss of independence. In the extreme formulation of this contrast between autonomy and family, many reject marriage for women altogether, since they see only the economic dependencies of marriage. And as Freud and Woody Allen told us, even for married men, we see marriage as a loss of freedom and independence.

We know why children should live in families; we need to find out why adults should, and how to construct families to benefit their members. There is a vast research literature developing that demonstrates that family life provides social support and by so doing, increases mental and physical health (see, e.g., House, Landis, & Umberson, 1988). To highlight how difficult reinforcing family life will be, however, I present the following vignettes:

1. An elderly Korean woman was quoted as saying that she lived with her son and daughter-in-law even though she had enough money to

maintain her own apartment and did not particularly care for either of them, because she did not want them to lose face with their friends, who would think that her children were selfish and irresponsible if she lived separately.

2. A graduate student did a survey of professionals in gerontology, asking, among other questions, "When you become old, if you were unable to maintain yourself alone, which would you rather do, go to an institution, move in with family, or other?" The majority of *professionals* indicated their answer as "other"—that they would kill themselves.

I am normally an optimist about the family. However, when I consider these two vignettes, I become somewhat pessimistic that the family will be flexible enough to respond to the life course challenges of the 21st century.

CONCLUSION

This chapter provides an assessment of how past and current trends in demographic rates, particularly the increase in life expectancy, are reshaping intergenerational and gender relationships and will continue to do so in the future. The enormous increase in joint survival—the likelihood that a family relationship will last many years—is shown to mean that parenting minor children will become less central in the construction of both male–female relationships and parent–child relationships. The lives of marital partners will become more similar as the justification for the "separate spheres" relationship weakens; the relationships between parents and children will become more egalitarian as an increasing proportion of their length is spent when each is an adult. The potential implications of these changes for the construction of careers, both in terms of paid employment and of caregiving, are considerable.

REFERENCES

Dornbusch, S., Ritter, P., Leiderman, P., Roberts, D., & Fraleigh, M. (1987). The relation of parenting style to adolescent school performance. *Child Development, 58*, 1244–1257.

Glick, P., & Parke, R. (1965). New approaches in studying the life cycle of the family. *Demography, 2*, 187–202.

Goldscheider, F., & Waite, L. (1991). *New families, no families: The transformation of the American home.* Berkeley, CA: University of California Press.

Heilig, G., Lutz, W., & Wolf, D. (1987). Aging and the family. *Popnet–IIASA, 11*, 1–6.

Horn, J. (1977). Mortality: The life-giving properties of marriage. *Psychology Today, 10*, 20–22.

House, J., Landis, K., & Umberson, D. (1988). Social relations and health. *Science, 241*, 540–545.

Keyfitz, N. (1973). Individual mobility in a stationary population. *Population Studies, 27*, 335–352.

Kobrin, F. (1966). The American midwife controversy: A crisis of professionalization. *Bulletin of the History of Medicine, 40,* 350–363.

Kobrin, F. (1976). The fall in household size and the rise of the primary individual in the United States. *Demography, 13,* 127–138.

Luker, K. (1984). *Abortion and the politics of motherhood.* Berkeley, CA: University of California Press.

Mencken, J. (1985). Age and fertility: How late can you wait? *Demography, 22,* 469–483.

Myrdal, G. (1940). *Population: A problem for democracy.* Cambridge, MA: Harvard University Press.

Norris, J., & Tindale, J. (1994). *Among generations: The cycle of adult relationships.* New York: Freeman.

United Nations. (1989). *1987 Demographic Yearbook.* New York: United Nations Press.

Waite, L., & Goldscheider, F. (1989, November). *Sharing responsibility for housework: Differences between younger and older couples.* Paper presented at the annual meeting of the Gerontological Society of America, Minneapolis, MN.

5

MARITAL INTEGRATION
IN THE DUAL CAREER FAMILY

Anna F. Steyn
Rand Afrikaans University

In South Africa, as is the case worldwide, the rate of married women entering the labor market continues to rise, thus creating one of the most significant social trends of our times which could affect marital adjustment and family stability. Conventional wisdom holds that employment of married women and marital dissolution are causally related—a view supported by some of the earlier as well as more recent research results.

However, increasingly more of the recent studies were unable to confirm these findings, pointing to intervening variables alleviating this situation and actually contributing to a more positive functioning of the employed wife's marital life.

Research undertaken in South Africa, in which scales were developed to measure a number of work related and family related variables, shows inter alia a high significant correlation between the working wife's experience of her husband's support and marital integration.

A multiple regression analysis shows that the working wife's experience of her husband's support, her commitment to growth in marriage, and her career ambition are statistically significant predictors for marital integration. It appears that in the life of the working wife there are a number of interwoven variables which could have a positive influence on marital integration.

THEORETICAL BACKGROUND

One of the most significant social trends of our times, manifesting itself worldwide and affecting family life extensively, is the continuous rise in the rate of married women entering the labor market. Not only is an increasing proportion of married women doing paid work outside the home, but married women are also moving into the professional occupations which were previously reserved for men. This is mainly due to the improvement in their educational and academic qualifications together with pressure from the feminist movement for parity between men and women.

As high demands are made on the time and commitment of professional people, it stands to reason that the commitment of married women to a professional career could have a profound influence on their marriage and family life. This is attributable to the possibility of role conflict between work and family roles, since women in such occupations are likely to view work as a second primary role beside that of the family.

Consequently this added role is not only a quantitative increase in role obligations, but qualitatively the added role may effect all the role relationships within the family as well as relevant role relationships outside the family. By entering the labor market the wife's career activities may lead to an increasing interface between work and family life. This could affect the intimate daily interactions of family life and necessitate profound changes in the roles of married women and the members of her family if her work role is to be accommodated successfully and an integrated family life is to be maintained.

This transformation in family life which may be caused by a woman fulfilling a work, as well as a family role, has led to an increased societal concern for a whole range of phenomena, for example, women's health and wellbeing, marital adjustment, marital integration and family stability in general.

Moreover, the concern about the implications of women's work for family life is heightened by the fact that increasingly higher family demands are made on people—men as well as women—in the labor force, thereby aggravating the difficulties of combining occupational and family roles and causing conflict and tension in their families.

The concern with the impact on the family of married women entering the labor market, can partly be attributed to the conventional belief that female employment and marital dissolution are causally related and that the increase in labor force participation contributed to high levels of divorce in advanced societies (Edwards & Fuller, 1992). On the whole this could imply that the wife's participation in the labor force affects her family detrimentally, and that even in those marriages not ending in divorce there might be a higher degree of dissatisfaction and stress for family members and a lower level of marital integration than in families in which the wife has not taken up employment outside the home.

Some of the early research bears out this view. Vannoy and Philliber (1992), pointed out that early research by Axelson (1963), Nye and Hoffman (1963) and Bradbane (1964) found that when the wife is employed, poorer marital adjustment is experienced, particularly by the husband. Some of the research done more recently also shows that female employment (i.e., women working for a wage or salary) is generally associated with a higher risk of marriage or union dissolution. This finding must, however, be qualified. The risk seems to be higher for families in certain contexts than in others. Edwards and Fuller (1992) for example found that the wife's employment has an effect on marital instability only for the working class in Bangkok and not for the middle class. For the middle class the only employment-related variable that has an independent effect is family income, which—as in Western societies—has a positive effect on marital cohesion. For the working class, however, the number of working hours has a significant direct effect on instability even after controlling for intervening variables.

In a study done in Puerto Rico, Carver and Teachman (1993) found that female employment is generally associated with higher risk of union dissolution. This effect, however, is significant only for women who work for wages or a salary. Women who work in a family business or who work out of their houses are no more likely to experience union dissolution than women who have no outside job.

From the results of this research it seems that the effect of women's employment on marital stability is not necessarily a negative one, and that it could vary according to a number of factors. In studies carried out more recently, researchers are no longer concentrating only on the detrimental effects of the dual roles of the working wife on family life in general, but they are increasingly investigating intervening variables which alleviate the stress in a dual career family and which may actually contribute to a more positive functioning of the marital relationship. Some of the salient family related variables that have been found to exert an influence on individual well-being as well as on marital and family stability of the working wife's family include the following.

Opposition of Husband to Wife's Employment

Ulbrich (1988) pointed out that men who oppose their wives' employment reported more symptoms of depression than those who favor their wives' employment. Those who oppose their wives' employment are more depressed if their own earnings are comparatively low than if their earnings are high. Husbands who favor their wives' employment are less depressed regardless of their earnings.

Husband Participation in Family Tasks

In summarizing research with regard to husband's participation in family tasks, Menagahn and Parcel (1990) pointed out that the husband's participation in family tasks appears to be important in moderating and qualifying any effects of the married mother's employment. This effect is not limited to employed wives, as both employed and nonemployed wives were less distressed when their husband did an equal share of the household work. However, sharing was rare—it was shared equally among only 20% of dual career couples and 7% of couples in which only the male follows a career, although studies quoted by Menagahn and Parcel (1990) showed that this trend has been increasing to some extent.

Closely related to husbands' concrete participation in household duties, are some of the following variables, with a more symbolic value, that contribute to an alleviation of the effects of female employment on family life.

Fairness in Division of Household Labor

In surveying the literature, Blair and Johnson (1992) quoted a number of studies in which a strong association was found between overall levels of marital happiness and satisfaction and the perception of fairness in the division of labor and childcare tasks. They also found that the employed wife's perception of fairness is strongly associated with her perception of whether her household labor is appreciated. Employed wives who perceive their housework to be appreciated are more likely to believe that housework in their home is fairly divided than those who believe their housework is unappreciated. Thus, perception of fairness is based on more than merely relieving the wife of onerous labor, and probably more with the symbolic value of men's demonstration of their appreciation of their wives' domestic efforts as well as a concern with fairness by actually contributing to household labor.

Sensitivity of Husband to Others

The sensitivity of the husband is one of the variables that could lead to the experience of enhanced marital quality for both marriage partners. Vannoy and Philliber (1992) stated:

> The marital quality experienced by the husband is more closely related to his sensitivity . . . Irrespective of his wife's relative status, the stronger his sensitivity, the more positive his marriage . . . For the wife, a husband's sensitivity is more important when her husband's status is higher . . . wives who find themselves in an occupation of lesser status may have a greater need for a supportive husband. (p. 396)

Emotional Support, "Emotional Work," and Intimacy

Closely related to the sensitivity of the husband are a number of aspects used by researchers which could be grouped together as one variable, that is, that of emotional support, "emotional work," and intimacy. Erickson (1993) pointed out that most researchers on family life classified emotional support as an aspect of marital and family intimacy. His means of measuring what he called "emotional work" consisted of a composite scale score developed on a number of items related to the amount of perceived emotional support demonstrated by the husband. Erickson's results suggest that the performance of "emotional work" has a significant impact on women's perceptions of marital well-being and feelings of marital burnout, as well as being a more powerful predictor of these outcomes than is the husbands' assisting with housework or child care. "Emotional work" by the female respondents themselves also tend to lessen the likelihood of their experiencing feelings of marital burnout. This seems to suggest that the more "emotional work" is done, the higher the quality of the marriage.

Piña and Bengston (1993) also found that emotional support together with help with household duties are relevant to the enhancement of marital quality. They found the wife's happiness to be affected indirectly by the division of household labor through the degree to which she perceives her husband as providing her with emotional and instrumental support. For wives with more egalitarian beliefs about marital roles and those employed full-time in the paid labor force, more equal division of labor with husbands is linked with greater feelings of support from husbands. Greater feelings of support are in turn associated with the wives' experience of a higher marital quality and increased psychological well-being.

Apart from the these family-related variables, some work related variables were considered which could have an impact on the quality of family life in the dual career family. The following have been investigated.

Interpersonal Conflicts at Work

Bulger et al. (in Monaghan & Parcel, 1990) found that interpersonal conflicts at work—arguments with supervisors, coworkers or subordinates at work—clearly showed a spillover from work to home, with arguments at work during the day likely to be followed by spousal arguments at home that evening. In addition, interpersonal conflicts, both at home and at work, emerged as a potent source of daily fluctuations in emotional distress and the tendency to depression.

High Pressure for Output and Low Supervisor Support

Hughes, Galinsky, and Marris (1992) found that workers in jobs with high pressure for output and low supervisor support report more frequent marital arguments, because such pressure results in competing work and family demands and negative affective states. They furthermore found that having

an enriching job was directly associated with increased marital companionship, independent of reported difficulties in meeting job or family demands.

Women's Work Stress Through Overload,
Low Reward, and Work Status

The results arrived at by Sears and Galambos (1992) suggest that women's
work experiences spill over into their marital adjustment through their
perception of work stress and global stress. Women experiencing more work
stress reported higher levels of global stress and lower levels of marital
adjustment than those experiencing less work stress. They also point out
that it is worth noting that these results are consistent with the notion that
positive work conditions may spill over into more positive marital relations.

Flexibility of Work Schedule and Working Hours

Guelzow, Bird, and Koball (1991) found that the larger a man's family and
the more inflexible his work schedule the higher are his levels of role strain.
In the case of women, working longer hours was related to higher levels of
role strain. Once role strain was perceived, its effect was pervasive throughout the stress process. This stress can, however, be alleviated by coping
resources, such as role reduction, involving reducing responsibilities in
major life roles, and marital relationship equity, involving mutuality of
spousal support whereby the perception of fairness, based on an overall
balance of rewards and constraints within a relationship, is assessed. We
came to the conclusion that their results add evidence to the growing body
of research demonstrating that multiple roles are not necessarily related to
high levels of stress. The fact that the wife has a professional career thus
need not have a detrimental affect on the quality of marital life.
    These findings suggest the necessity of further research to determine
which variables have a positive impact on the marital relationship.

MARITAL INTEGRATION AMONG MARRIED
WHITE WORKING WOMEN IN THE REPUBLIC
OF SOUTH AFRICA

In South Africa, as is the case worldwide, the rate of married women entering
the labor market—also in professional fields—continues to rise. For example,
in 1944, of all the White women in paid labor, only 19.7% were married; in
1960, 44.8% were married; in 1980, 60.2% were married; and in 1991, 61.04%
were married (du Toit, 1992). Of all the married White women in South Africa
in 1991, 48.4%—a substantial proportion—were in the labor market.

Initially, during the early 1940s and the 1950s, when this trend was becoming apparent, there was an outcry voicing concern that married women entering the labor market would have a detrimental effect on child development, on marital stability, and the quality of family life. Strong pleas were made that married women with small children should not do paid work outside the home and that women should be full-time mothers and homemakers (Steyn, 1982). By the mid 1960s, social scientists were approaching this phenomenon more objectively and doing more objective research, albeit on a more descriptive level, on the dual-career family, paying specific attention to the changing role of women, child neglect and the nature of child care in the dual income family, the influence of the mother's work on family life, and role conflict.

Recent Studies in the Republic of South Africa

Since the late 1970s and early 1980s there was a shift in the focus of studies of the family. The dual-income family remained an area of concern, but the research became more analytic in nature concentrating on marital integration in the dual career family and analyzing the relation between marital integration and some work- and family-related variables.

Two of the work-related variables which were used in these analyses—and which have received scant attention in the literature thus far—are the extent to which married women (a) are professionally oriented and (b) experience satisfaction with their work involvement. A relevant question which might be asked with regard to satisfaction with work involvement is the following: Do women with a higher degree of satisfaction with work involvement experience higher marital integration?

With regard to the relation between professional orientation and marital integration the following questions arise: Is it possible that women with a strong professional orientation could combine a career with a highly integrated marriage? Is it possible that women with a high professional orientation could be committed to growth in their marriage? Are there other family related variables, like the wife's experience of her husband's support, her time management and her experience of interrole conflict, which could have a positive (or negative) influence on the professional orientation of the wife on the one hand, and her marital integration on the other hand?

In an attempt to reach answers to some of these questions, a series of studies was executed at the Rand Afrikaans University, among working wives in the White population group. The first step in these studies was to develop and standardize scales to measure some of the work-related and some of the family-related variables.

The following scales measuring work-related variables were constructed and rated on a 5-point Likert Cronbach's scale:

1. *Married women's career involvement (Cronbach's* α *= .92)*. This scale had 22 items, asking, for example, whether the wife feels enriched by her work and to what extent she is prepared to spend of her leisure time on her work activities (du Toit, 1992).

2. *Married women's career ambition (Cronbach's* α *= .93)*. This scale had 10 items, asking, for example, about the wife's willingness to continue her training to supplement her knowledge about her work, and whether she is aiming to reach a top position in her work in the long run (du Toit, 1992).

3. *Wife's satisfaction with her career involvement (Cronbach's* α *= .92)*. This scale had 27 items asking, for example, whether the wife is looking forward to going to work in the morning, and whether her work offers a feeling of personal fulfillment (Swanepeol, 1990).

The following scales measuring family-related variables were con-structed:

4. *Marital integration (Cronbach's* α *= .93)*. *Marital integration* was defined as when the process of interaction is cooperative and emotionally supportive to the extent that the different areas of marital activities are accompanied by a minimum of destructive conflict, thus leading to the maintenance of the marriage as a unity. This scale had 20 items, asking the wife, for example, how often she and her husband discuss issues that could cause problems in their family, how adequately they deal with problems arising in their marriage, and to what extent the wife considers her and her husband to be good friends (du Toit, 1992).

5. *Commitment to growth in the marital relationship (Cronbach's* α *= .90)*. This scale was composed of 16 items, asking the wife, for example, to what extent she was prepared to support her husband through thick and thin, to what extent she was prepared to take her partner's feelings into considera-tion, and to what extent she was prepared to work towards a better under-standing of her husband as a person (de Waal, 1990).

6. *Commitment to a long term maintenance of the marital relationship (Cron-bach's* α *= .89)*. This scale had 14 items, asking the wife, for example, to what extent she was willing to maintain the marital relationship in spite of a number of negative conditions in the marital relationship, like personal unhappiness of one of the marriage partners, unsatisfactory sexual relation-ship with the partner, and alcohol abuse by the partner (de Waal, 1990).

7. *The wife's experience of her husband's support (Cronbach's* α *= .94)*. This scale was composed of 24 items. The items designed to measure this con-struct included not only support by doing various household tasks and by taking care of the children but also moral support, by showing appreciation,

serving as a sounding board for the wife's problems, giving emotional support and encouragement for the wife's occupational activities (du Toit, 1992).

8. *Wife's experience of positive time management (Cronbach's α = .94).* This scale consisted of 16 items. It measured the extent to which the wife felt that she had sufficient time to manage her household and familial obligation by asking, for example, whether she had sufficient time to spend casually with the family, and whether she had sufficient time to play with and enjoy the children. (Swanepoel, 1990; du Toit, 1992).

9. *Wife's experience of interrole conflict (Cronbach's α = .82).* This scale consisted of 11 items. It measured the conflict the wife experienced between her work and family roles, by asking, for example, whether she experienced inner conflict if she had to go to work if a member of her family were ill, whether she would experience conflict between her work and family roles if she had to do office work at home, and if she would experience inner conflict if she were to decrease her job involvement in order to satisfy the needs of her family (du Toit, 1992).

To test the relationship between family integration, the work-related variables and the other family-related variables, two studies were undertaken. In the first of these studies done by Swanepoel (1990) the focus was on the relation between the wife's perception of family integration and the wife's satisfaction with her work involvement, together with the wife's perception of her husband's support and her time-management.

Swanepoel's sample consisted of 250 White working wives with dependent children in Johannesburg and vicinity. The sample was drawn by means of a snowball technique. Organizations, schools, and nursery schools were contacted personally or by letter to obtain names of respondents who were contacted to complete the questionnaire. These respondents supplied further names and addresses.

The intercorrelation matrix (Table 5.1) shows statistically significant correlations between a number of the variables. Table 5.1 shows that the family variables, marital integration, and the wife's experience of the husband's support are highly positively correlated. Similarly, marital integration and husband's perceived support, are both moderately correlated with time-management in the family context.

It is interesting to note that family- and work-related variables tend to complement each other. Hence, the wife's experience of work satisfaction is highly, significantly, and positively correlated with time-management in the family context, as well as being moderately correlated with marital integration and perceived spousal support. These finding suggest that work satisfaction is positively related to family variables like time-management and couple harmony, contradicting earlier findings, as well as the popular view that work and domestic realms clash with each other.

TABLE 5.1
Intercorrelation Matrix Between Work Satisfaction and Family-Related Variables

	Work Satisfaction	Marital Integration	Time Management
Marital Integration	$r = .15$ $p = .02$		
Time Management	$r = .58$ $p = .00$	$r = .17$ $p = .01$	
Husband Support	$r = .16$ $p = .01$	$r = .76$ $p = .00$	$r = .17$ $p = .01$

In summary, it appears that not only do different family variables interact with each other, but also that family- and work-related variables complement each other and contribute to working wives' experience of a higher degree of marital harmony and family time-management, as well as to positive work satisfaction. This suggests that family life may not only positively influence work adjustment, but work adjustment may positively affect the effectiveness of family life.

These results of Swanepoel's study were to some extent verified by a subsequent study done by du Toit (1992), although some of the variables employed differed from those used by Swanepoel. Regarding family related variables, du Toit also used marital integration, time-management and the wife's experience of her husband's support, but, in addition, she included the variables of commitment to working on the marital relationship (de Waal, 1990) and the experience of role conflict. As far as the work-related variables are concerned, she employed different variables—those of involvement in the career and career ambition, which were the two dimensions of professional orientation developed by du Toit (1992). The rationale for using professional orientation as a work related variable, is that this scale reflects more definitely the degree of involvement of women with their career role— which might compete successfully with the family role—than the variables of work satisfaction and hours of work or independence in their work role.

To gather the data, a combined telephone–postal survey was used. A proportional sample of 2,000 telephone numbers were drawn from the larger Johannesburg–Pretoria–Vaal triangle area. These telephone numbers were dialed to determine whether the women living there would qualify to be included in the sample (i.e., being working wives with dependent children at home) and, to determine whether they would be willing to participate in the research. On the basis of this information 1,156 questionaires were sent out. Altogether 731 respondents returned their questionaires and of these 642 could be used for the analysis of the data.

Table 5.2 shows that most of the family-related variables are positively and significantly correlated. The highest positive correlations obtained were between marital integration with the wife's perception of her husband's support, as well as with her commitment to marital growth. Other correlations reported below are also significant but more moderate. Time-management in the family context was found to be related to the perception of the husband's support, marital integration and commitment to marital growth, in that order. However, it was also found to be negatively related to interrole conflict (i.e., poor time management was related to more interrole conflict between the work and family spheres).

As for the intercorrelations between the family- and work-related variables, in accordance with "traditional" expectations a negative significant, but low correlation was obtained between the wife's career ambition with her time-management, that is, the higher her work ambition, the poorer was her time management in the family context. Surprisingly, however, the work arena tended to complement family functioning in other areas. Hence, career ambition was found to be significantly and positively correlated with commitment to growth in the marriage, as well as to perceptions of spousal support. Similarly, both career ambition and involvement were significantly and negatively related to interrole conflict, that is the higher the ambitions and the involvement of these mothers in the occupational sphere, the lower

TABLE 5.2
Intercorrelation Matrix of Work-Related and Family-Related Variables

	Career Involvement	Career Ambition	Marital Integration	Commitment Marital Growth	Husband's Support	Time Management
Career Ambition	$r = .53$ $p = .00$					
Marital Integration	$r = .07$ $p = .03$	.06 .06				
Commitment Marital Growth	$r = .09$ $p = .00$	.13 .00	.70 .00			
Husband's Support	$r = .18$ $p = .00$	.13 .00	.72 .00	.47 .00		
Time Management	$r = .09$ $p = .01$	-.10 .00	.24 .00	.15 .00	.25 .00	
Interrole Conflict	$r = -.24$ $p = .00$	-.16 .00	.04 .13	-.15 .00	-.11 .00	-.16 .00

was the amount of perceived conflict between the family and the occupational arenas. These findings once again are indicative of complementarity between domestic and career roles. Hence, the professional orientation of the wife may contribute positively to family adjustment, while family adjustment may also be related to positive functioning in the occupational sphere.

In the light of the positive effects evidence between these family- and work-related variables in working women du Toit (1992) developed a multiple regression model to determine the predictors for marital integration. All the scales were used in the development of the model.

From Table 5.3 it is clear that the wife's experience of the husband's support is by far the most significant predictor for marital integration, the second most important one being her commitment to working on the marital relationship. Career ambition, although making a low contribution, is also a predictor. These three predictors explain a total of 69% of the variation in marital integration, which is remarkable.

The fact that career ambition was a significant predictor for marital integration came as a surprise, as there was no significant correlation between these two variables. The question to be asked here, and which needs further research, is to what extent the personality of the woman plays a role in her general willingness to make a success of both her marriage and her career. If she succeeds in these spheres, is she not the type of person who is committed to achieving success in many varied spheres of her life?

Looking at the situation of the married working women as a whole, there is suggestive evidence that having a career outside the house does not necessarily have a detrimental effect on the family. These findings focus attention on the fact that in doing research on the quality of marital life and family integration in the dual career family, the question to be asked should not be: to what extent is family life detrimentally influenced by the wife's employment but rather: under what circumstances could the wife's experience of her dual role be related positively to her personal well-being, her

TABLE 5.3
Multiple Regression Model for Determining Predictors for Marital Integration

Step	Predictor for Marital Integration	R^2	Increase in R^2	F^4
1	Experience of husband's support	.5226	.5226	700.5920
2	Commitment to growth in Marriage	.6860	.1634	332.4210
3	Career ambition	.6902	,0043	8.87787

marital relationship and the interaction patterns in her family? In other words, how do work- and family-related variables interact to contribute to a positive impact in both the domestic and occupational spheres?

Knowledge of the variables contributing to an enhanced marital integration and quality of family life of the dual career family could be of invaluable importance in the 21st century. The tendency is for an increasing percentage of families to become dual career families—a tendency that might well be continued in the 21st century. This knowledge could therefore find an increasing application by being included in programs on family enrichment, family guidance, and family counseling—thus contributing to the upgrading of family life in the 21st century.

REFERENCES

Blair, S. L., & Johnson, M. P. (1992). Wives' perceptions of the fairness of the division of household labor: The intersection of house work and ideology. *Journal of Marriage and the Family, 54,* 570–581.

Carver, K. P., & Teachman, J. D. (1993). Female employment and first union dissolution in Puerto Rico. *Journal of Marriage and the Family, 55,* 686–698.

de Waal, M. (1990). *The commitment of White married persons to marriage.* Johannesburg: Ongepubliseerde D. Litt. et Phil. proefskrif, RAU.

du Toit, D. A. (1992). *The professional orientation and family life of working married women.* Johannesburg: Ongepubliseerde D. Phil et Litt. Proefskrif, RAU.

Edwards, J. N., & Fuller, T. D. (1992). Female employment and marital instability: Evidence from Thailand. *Journal of Marriage and the Family, 54,* 59–68.

Erickson, R. J. (1993). Reconceptualizing family work: The effect of emotion work on perceptions of marital quality. *Journal of Marriage and the Family, 55,* 888–900.

Guelzow, M. G., Bird, G. W., & Kobalt, E. H. (1991). An exploratory path analysis of the stress process of dual-career men and women. *Journal of Marriage and the Family, 53,* 151–164.

Hughes, D., Galinsky, E., & Morris, A. (1992). The effects of job characteristics on marital quality: Specifying linking mechanisms. *Journal of Marriage and the Family, 54,* 31–42.

Menaghan, E. G., & Parcel, T. L. (1990). Parental employment and family life: Research in the 1980's. *Journal of Marriage and the Family, 52,* 1079–1098.

Piña, D. L., & Bengston, V. L. (1993). The division of household labor and wives' happiness: Ideology, employment, and perceptions of support. *Journal of Marriage and the Family, 55,* 901–912.

Sears, H. A., & Galambos, N. L. (1992). Women's work conditions and marital adjustment in two-earner couples: A structural model. *Journal of Marriage and the Family, 54,* 789–797.

Steyn, A. F. (1982). Family sociology in South Africa. *Humanitas, 8,* 89–104.

Swanepoel, M. *Marital integration in the dual income family.* Johannesburg: Ongepubliseerde M-verhandeling, RAU.

Ulbrich, P. M. (1988). The determinants of depression in two-income families. *Journal of Marriage and the Family, 50*(1), 121–130.

Vannoy, D., & Philliber, W. W. (1992). Wife's employment and quality of marriage. *Journal of Marriage and the Family, 54,* 387–398.

THE EXTENDED FAMILY AND ALTERNATE FAMILY FORMS

6

THE FALSE ASSUMPTIONS
OF TRADITIONAL VALUES

Annette B. Weiner
New York University

As an anthropologist, I know that families—even nuclear families—do not exist in isolation. As an American, I know that nuclear families in the United States are very isolated. Yet current debates about the American nuclear family emphasize attributes such as self-sufficiency and independence rather than isolation, suggesting that there is something inherently natural and positive about isolation. In reality, however, the American nuclear family model has never worked as an emotionally and economically self-contained kinship unit. In societies throughout the world, regardless of the type of family organization, each individual is linked to other extended kin through a vast array of mutual obligations that continue throughout each person's life. Reciprocal exchanges solidify connection between generations, establishing continued support for young and old.

In the American kinship system, this locus of reciprocity began to shift in the early years of the 20th century. The continual obligations due extended kin and community diminished in importance as the government, unions, and corporate America replaced kinship support. As upper middle class cultural and economic values became the model for all those aspiring to climb the American ladder of success, deeper political and economic needs were at work. The advantage of having a controllable and profitable labor force had wide-ranging repercussions on the nature of the family unit. Once severed from the vast demands of kinship, the nuclear family provided the economy with an ever expanding and ever more commodities-dependent consumer population.

There is nothing "natural" about the growing isolation and self-reliance of the nuclear family. Contrary to what many politicians claim, self-sufficiency is not an innate characteristic of the nuclear family. In fact, the development of the nuclear family is a direct result of state and economic interests. Today, the nuclear family—often a single-parent unit—is not foundering on a breakdown of traditional values but on the vast changes in corporate interests and transnational economies that no longer depend on the United States for labor forces or domestic markets.

Neither government nor big business, however, could proclaim or legislate the nuclear family as a labor force and as a primary source of domestic consumption. Instead, the values and form that the 20th-century American nuclear family took were shaped by widely circulating pronouncements about what a proper family should be. To be effective, national myth-making about the appropriate American family form had to seem distinct from state and economic interests. Family values, to be seriously inculcated, had to be understood as a natural expression of the needs and concerns of individual families. Such consensus today would be difficult to sustain. Today, national myth-making and media messages are no longer so homogenous nor so easily believed. It is easy to forget the power national myths once had in generating common, local interests and decisions for national economic and political ends.

Assumptions of what a family should be had strong appeal and support because they were rooted in three pervasive American ideals. One was an interpretation of American history that stressed the frontier-breaking cowboy qualities of individualism and self-reliance. Another was a perception that the country should be homogenous, a Melting Pot image that allegedly erased differences between people of varied backgrounds and classes. Third, the country's shifting economic interests required that families continually increase their purchasing power even when such consumption undermined other kin and community obligations. This is the problem that many people in Third World countries face today, as capitalism undermines a society's long-standing commitment to mutual obligations to a wide spectrum of intergenerational family. The pull between the purchasing power of hard currency and the demands of kin-based reciprocal exchanges that produce, not commodities, but future support and sustenance is a dilemma that is undermining many different kinds of family structures.

This chapter looks at the major changes of the American nuclear family over the past hundred years. I believe the most critical influences behind the development and the demise of the nuclear family form of the 20th century include a social and political movement called *Americanization*, an industrialization process called *Fordism*, a national drive to hasten domestic market expansion, and changes brought by the rising prominence of transnational interests over national ones. In contemplating the family on the threshold of the 21st century, we must study these processes to learn how the myth about the nuclear family's historical depth and stability has been generated. Only then can we consider its future.

BECOMING A GOOD AMERICAN

I begin my critique by discussing the end of the 19th century, when the American nuclear family model was embraced by the state as a useful tool in its campaign to make "good Americans" out of thousands of newly arrived immigrants (Berkson, 1969; Gavit, 1922). Before the 1880s, the majority of immigrants to the United States were northern Europeans of Protestant background. By the end of the 1880s, however, most immigrants hailed from southern or eastern Europe. They were darker complected, more religiously diverse, and often poorer than those who preceded them (Carlson, 1975). They were perceived as "more foreign" and were thought to be unskilled, undisciplined workers, and therefore a potential threat to an increasingly stable American work force.

These immigrants were described in the media, from pulpits, and in schools as a national problem, one addressed at several levels. Many disparate sources stressed similar versions of American behavior and values for immigrants to imitate, and thus set into motion a thorough process of homogenous myth-making. Immigration laws grew more restrictive than ever before (Bradshaw, 1925). An increasingly popular eugenics movement promoted sterilization as a way to control "bad" genes and therefore behavior (Ross, 1994). The wives of successful businessmen founded charities like the Children's Aid Society and the Association for the Improvement of Conditions of the Poor (Stansell, 1987) to socialize immigrant children into appropriate American behavior.

The emphasis on appropriate American behavior was formalized in a new, national movement called *Americanization*, which sought to institutionalize the mechanisms whereby immigrants would be transformed into good Americans. A proper American, these cultural canons taught, could speak English (preferably without an accent), had an education, was a citizen, and demonstrated a wish to endorse, even imitate, the lifestyles of the rich and influential, even if those lifestyles were beyond the means of most (Berkson, 1975; Stansell, 1987). To transform immigrants into Americans, the Americanization movement was soon attracting articulate proponents in cities across the country. Chambers of Commerce, manufacturers' associations, Rotary and Kiwanis Clubs, the YMCA, YMHA, and Daughters of the American Revolution lent support, as did clergy, teachers, merchants, and politicians.

Immigrants were targeted wherever they were found: in schools, churches, synagogues, factories, sports clubs, jails, libraries, hospitals, and boarding houses (Roberts, 1920). The movement's most obvious goal was to smooth the rough edges of diversity brought by representatives of dozens of ethnicities and nationalities. Americanization stressed how important it was for immigrants to become members of the national culture. A country-wide drive soon focused on every aspect of American life. State committees were formed, headed by regional directors who organized teams of teachers, translators, and lecturers. By the early 1920s, the Americanization Committee of the Motion Picture Industry, headed by a former Secretary of the Interior, had made movies for distribution to theaters, schools and philanthropic organizations with titles like *Epochs in American History*, *American Customs*, and *Lives of Great Americans* (Roberts, 1920).

Built into this project of inculcation was a goal to shrink the size of immigrant families, and rearrange older relationships of economic cooperation among family members and between family groups that often blended their incomes to survive. In its place, the nuclear model was upheld as the ideal. This, after all, was the pattern followed by "native Americans"—a phrase that in the 1920s meant Whites born on U.S. soil. Contrary to the family downsizing urged on immigrants, President Theodore Roosevelt encouraged all "natives" to have more children and thus preserve the racial purity of the country (a trend that found its apotheosis in Hitler's Germany two decades later).

The model for the appropriate family was created by elites. By the 1920s, elite urban families functioned not as external economic producers but as emotional centers that tried to keep the family unit self-contained and self-fulfilled, dedicated to personal happiness, privacy, consumption, and the proper raising of children. It is not mere coincidence that at about the same time, department stores, women's self-help magazines, and increased advertising aimed at women, the primary buyers in most elite households, all became more prominent (Stansell, 1987).

The Americanization movement gave approval and support for decisions that altered family structure away from obligations to extended kin and toward independent, geographically isolated households. The mythology developed by the state and popular culture in early 20th-century America stressed traits of self-sufficiency and independence. These traits further penetrated the ideology of the family as the Americanization movement tried to shape a controllable work force that could be used without fear and a market that could expand significantly by guiding families to reconfigure themselves in nuclear patterns, with women responsible for domestic spending and therefore for family well-being (Coontz, 1988; Lipsitz, 1986; Stansell, 1987).

TRANSITION

World War I marked a significant shift. The Americanization movement reached its height when wartime hysteria fueled xenophobia and racism. But it started losing momentum after the war, when criticism was finally raised against its sometimes vicious insistence on homogeneity. Strengthening labor organizations also cut into some gains of the movement, which had successfully discouraged unions as un-American. Unions came into their own during the Depression as desperate conditions forced workers to organize for better wages, job security, and safer working conditions.

Unions also rose to safeguard workers' rights in the face of a new demand on labor. The assembly line had been introduced by Henry Ford in 1914, and as it became common across many industrial sectors, its novelty required changes at every level of working life. Fordism, as it was known, aimed at perfecting a scientific approach to production. It simultaneously changed labor organization, management and control as factory work became a series of piecemeal tasks, rather than a collective effort. Equally important, Ford's innovations changed the process of domestic consumption (Harvey, 1992).

This was intentional. When Ford offered his $5, 8-hour working day, the higher wage and lowered hours were intended to create good consumers, not just good workers. He understood that not all laborers would know the best way to direct their new financial and leisure resources, so in 1916, borrowing from the Americanization movement, he sent social workers into the homes of his mostly immigrant work force. He wanted to insure that they had "the right kind of moral probity, family life, and capacity for prudent and 'rational' consumption" to become the first of a new generation of consumers (Harvey, 1992, p. 126). Intense corporate interest in family stability dates from this time; it suited industry to foster family structure that was private, separate, and based on purchased commodities.

Unions also participated in these processes when they promised management greater productivity in exchange for wage hikes, thereby increasing both production and consumption, just as Henry Ford had envisioned. Antonio Gramsci noted that Fordism implied changes "inseparable from a specific mode of living and of thinking and feeling life" (1971, p. 43). Mass produced commodities created an entirely new aesthetic as culture itself became commodified, and the assembly-line organization of the factory created a new worker, new family dynamic, and two new social muscles to flex: purchasing power and increased leisure time.

By the end of World War II, increased wages, altered working hours and practices, more leisure time, unprecedented postwar industrial strength, and the new cultural aesthetic together changed the face of the American family. The nuclear unit could afford to indulge in luxuries unheard of by immigrant forebears, at the same time separating families from each other in ways equally unimagined by previous generations. Most significantly, the family no longer gave high priority to those things that marked generational continuity. Increasing mobility separated generations from each other so that the long-term support and symbols of identity, such as land and other possessions, were greatly diminished or even eradicated. Without the need for or access to external material or emotional support, the family completed its focus inward, meeting the larger world as continually spending consumers while becoming the site of an intensely atomized acquisitiveness. Even the geography of family life changed as wage-earners followed the factory exodus from city to suburb.

Families living in geographic and social isolation from other families and from extended kin networks found many sources of reassurance that they were making the right choice. External forces imprinting family life with common values came from the union, the corporation, and from the new license to spend money like never before. The invention called television echoed and encouraged these trends, with influential early programs like "Mama" and "The Goldbergs" highlighting the importance of the ideal—a mother at home, a father at work, and children benefiting from consumer goods (Lipsitz, 1986). Never mind that the ideal was unrealistic, because only middle and upper class families could afford it. Poor families always needed dual incomes, making women significant parts of the work force for generations (Stansell, 1987). But that was not the vision presented by television. Advertisers, who suddenly penetrated family life with an intimacy and immediacy radio had not allowed, bolstered the appeal of the nuclear family myth.

By the end of the 1950s, nuclear family members relied on each other almost exclusively for intimacy and nurture, whereas their connection to the larger world was increasingly dependent on the marketplace. Union strength insured that workers continued to bring home comfortable pay checks, and job security promises seemed to mean that a materially comfortable lifestyle could be perpetuated indefinitely. The Americanization movement had become marginalized, except in fitful and devastating guises like the anticommunism persecutions of the McCarthy era and more recently in a referendum passed in California called Proposition 187, making it legal for the state to deny undocumented immigrants access to schools, medical care, or other state services (at the time of this writing, it is undergoing appeal).

The myth of the American nuclear family promoted the illusion that greater purchasing power could compensate for greater anomie and separation. People living in nuclear families were told by every source that they were living the way they were supposed to be. For a while, it seemed to work. The country was prosperous, peaceful, almost swollen with a sense of well-being, of better living through commodities. American capitalism was unflinchingly linked to patriarchy and consumerism, a combination that defined patriotism. The fifteen years after the Second World War seemed to be the beginning of a bountiful and pacific second half of the 20th century.

WHAT WENT WRONG

The model, however, was flawed. The imprinting of support and approval that came from most sectors of society could not accommodate the transience of the post-War boom, nor the lengths to which capitalism would go in pushing for ever greater profits. Starting in the 1960s, many companies moved operations to cheaper labor sources overseas. Unions, rapidly losing their earlier powers, were forced to accept scaled down wages, fewer benefits, and thinner security packages for uncertain job guarantees; thousands of blue-collar workers lost their jobs. Those women who had always been in the labor market were joined by growing numbers of additional middle class women as inflation and a weakening dollar made two wages necessary to maintain a consuming lifestyle. The women's movement in the 1970s brought some public sanction and a call for pay equity to women's wage labor, but women in the work force—at all levels—still face wage discrimination (Lebow, 1993; O'Neill, 1977).

The nuclear family model created strong dependence on market forces that failed; at the same time it discouraged dependence on extended kin and neighbor ties that throughout history have proven effective in time of need. Economic and political supports of disconnected domestic arrangements also failed to take into account those who were not configuring their families in a nuclear pattern. For middle class suburban women, the family was sometimes the locus of oppression, but for people caught in cycles of structural poverty, the family was a strategic means of survival (Zinn, 1989). African American families looked more like immigrant families of the past century in which members turned to each other for opportunities in jobs and housing, as the source of short-term loans and child care, even for the use of furniture and clothing (Stack, 1974). The very need to rely on family members underscored the importance of kin ties; however, it was not a pattern given social sanction. Success, which required financial security unavailable to many, meant moving away from extended kin obligations.

The urban riots of the 1960s vividly demonstrated just how many people had been denied access to the dominant ethos of private commodity acquisition. Particular configurations of race, gender, class and ethnicity gave to some groups the security of decent wages and significant commodities while denying both to entire segments of society. These political and cultural discontentments opened a new atmosphere of anti-establishment protest. Even upper middle class children revolted against the nuclear family model with the creation of communes that tried to replicate extended family structures.

The welfare system, in part a response to the rage that burst into the streets of Los Angeles, Detroit, and Newark, was a formal, legislated attempt by the government to repair the social and economic damage that the mythology of a "traditional" American nuclear family had perpetuated in the face of other realities. The racial and class divisions within American society were largely ignored in the great American dream. Only as the labor force substantially shifted from an unskilled to a highly skilled work force did the impact of poor education, failing job support, and desperate housing situations expose the enormous economic and social divides within the United States.

Among many African Americans, the nuclear family shrunk to the most basic family unit—mother and children—even as divorce rates escalated among middle class families, so that single-parent families were no longer unusual. Yet from similar situations in other parts of the world, we know that single-parent families do not suffer undue hardships, nor are they considered a problem, if they are surrounded by extended kin and a nurturing community that have a stake in the well-being of children. But today, the government is left to manage those whose lives were most jeopardized by the changes in American economics. Middle class America is also left afloat as its own secure economic base begins to erode, making the gap between rich and poor wider than it has ever been. With this middle class economic crunch, taxpayers now are resentful of the dollars spent on housing projects and welfare benefits. Congress has approved a monumental retreat from most federally funded supportive strategies. The myth that nuclear families must be self-sufficient and independent circulates without reference to the way government, unions and corporations once did so much to support the nuclear family. Few recognize that these notions about the nature of the nuclear family were and continue to be based on illusions that capitalism would always protect workers' interests; that Fordism was infinitely expandable; that an atomized family structure bound to commodities was in the national interest and worth perpetuation; that those who did not achieve the wealth and isolation of the middle class had only themselves to blame.

The Americanization movement strove for a false uniformity that found expression, among other places, in a family pattern that eventually found itself cut off from larger networks of kin, of exchange, of rapport, and finally from its own family members. The very gains that made factory labor in the United States attractive to large numbers of workers drove profit-greedy corporations to other countries for cheaper labor. The shift in today's labor force from skilled workers to technologically competent management has set thousands of American families adrift.

Today, politicians of all stripes, from Bill Clinton to Phil Gramm, are clamoring for a return to traditional family values, but those were the very values that got us into trouble in the first place (Gordon & Hunter, 1977). As nation-state agendas give way to the larger demands of global labor forces, transnational industrialization, and third-world markets, families find themselves rootless. Satellites, television, tourism, computer communications, cheap oil, cheap transport—these have brought images, foods, clothing, entertainment from various corners of the world into one place, collapsing distance, eliding space, compressing time, and glossing over cultural difference (Harvey, 1992). Values that were passed across generations are now dismissed inside decades; history is ignored because families no longer feel connected to it. The political demise of American labor is nearly complete: A proudly patriotic, unionized work force once strong in the certainty of its family roots has become a transnational, amorphous, unorganized body that gives no coherent voice to anything, except occasionally to its own oppression. The family, especially in its nuclear shape, is tossed upon this sea of change like the rest of the flotsam of postmodern life—commodified, uncertain, outmoded, and insecure.

FACING THE NEXT CENTURY

Any attempt to predict, understand, structure or guide the family in the 21st century must acknowledge the influence of government and corporations that created the configuration of the nuclear family for most of this century. The family unit is not separable from the economics and politics of national and transnational interests. In the United States, the values that defined the nuclear family only offered a solid foundation for society when the family was supported as a major labor force and a major consumer power. To be successful, however, those values made the nuclear family appear self-sufficient and independent. Now that the American nuclear family is competing for resources and jobs with the rest of the world, and national corporate interests are secondary to transnational ones, it has little internal support to fall back on.

In the 1990s, generations are disconnected from each other so completely that now each gets its own label, like independent age sets unrelated to who went before. Witness the most recently named group, poignantly but appropriately called *Generation X*. Anthropology teaches that families throughout the world have always relied on two principles: supporting networks of relationships and a historical grounding so that generations might see themselves connected to something larger than individual lives. But the history of the American nuclear family in the 20th century is one in which these principles were replaced by national economic interests under the myth of independence and autonomy. This myth must be revealed for what it is—a fiction—so that new support structures for new kinds of family units will flourish in the 21st century.

Familial diversity is a major challenge of the next century and to meet it families must be allowed their different shapes without societal fear of those differences. Throughout history, families have always evolved and changed; they have never been stable. Even the great social evolutionist Lewis Henry Morgan (1985/1877), writing in the last century, believed that the Western nuclear family was only one moment in human history.

The family in the 21st century will face challenges we cannot yet predict; no doubt our children's children will confront many we cannot even imagine.

I do not offer a prescription for how to hand these yet-unknown trials or triumphs. But I do know that unless we recognize how myths about the fundamental nature of the nuclear family as self-sufficient and autonomous generated by state and market forces gave rise to the currently withering nuclear family model, the family structures that take its place will likely be just as affected by powers outside its local spheres or interests. If a society is built of the families that comprise it, the 21st century offers a rare opportunity to confront and reshape the family structure more thoughtfully and more self-consciously than we have ever been able to do in the past.

ACKNOWLEDGMENT

I am deeply indebted to my colleague, Robin Nagle, for her editorial work on this essay.

REFERENCES

Berkson, I. B. (1969). *Theories of Americanization: A critical study.* New York: Arno Press.
Berkson, I. B. (1975). The Community Theory. In R. Meister (Ed.), *Race and ethnicity in modern America* (pp. XX–XX). Lexington, MA: D. C. Heath.
Bradshaw, I. (1925). *Americanization questionnaire: The questions usually asked of aliens applying for citizenship papers.* New York: Noble and Noble.
Carlson, R. (1975). *The quest for conformity: Americanization through education.* New York: Wiley.
Coontz, S. (1988). *The social origins of private life: A history of American families, 1600–1900.* London: Verso.
Gavit, J. P. (1922). *Americans by choice.* New York: Harper & Brothers.
Gordon, L., & Hunter, A. (1977). Sex, family and the new right: Anti-feminism as a political force. *Radical America, 11*(6)–*12*(1), 9–25.
Gramsci, A. (1971). *Selections from the prison notebooks.* New York: Columbia University Press.
Harvey, D. (1992). *The condition of postmodernity.* Cambridge, MA: Blackwell.
Lebow, E. (1993). *Tell them who I am.* New York: Free Press.
Lipsitz, G. (1986). The meaning of memory: Family, class, and ethnicity in early network television programs. *Cultural Anthropology, 1*(4), 355–387.
Morgan, L. H. (1985). *Ancient society.* Tucson: University of Arizona Press. (Original work published 1877)
O'Neill, L. D. (1977). The changing family. *The Wilson Quarterly, Winter,* 73–104.
Roberts, P. (1920). *The problem of Americanization.* New York: Macmillan.
Ross, L. (1994). Sterilization and "de facto" sterilization. *Amicus Journal, Winter,* 92.
Stack, C. (1974). *All our kin.* New York: Macmillan.
Stansell, C. (1987). *City of women: Sex and class in New York, 1789–1860.* Chicago: University of Illinois Press.
Zinn, M. B. (1989). Family, race and poverty in the eighties. *Signs, 14*(4), 856–874.

CHAPTER

7

FAMILY, NETWORKS, AND SURVIVAL ON THE THRESHOLD OF THE 21ST CENTURY IN URBAN MEXICO

Larissa Adler Lomnitz
National University of Mexico

THE GRAND-FAMILY

In cultural terms, the *grand-family* represents a value idea, a cultural category that implies a set of norms governing expected behavior between kin. It is a part of the "grammar" of behavior that reinforces the economic, social, and ritual aspects of solidarity. This idea is shared by members of the culture who attempt to conform their lives through repeated acts of ritual, exchange, and ideological commitment, although actual behavioral manifestation is subject to variations resulting from class differences and the specific conditions of an individual's life.

A grand-family is composed of a couple, their children, and their grandchildren, so that the person's "meaningful others" include parents and siblings as well as spouse and children. There is no drastic change in parent–child relations or in married children's forming homes of their own. Solidarity and ritual assistance continue. Each person adjusts to the expectations of the members of the grand-family and expects their support in return. Basic family obligations include economic support, participation in family rituals, and social recognition. The latter involves the impact of individual status changes on the entire grand-family and, perhaps more important, the corporate sharing of social networks. That is, the social relations of all members form a resource to be tapped when the need arises. One important consequence of having a three-generational family unit as the building block of society is the life span of the unit in comparison to that of the Anglo-Saxon family (Firth, 1964; Macfarlane, 1979; Schneider, 1968; Schneider & Smith, 1963).

The two-generational nuclear family is only operational for 20 to 30 years, as each son or daughter forms his or her own family unit at marriage. In the three-generational grand-family, the operational life span of the family is the life span of the grandparents and even of the great-grandparents. As long as one grandparent is alive, the family exists as an effective unity of solidarity. Only after both grandparents are deceased does each son or daughter become the head of a grand-family. This means that grand-families remain operational during the entire life of the individual, because there is no switching of allegiance at marriage. Nor do children "leave home" in a final sense in their parents' lifetime, even when they set up a separate household.

Solidarity is expressed in different forms, depending on social position, economic resources, geographical location of members, and historical or individual circumstances. In general, economic resources facilitate the expression of family solidarity, and the lack of them tends to impede such expression to a greater or lesser degree. In all cases, however, unconditional solidarity is the ideal among members of the grand-family. Such kin solidarity is expressed in four domains: social life, rituals, economic relations, and ideology, which I discuss below:

The fact that the grand-family is the basic unit of solidarity has deep implications for Mexican society. In fact, I claim that the grand-family is the metaphor for the way Mexican society is organized. A child is usually born into a large social group that, due to the demographic characteristics of Mexico, may easily number 50 to 70 people. In addition, there is the immediate kin beyond the grand-family: parents, uncles and aunts, second cousins, and so on, bringing the total number of significant relatives to 100 or more.

The size of this human group tends to grow in time, as children are born to members of both families and in-laws are acquired. This is the reference group of an individual Mexican for life. It determines social status, and supplies social control and economic and emotional support. It also provides basic social networks. In fact, kinship is the basic group from which an individual constructs his or her social networks: It is the basis of his or her social capital.

AFFINAL RELATIONS

In Mexico the kinship system is bilateral. That is, any given individual belongs to two grand-families and, by extension, to two family stocks. There are no formal norms that prescribe the choice of a mate, as marriage is supposed to be the result of free choice based on love between partners. However, there are many factors that influence the selection of spouse in an urban, social-stratified environment, in which young people are apt to meet many potential partners for marriage. In general, there is some social pressure to conform to certain social, occupational, and religious criteria. The individual actors may not be conscious of such restrictions and may believe in love as the guiding principle of mate selection unless they happen to transgress the unspoken norms, in which case they may find themselves subject to considerable social pressure.

Institutionalized matrimony is the union between two marriage partners. It also may institute a structural conflict between spouses and their respective in-laws. Most conflicts relate to kin solidarity. Each spouse is expected to continue fulfilling his or her obligations toward parents and siblings, in addition to the new set of formal obligations contracted toward the parents and siblings of the spouse.

Beginning with the wedding, a couple finds itself to be a focal point of competition between the two affinal families. Open or undeclared, this rivalry is nearly always present, and it takes place at all levels: social, economic, moral, ritual, residential, and so on. When the affinal kin live outside the city or the parents are both deceased, or belong to an inferior social stratum, there is no contest. Otherwise, the ascendency of one kin group over the other emerges gradually. Loyalties and obligations toward consanguineous kin are recognized by both sides, but the final test of ascendency is probably to be found in the lifestyle adopted by the new nuclear family. Both sets of kin usually realize this and attempt to win the new household over to their own patterns, particularly regarding the education and the world view of their grandchildren. The stronger families (economically and ideologically) exert a firmer pull over their descendants and emerge more powerful.

Open conflict, however, is averted through ritualization of affinal relations. For example, in the area that represents the most important source of potential friction—namely, the raising of grandchildren—problems are diluted through the institution of godparenthood where a male and female godparent must be chosen for each ritual situation (baptism, first communion, confirmation, or marriage). Often, a godparent is chosen from each of the affinal grand-families so that in-laws become involved in a sacred bond of cogodparenthood. In other arenas, such as ritual celebrations, Christmas presents, and ritual presentations, the relations between two sets of parents tend to be formal and ritually correct.

SEGMENTATION AND EVOLUTION

Each individual belongs to two grand-families: the family of origin of the father and that of the mother, until, eventually, each forms his or her own family and later becomes the head of his or her own household. An individual continues to belong to the remnants of the original grand-families after the death of both parents. These remnants include siblings, aunts, uncles, cousins, nieces, and nephews. The children of one set of parents grow up with the experience of solidarity with uncles, aunts, and first cousins who, though they do not belong to the individual's grand-family, still require a prescribed amount of loyalty and affection.

How and When Are the Limits of Kin Solidarity Defined?

Clearly, solidarity relations and obligations are created first between children and their parents and siblings, later they extend to both parents' consanguineous kin, to one's spouse, one's children and, eventually, to one's grandchildren. Linear relations have priority over collateral relations. This rule is reflected in the inheritance laws.

The next highest order of solidarity in the kinship system is logically found in the fourth young generation's descendance group—namely, the group of all linear descendents of a common great-grandfather. We call such a group a *branch*. The level of solidarity among members of a branch is lower than among members of a grand-family, but it is still considerable.

It is also helpful to use the concept of *stock*, defined as all the descendants of a man and his wife, counting descent through females as well as males, regardless of the interactions that exist between them. In a kinship system based on the grand-family, individuals who are members of the same stock are more likely to meet and engage in significant social interactions among them than, for example, in a kinship system based on a two-generation nuclear family. In fact, each individual is considered to belong to four stocks: those of his or her four paternal or maternal grandparents. The four corresponding family names are often known by each member and members of any of the four stocks are recognized as potential relatives: They are the members of the kindred of a given individual.

In conclusion, the segmentations and evolution of stocks are based primarily on the principle of linear descent and secondarily on solidarity between descendents of a common ancestor. The more distant the common ancestor, the less intense is the solidarity: from the nuclear family (two generations), to the grand-family (three generations), to the branch (four generations), to members who acknowledge belonging to a common stock, to the boundaries of the cognitive map of one's kindred.

KINDRED

If a stock is composed of all the descendants of a man and his wife, a kindred consists of all one's bilateral consanguineous relations. The kindred is a cognitive category that takes the individual self as a point of reference; in practice an ego's kindred consists of the members of his or her stocks that he or she knows.

In order to understand the process of kinship in nonunilineal societies—meaning the actual behavior as opposed to the formal structure—the theory of social networks is useful. Firth (1964) pointed out that a kindred in a modern complex society is not a true social group because its membership is based on recognition by the individuals. But the criteria of inclusion and exclusion are not entirely governed by personal whim; rather the development of exchange relations plays a mayor role of the constitution of the kindred. The main forms of exchange among kin are exchanges of information and exchange of goods and services. Kindred grows through personal contacts with members of the kindred, or shrinks through the lack of information and loss of contact.

The flow of information is largely transmitted in social encounters—both formal and informal. The information is updated in an institutionalized arena—ritual family get-togethers at which attendance becomes tantamount to a mutual acknowledgment of family affiliation. A prolonged absence from family rituals, however involuntary, may mean a weakening of family links and the eventual estrangement of the individual concerned.

In the case of upper class families, the social acknowledgment of kinship of distant relatives is conditioned by criteria like prestige, class, politics, social behavior and personal preference. Relatives who have sunk below a "decent middle-class" socioeconomic level, or who have committed some social breach of the norm, are ignored or deliberatedly excluded from the kinship network. They are no longer invited to family reunions with the result that such individuals disappear from the kinship map of younger family members.

Business and family interests are inextricably interwoven; it may be said that the system of economic exchange is embedded in a matrix of family recognitions. The factors that determine the intensity of exchange between members of the kindred are the following:

1. *Physical distance.* Families living in close proximity have more opportunities to share experiences and exchange communications, goods, and services.

2. *Genealogical distance.* This is the ideal model of kinship relations, as internalized by members of the culture. It implies a set of rights and obligations that depend on the specific degree of kinship.

3. *Economic distance.* This may be of two kinds: differences in the type of economic activity and differences in the amount of capital.

4. *Age difference.* These generation gaps imply changing viewpoints, interests, and ideologies, tending to increase social distance.

5. *Ideological distance.* Ideological differences such as political and religious differences also increase the social distance among its members.

All these factors determine the degree of *confianza* or personal trust that expresses or measures the capacity and disposition to exchange information and favors between two particular individuals. Physical, genealogical, socio-economic, ideological, and generational closeness promote a level of *confianza* that determines the intensity of exchange between the kinship network.

SOCIAL NETWORKS

The family, as understood in all of the broad meanings I defined, is basic to the construction of social networks which ensure physical and class survival among upper, middle, and lower classes. Thus, one might visualize social networks as a sort of capital, usable to build economic enterprises—formal and informal—and social security mechanisms.

A social network is a social field of relationships between individuals as defined by some underlying variable (Barns, 1954; Mayer, 1968; Mitchell, 1969; Wolf, 1969). This variable may refer to any specific aspect of the relationship (e.g., kinship, mutual help, drug trafficking, political activism, etc.).

My own interest is the study of social networks as defined by an exchange of goods, services, and economically relevant information among members. This use of social resources for economic ends is what I call *social capital*, and it is found among all social strata, as this chapter shows.

MIDDLE-CLASS NETWORKS

In Latin America, the middle classes have developed since the latter part of the 19th century, but particularly grown since the 1930s, when the state apparatus took over the modernizing project of industrialization. The middle class is characterized by its heterogeneity and by the lack of clear criteria to define itself. Although there is a growing sector of middle class business-men, the Latin American middle class is mainly composed of members of the state apparatus, such as civil servants or public university professors. The new elite, which in effect rules the public life, come mainly from this middle class, among whose ranks are the politicians, technocrats, intellec-tuals, and upper echelons of the armed forces, who cooperate or compete among themselves for the control of the state apparatus.

To acquire the skills to occupy different positions it is necessary for individuals to go through a period of training in educational institutions. That includes also the professional people working for private corporations. There is thus a direct relationship between the development and evolution of the new middle class elites and the university, because the latter not only transmits the knowledge allowing an individual to legitimize his or her position in the state apparatus, but it also trains the technological leaders of the future.

Political leaders and technical *cadres* are socialized in the same political culture, learning the art of negotiation and establishing the social networks that will form the bases of the principles and alliances of the national political culture. Hence, the national universities are the breeding grounds for the political and technical elites for the state apparatus, and the arena where permanent cliques and social networks are being formed.

The social survival of this middle class group (that is, maintaining the status and way of life suitable to that category) depends, to a great extent, on its access to a close knowledge of the bureaucracy, in order to use social resources for economic ends. For an individual, access to the state apparatus depends to a large extent on a network of political, social, and family connections. These networks operate as systems of reciprocity that consist of a continuous exchange of favors. An ideal of friendship, reinforced by social closeness, motivates the exchange. The favors tend to be bureaucratic in nature, consisting usually of preferential treatment in dealing with red-tape procedures and priority access to the services offered by the state. This social institution allows people to maintain certain privileges, and to have access to jobs and to services that the state offers but not always is able to provide to all society members.

This social institution which has euphemistical names in different countries (*compadrazgo, palanca, pitutos, sociolismo, relaciones*, etc.) operates usually among social equals—men and women—and among people that have gone to the same school, who have undergone similar political experiences, and who move in the same social circles.

The most typical favor obtained through social relations is getting a job, which entails a mental revision of all personal relationships until one hits on a friend with some link to the personnel department of the specific agency where employment is sought. In the same way, when candidates for some vacancy are required, a list of friends and relatives is gone over until the appropriate person is found. Other typical favors include the expedition of obtaining certificates, licenses, permits, or passports and simplifying bothersome red-tape procedures.

Most of the services entail economic advantages for the individuals who receive them as a guarantee of a higher level of material life. Salaried middle-class people typically do not have savings, and the economic difficulties can typically recur in a situation of chronic inflation.

Middle class people live in economic limitation. They must conform to insufficient salaries, sometimes equal to those of manual workers, yet their actual standard of living must be patterned like that of the middle classes of the more prosperous societies. Money may be scarce, but a well-placed friend or relative in a loan association or a bank facilitates getting money or the access to an apartment in a public housing project. Friends and relatives might be helpful in getting one's children admitted to public—but prestigious—schools, where they can meet other children who will become members of their lifetime networks. Friends may give advice and job openings, scholarships, medical services in public hospitals, and so on. The ideal of such a middle class member is always to have "the right person at the right place and the right time" (Lomnitz Adler, 1971, p. 96).

The social network of people one can trust to ask for such favors begins with the immediate grand-family, continues through friends and close members of the kindred group, and extends also to other relevant personal social networks. Hence, kinship is again the building block of a person's network, although friendship is also important.

Women provide an important part of a family's network through their own grand-families and kindred and also through their own friends. Furthermore, they are the ones that organize the social life of a nuclear family by being in charge of social parties and rituals.

UPPER CLASS NETWORKS

Entrepreneurial groups based on kinship affiliation (family enterprises) were the basis of the Mexican industrial development until the end of World War II. They are still so—although non-kinship-based corporate organizations are increasing.

Traditionally, the Latin American entrepreneur depends to a considerable extent on social resources for economic ends (Aubey, 1977; Greenfield & Strickon, 1979; Lipset & Solari, 1967; Lomnitz Adler & Pérez Lizaúr, 1987; Long, 1977; Strickon, 1965).

Social relations that engender confidence and trust are critical resources in the entrepreuneurial venture. Three major aspects of the economic utilization of social resources may be singled out: action groups, social networks for the circulation of information, and social networks for facilitating access to economic resources.

1. *Action groups* refer to the pattern of diversification typical of Latin American industrial development, in which a state of insecurity is generally the norm. Initially, an entrepreneur may attend his business personally in all aspects, but with growth and diversification "people of *confianza*" are placed in a position of trust. Usually they are brothers-in-law, nephews, and later sons of the entrepreneur, who often become the owners of the inherited enterprises. Eventually, all these owners and their kinship clients become a corporate group centered around the *patron*. In effect, the entrepreneurs become brokers between the family enterprise, their kinship groups, and

the national system. The entire kinship network of each entrepreneur represents a pool from which managerial personnel is selected, as well as constitutes a network of peripherally related enterprises, which though privately owned by members of the family, act as a corporation.

2. *Access to information.* Economically valuable information is circulated constantly among kinship networks and their allied networks beyond family boundaries. Occasions are provided by innumerable ritual family gatherings and the membership of entrepreneurs in formal and informal organizations. Information is a primary resource in the Latin American economy. However, as public information is scarce and not always reliable, networks represent the main source for business intelligence. In family parties it flows freely, and business conversation is quite active even among women. Hardly any social occasion goes by without a new business deal being made.

3. *Access to economic resources.* An entrepreneur is a businessman who is also an innovator. In the traditional literature the innovations introduced by the entrepreneur consists in identifying and using new technologies, developing new products, or opening up new markets. In the case of Mexico, the most remarkable and novel aspect refers to the development and use of social networks for tapping the economic resources.

In the case studied, family contacts with the church hierarchy during the last decades of the 19th century allowed the first entrepreneur to get access to capital; his son became attached to the postrevolutionary regime from which licenses and financial support were obtained. Later on, contacts with the banking Spanish community allowed a member of the family to get access to more capital. It is interesting to note that in those families there are several "centralizing" women who maintain the family's spirit and solidarity through the transmission of social and economic information within the family network. In fact, they become intermediaries between members of the different branches, including the less affluent ones (whose members often are in need of jobs or loans) and the entrepreneurs. During social gatherings and through almost daily telephone conversations, these "centralizing" women inform their closer relatives of the latest events and gossip gathered in their daily rounds, including economic information. Like in the case of the middle class families, women are also the organizers of family rituals, which are veritable arenas of communication among the kinship network.

THE NETWORKS OF THE URBAN POOR

For decades, the term informal economy referred to the urban poor or the "informal sector" of Latin American cities. It is the sector of the working class characterized by a chronic state of economic insecurity, both regarding income and permanent employment.

The informal sector is composed of urban workers who are not contractually articulated to the formal, modern sector of society, thus lacking job stability, the benefits of modern labor legislation, and welfare. This stratum is typically composed of migrants and their descendents—often all from the landless peasantry. It also includes small family enterprises, usually unregulated economic activities, criminal or legal (Castells & Portes, 1986; de Soto, 1987). All those activities are made possible by using social networks through which a substratum of trust has been built among its members, allowing for unregulated or sometimes illegal exchanges to take place (Lomnitz Adler, 1988).

In order to be able to survive during recurrent periods of unemployment, members of the informal sector make full and varied use of their social resources. Lomnitz Adler (1977) showed the way the stratum generates their own security mechanisms by means of reciprocity networks, mainly among neighbors and kin. Among the social resources utilized are intrafamily cooperation (for example, wives prepare food for sale, children shine shoes, wash cars, or beg in the streets, old people raise animals or become water carriers) to complement the wages of the heads of the households. A network typically consists of four or five nuclear families who dwell in adjoining quarters or even under the same roof. Nonkin neighbors may also be incorporated into such informal networks by means of an intense exchange of goods and services, which usually leads to the establishment of fictive parenthood (*compadrazgo*). In addition to physical and social proximity, one key variable governing membership into networks is, once again, *confianza* (trust), which is born first out of sociability. It is generally kinship among extended families through which this trust appears as part of a cultural norm. Women request cooperation on a daily basis from neighbors, such as the frequent borrowing of small amounts of food or money or baby-sitting. Hence, women in the shantytown are the basic agents in the formation of the network structure. Lomnitz Adler (1977), in her study of a Mexican shantytown, found that to an important degree exchange networks were organized around a forceful female figure (usually the mother) who would set the tone for mutual assistance. In the absence of such a female moral leader, the network tended to disintegrate.

THE CRISIS OF THE 1980s AND FAMILY SURVIVAL ON THE THRESHOLD OF THE 21st CENTURY

It is recognized that during the decade of the 1980s most Latin American countries underwent what is known as the "foreign debt crisis." During the decades following World War II, the *desarrollista* (developmental) state was the sociopolitical and economic pivot of the model of growth and partial modernization was implemented. The state expanded and assumed varied functions: job creation, capital accumulation, the creation of public enterprises, and the provision of social services (health, education, housing, social security). It also provided private enterprise by means of subsidies, protection, and credit (Sunkel, 1988).

All this was done on the basis of industrial development already achieved and the surplus generated by traditional exports income. However these measures were not enough to sustain growth and fulfill all the functions the state had assumed. Society was coming to demand more and more: As the surplus run out, the government increasingly resorted to inflationary financing and later to taking out loans from foreign sources, the latter process reaching a feverish climax during the 1970s.

The spectacular level of foreign borrowing came to an abrupt end in 1982 when the foreign debt crisis curtailed the state's accumulating and redistributing role. At that point, not only was that a source of credit loss, but there was now the need to send large remittances abroad. The policies of economic adjustment were the reply to this situation. They included, on the one hand, an attempt to increase exports with the aim of generating income in foreign currency, and on the other, the cutting back of the public sector as a whole, dismissing public servants, keeping salaries depressed, reducing expenditure on public social services, eliminating subsidies, decreasing public investment, and privatizing public enterprises, while attempting to increase the government's revenue.

This is what is known as the *neoliberal model* which was implemented under the following assumptions: Efficient resource assignment must incorporate a free market and the opening up of the economy to foreign competition; public enterprises are less efficient than private ones; economic freedom is the basis of and the prerequisite for political freedom, and the growth of the economy will necessarily benefit all social groups in the country.

The idea that the free market will automatically produce correctives to the early defects of neoliberal restructuring has not been demonstrated in practice. Though not openly, unemployment is incessantly growing. As the lack of a steady income makes it impossible for families to survive, the growth of the informal sector has also grown. This sector, composed of independent workers (artisans, craftsmen), small family enterprises (comprising fewer than 5 family members), and underemployed salaried workers, has increased to approximately 51% of the urban population in Mexico. Furthermore, middle class groups of public and private employees have been dismissed, increasing the level of unemployed or private economic activities such as taxi driving, door to door sales of homemade products, book vendors, and so on.

Finally, traditional industrial enterprises, which previously represented the upper echelon of the bourgeoisie, have lost their ability to compete for the consumers market. This follows, because these businesses lack capital to introduce technological innovations that would allow them to compete with foreign corporations displaying superior organization and technology.

In summary, the crisis at the end of the 20th century is affecting all levels of the population, except for a small number of corporations and the privileged employees that work for them. In this setting, the importance of what I call *social capital* becomes paramount: As I have shown, individuals rely more and more on their personal networks to cope with the ups and downs of their privatized economy. The family is not only the basic building block of an individual's social networks but also the only group a person can rely on for help in moments of crisis. Therefore, in Mexico the traditional extended family—or grand-family—is not on the verge of disappearing, as has been predicted by the modernization theorists, but, quite the opposite, it is entering into the 21st century more fortified than ever.

ACKNOWLEDGMENT

I thank Ms. Narda Alcántara Valverde, of the Applied Mathematics and Systems Research Institute of the National University of Mexico, for editing this chapter.

REFERENCES

Aubey, R. T. (1979). Capital mobilization and patterns of business, ownership, and control in cultural context. In S. Greenfield, A. Strickon, & R. Aubey (Eds.), *Entrepreneurs in cultural context*. Albuquerque: University of New Mexico.

Barnes, J. A. (1954). Class committees in a Norwegian Island. *Human Relations, 7*, 39–58.

Castells, C., & Portes, A. (1991). The informal economy. In C. Castells, A. Portes, & L. Benton (Eds.), *The informal economy: Studies in advanced and less developed countries*. Baltimore: Johns Hopkins University Press.

de Soto, H. (1986). *El otro sendero. La revolución informal* [The other path]. México: Diana.

Firth, R. (1964). Family and kinship in industrial society. *Sociological Review, 8*, 65–87.

Greenfield, S. M., & Strickon, A. (1979). Entrepreneurship and social change: toward a populational decision-making approach. In S. Greenfield, A. Strickon, & R. Aubey (Eds.), *Entrepreneurs in cultural context* (pp. 329–350). Albuquerque: University of New Mexico.

Lipset, S. M., & Solari, A. (Eds.). (1967). *Elites in Latin America*. London: Oxford University.

Lomnitz Adler, L. (1971). Reciprocity of favors in the urban middle class of Chile. In G. Dalton (Ed.), *Studies in economic anthropology* (pp. 93–106). Washington, DC: American Anthropological Association.

Lomnitz Adler, L. (1977). *Networks and marginality: Life in a Mexican shanty town*. New York: Academic Press.

Lomnitz Adler, L. (1988). The social and economic organization of a Mexican shanty town. In *The urbanization of the Third World*. Oxford, England: Oxford University.

Lomnitz Adler, L., & Lizaúr, M. P. (1987). *A Mexican elite family, 1820–1980: Kinship, class and culture*. Princeton, NJ: Princeton University.

Long, N. (1977). Commerce and kinship in the Peruvian highlands. In E. Mayer & R. Bolton (Eds.), *Andean kinship and marriage* (pp. 123–158). Washington, DC: American Anthropological Association.

Macfarlane, A. (1979). *The origins of English individualism.* Cambridge, England: Cambridge University Press.

Mayer, A. (1968). The significance of quasi-groups in the study of complex societies. In M. Banton (Ed.), *The social anthropology of complex societies.* London: Tavistock.

Mitchell, C. (1969). *Social networks in urban situations.* Manchester, England: Manchester University Press.

Schneider, D. M. (1968). *American kinship: A cultural account.* Englewood Cliffs: Prentice-Hall.

Schneider, D. M., & Smith, R. T. (1973). *Class differences and sex roles in American kinship and family structure.* Englewood Cliffs, NJ: Prentice-Hall.

Strickon, A. (1965). Class and kinship in Argentina. In A. D. Heath & R. Adams (Eds.), *Contemporary cultures and societies of Latin America* (pp. 324–341). New York: Random House.

Sunkel, O. (1988). *Perspectivas demográficas y crisis de desarrollo* [Demographic perspectives and crisis of development]. Unpublished manuscript.

Wolf, E. (1969). Kinship, friendship and patron-client relations. In M. Banton (Ed.), *The social anthropology of complex societies.* London: Tavistock.

CULTURE, SOCIETY, AND THE FAMILY

8

VIOLENCE-FREE FAMILIES

Beverly Birns
State University of New York at Stony Brook

Susan Birns
Syracuse University

The home, perceived as a safe haven of love and intimacy, is frequently a dangerous place. In the United States, violence in the family has been declared a major public health problem. Millions of women and children are assaulted each year. Women are more likely to be injured by male partners than by strangers, and most sexual abuse of children is perpetrated by male family members or friends.

We document the extent of abuse of women and children and use common myths to demonstrate the negative effect of false theory on clinical treatment and intervention. The myths concern individual pathology, gender symmetry regarding perpetrators, and women's freedom to leave abusive relationships. We propose that to progress towards violence-free families in the next century, changes need to be made in all the relevant social institutions. An imperative social change concerns the existing power structure within society that supports male dominance.

VIOLENCE-FREE FAMILIES

On July 8th, 1992, Kathy Germaine, a successful businesswoman and mother of two sons was murdered in Holbrook, a suburb of New York City. She was shot 5 times with a semiautomatic gun (Taylor & Gallagher, 1992). She was not a victim of random street violence, nor was she killed during a robbery or while fighting off a rapist. Kathy was one of the 1,200 American women killed annually by their male partners (Novello, Rosenburg, Saltzman, & Shosky, 1992). Prior to her death, she had been one of the 2,000,000 to 4,000,000 women beaten or seriously threatened by their male partners each year (Browne, 1992).

Kathy's husband, Thomas Germaine, a man with a stable work history, had been perceived by many to be a responsible but very demanding husband. Less well known was his history of threatening behavior. Kathy was not the only victim in her family. Thomas also beat one of her two sons, his stepson, Michael (Vitello, 1993). Michael was one of the 3,000,000 reported seriously abused children in the United States each year (Department of Health and Human Services, 1996).

Thomas's final rage was triggered when he was served with divorce papers. In fact, several studies documented that women are most at risk for being murdered when they threaten to leave and when they actually do leave (Walker, 1989). Contrary to popular myths regarding victims, Kathy Germaine was not a passive victim. Nor was she a dependent, helpless, masochist. She worked, separated from Thomas, served him with divorce papers, and went to court to request an order of protection, a legal document ordering batterers to refrain from any further contact with the abused.

Despite Thomas' history of extreme physical violence towards her son, his stalking behavior, threats to her, and possession of many weapons, the judge postponed the order of protection. We cite this tragic case because it illustrates many of the issues we discuss in this chapter. There is a complex mythology surrounding violence within the family. We address three primary myths, their sources, and the need to reframe the issues in order to promote social change.

THE MYTHS

The myths are the following:

1. Violence within the family is relatively rare and reflects the psychopathology of both the perpetrator and the victim. Violence, according to the myth, is purely personal, not a social problem.
2. Family violence is gender neutral—each partner is equally likely to abuse the other.
3. Adequate help is available to battered women and abused children, for both treatment and prevention of the violence in their lives. When battered women, or the mothers of abused children, stay it is their free choice.

Many chapters in this volume discuss changes occurring as we approach the new century. Our topic, domestic violence, is ancient. However, research in this area is new, and the findings are shocking. We hope that everyone continues to be shocked by "the dark side of families" (Finkelhor, Gelles, Hotaling, & Straus, 1983); the violence that characterizes so many intimate relationships. We contend that its roots lie in the fundamental inequality between men and women in marriage as well as in all other social institutions (Okun, 1986; Schecter, 1982; Walker, 1984).

Domestic violence is a topic fraught with considerable emotion and misinformation. In order to envision violence-free families in the next century, we must begin with an accurate analysis of the violence currently documented. In order to generate social change, we must move beyond analysis of the individual to an analysis of society. Why does our society not only tolerate, but even foster violence in the home?

We argue that these myths must be dispelled if we are to diminish and ultimately end family violence. Violence against women and children, and indeed all violence, is a social problem (Birns, 1988; Birns, Cascardi, & Meyer, 1989; Koop, 1992). Although each act is an individual act, the magnitude of these acts makes domestic violence a major public health problem (Browne, 1992; Stark, Flitcraft, & Frazier, 1979) that must ultimately be solved at a societal level.

Second, we argue that *family violence* is a misnomer. By definition, most intimate violence occurs within a family context, but calling it *family violence* implies that all members of the family contribute equally to its occurrence and are equally victimized. We will demonstrate that most, although not all, family violence involves male perpetrators with women and children as victims.

Finally, we address the following question: Why don't women leave? Women who don't leave, as well as those who do, are often motivated by terror, fear for their lives, and fear for the lives of their children (Walker, 1989). Women also stay because they lack the appropriate resources, are often refused help, and, with the exception of shelters may have no place to go.

MYTH I

Violence seldom occurs in families. When it does occur, it is a personal, psychological problem. Abusive men are psychopaths or psychotic and the women they abuse are masochists.

But:

There is no evidence that Thomas Germaine had a mental health problem, nor is there evidence that Kathy either enjoyed or elicited his violent behavior. She actively tried to protect herself and her children.

American culture has traditionally presented the home as an island of safety in an otherwise harsh world. We teach children to be wary of strangers and to stay home at night in order to avoid being kidnapped or raped. We perceive the family as the source of love and trust. The notion that love and violence characterize the same relationship violates our idealized vision of family life (Straus, Gelles, & Steinmetz, 1980) and requires a reconceptualization of the family. National crime statistics and national studies demonstrate that violent acts in the home can no longer be viewed as rare isolated events (Straus et al., 1980; Straus & Gelles, 1986; DHHS, 1988).

Studies published in the *Journal of the American Medical Association* (1992) indicate that between one fifth and one third of all women are assaulted by a partner or ex-partner during their lifetime. Women are also more likely to be raped, injured, or killed by their male partners than by all other assailants (Browne, 1992). According to McFarlane, Parker, Soeken, and Bullock (1992), 17% of pregnant women, regardless of income or educational level, are assaulted during pregnancy, harming them and their fetuses. Other studies cite even higher rates of abuse during pregnancy (Helton, McFarlane, & Anderson, 1987). Furthermore 25% to 45% of women living with batterers are abused during pregnancy (Jones, 1993).

There are approximately 3,000,000 children reported to be seriously abused each year. Indications are that these numbers are underestimates and also that they are increasing (DHHS, 1996). Straus et al. (1980) initially described the high correlation between spouse abuse and child abuse. They claimed that 70% of children of "abusive couples" were abused. More recent research indicates that as many as 60% of children with injuries serious enough to have them brought to an emergency room had mothers who had also been abused (McKibben, DeVos, & Newberger, 1989; Stark & Flitcraft, 1988). In 1992 there were more than 1,261 child abuse fatalities in the United States, most at the hands of their parents or other caretakers. Futhermore, this number represents an increase from previous years (McCurdy & Daro, 1993).

Studies indicate that 70% of violent husbands are also violent fathers or stepfathers (Bowker, Arbitell, & McFerron, 1988). The belief that male violence against women and children is rare suggests a psychological analysis of perpetrator and victim. When the abuse of children, and the abuse of women, first became the object of scientific scrutiny, many believed that serious intimate violence could only be perpetrated by severely disturbed individuals. In fact, the search for specific psychological causes and profiles continues today.

Male perpetrators previously believed to be psychotic are now described as suffering from low self-esteem, emotional dependency, and poor ability to control anger because of childhood experience (Goldstein & Rosenbaum, 1985). Although it is true that many abusive men report having been abused as children, or having witnessed abuse, psychotherapy was proved to be unsuccessful (Adams, 1988; Tolman & Bennett, 1990). In fact, psychotherapy in many cases served to support and justify men in their violent behavior (Adams, 1988).

Whereas psychological analysis portrays violent men as either psychopathic or inadequate, it portrays the victims as passive or masochistic (Young & Gerson, 1991). The assumption is that normal people, when assaulted, remove themselves from situations threatening further danger. Because battered women, by definition, endure multiple attacks, some claim they provoke and enjoy the abuse.

Crimes of violence against women are one example of society blaming the victim. Since battering emerged as a problem, some have promulgated profiles of the typical battered woman. For decades, psychiatrists were taught that women were battered because of flaws in their character, usually labelled *masochism*. This was part of the Freudian interpretation of women as intellectually, morally, and emotionally inferior, that is, childlike, and inadequate. This discredited view sees the source of family violence as the result of female inadequacy and neurosis (Birns, 1988).

Belief that the root of violence against women lies in the psychic structure of women is basic to the most commonly asked question about abused wives: Why don't they leave? The following erroneous assumptions underlie this myth: Battered women don't seek help; battered women are free to leave—they have a place to go; battered women fail to protect their children; battered women become safe when they leave; and, generally speaking, battered women "choose to stay" (Okun, 1986). Because these assumptions are seldom true, treatment and intervention based upon them often lead to catastrophic results.

Trying to "fix" the problems of battered women and encouraging them to try to mend the marriage removes the responsibility for the violence from the perpetrator and may lead to escalation. Most men abuse not because of underlying psychopathology but primarily because their abusive behavior gets them what they want—the *control* of their partners (Pagelow, 1984; Schecter, 1982).

Individual causes cannot explain the epidemic of abuse. Each individual brings to every relationship some of their past and present conflicts, anxieties, attitudes, and behaviors. When behavior affects millions of individuals, it is obligatory to ask this question: What in the social fabric explains the epidemic? An example from medicine clarifies this point. In 1992, more than 52,000 cases of tuberculosis were reported to the Centers for Disease Control in the United States (Alland et al., 1994). Tuberculosis, a bacterial disease, is again becoming a major public health problem with primarily social roots. Although each patient requires medical treatment, it was well established that only public health measures aimed specifically at prevention will stop its rise. So it is with violence within the family.

In the case of violence, each victim requires protection that will prevent further harm, and every abuser requires intervention directed toward ending the violence. Ultimately, we must look at the environment in which both tuberculosis and domestic violence occur. What are the toxic social conditions that allow for millions of women and children to be seriously assaulted each year?

Just as poverty is the environment that fosters tuberculosis, the concentration of power and control in male hands in most social institutions provides the environment that fosters the battering of women and children.

MYTH 2

Family violence is gender neutral. Women and men are equally violent toward each other and toward the children.

But:

Kathy did not threaten to kill her husband, own a gun, or abuse her children. Thomas beat her son and terrorized her.

Academic research, clinical intervention, and public policy in the United States are all influenced by the debate over "gender neutrality" of violence in the family. Some claim that women are as violent or even more violent than men in marriage (McNeely & Robinson-Simpson, 1987; Steinmetz, 1977–1978). If this claim is true—that either spouse is equally likely to abuse the other or to abuse the children—then family violence is the appropriate label. If violence in the family is perpetrated primarily by men against women and child victims, as we contend, then *family violence* is a poor term. Despite the epidemiological data documenting pervasive male violence against women and children, the myth of gender neutrality persists. What is the source of this myth and why is it so dangerous (Dobash, Dobash, Wilson, & Daly, 1992)?

Prior to 1980, the primary data on violence within the family came from police and hospital records. Therefore, little was known about its incidence in the population at large. In 1980, Straus et al. published a landmark study, documenting the widespread incidence of violence within the American family. Using a random sample of more than 2,000 married subjects as well as Straus et al.'s newly developed measure, the Conflict Tactic Scale (CTS), the authors documented the widespread use of violence among family members.

They found that 16% of individuals they interviewed reported at least one violent act during the preceding year and that almost 10% described severe violent acts, such as kicking, biting, punching, or the use of gun or knife.

Sixty percent of parents reported hitting their children and severely abusive behavior toward children was admitted by 4% of the parents.

The CTS, an easily administered questionnaire, asks adults about their techniques of conflict resolution. Questions concerning violence range from verbal threats to the use of a knife or a gun. Based on their data they estimated that nearly 500,000 parents use a knife or a gun against their children.

The authors claimed that women are as violent as men and that the "marriage license is a hitting license." They stated that contrary to popular image, the home is as much a battleground as a safe haven. One member of the original team, Steinmetz, in subsequent publications, went so far as to claim that women are more violent than men and that the focus of research and service should be on battered husbands (Steinmetz, 1977–1978). This interpretation contradicts all other available data from government studies and medical records (Browne, 1992; McCleer, 1989; Novello et al., 1992).

In spite of the value of this sociological study in demonstrating the prevalence of violence within the typical American family, the research is seriously flawed. Problems with the CTS, coupled with errors in design, create and sustain the false conclusion concerning the absence of gender differences in violence within the home. One major design flaw consisted of only interviewing couples living together. Women most at risk for abuse, those who had taken steps to end the marriage by leaving their abusive husbands, were excluded. Walker (1989) cited United States Department of Justice data indicating that 70% of assaults of women by intimates occur when the women threaten to, or actually, leave. Straus et al. (1980) also excluded husbands and wives with children under 3 years of age, who are known to have high rates of family discord and probable high rates of aggression.

More serious than flaws in design are the problems inherent in the CTS. The CTS asks only whether or not specific actions occurred, ignoring who initiated the aggression and their consequences (see Dobash, Dobash, Wilson, & Daly, 1992, for full discussion). Few battered men appear in hospital emergency rooms, and probably equally few are afraid of their wives. Although Cascardi, Langhinrichen, and Vivian (1992) support the finding of equal episodes of husband and wife aggression, these authors stated that 95% of injuries sustained by couples requiring medical intervention are sustained by wives. Further, they report the physical injuries and psychological sequaelae of the violence are very different for wives and husbands.

Compare, for example, a man saying to his wife, "Clean this house, or I'll beat you," versus the wife saying, "Clean this house, or I'll beat you later." Many men report laughing at their wives when the women threaten or engage in acts of physical violence.

For women, threats or the use of violence are never a laughing matter, rather they cause dread and frequently physical and psychological ailments. High rates of suicide attempts, sleep disorders, and depression are all reported in women who are repeatedly physically abused and threatened (Stark et al., 1979; Cascardi et al., 1992).

Counting episodes of specific types of violence, an analysis that excludes precipitating events and consequences provides limited and faulty data. A shove from an angry spouse is different than a shove that is a means of self-defense used to protect oneself from violence.

The implications of research claiming husbands and wives are equally violent extends to treatment protocols, service provision, social policy, funding decisions, and ultimately to primary prevention. If violence is gender-neutral, the following interventions are both appropriate and sufficient to treat and prevent violence within the family. Couples counseling involves seeing the pair together assuming that each member contributes equally to the problem and that careful listening, support, and specific strategies will help the couple resolve their conflicts. Often the wife speaks honestly, the abusive partner minimizes or denies the violence, and after the session becomes even more violent towards his wife for exposing him. The National Center on Women and Family Law, Inc. (1993) cited several studies demonstrating the serious harm done when this approach is applied in therapy.

Teaching couples how to negotiate conflict successfully is a useful thing to do. However, assuming that each spouse contributes equally to the use of force implies that each member is required to change his or her behavior to end the violence. Years of experience with this approach (Adams, 1988) documented that wives are not equally violent and that women's changing their behavior does *not* successfully diminish the violence.

Assuming that men are equally battered implies that funding should be equally available for battered men. In 1985, then Surgeon General Koop declared that "violence against women is the number one health problem of American women" (Cascardi et al., 1992, p. 1178). Furthermore, in 1992 the Council on Ethical and Judicial Affairs of the American Medical Association declared that, "most evidence indicates that domestic violence is predominantly perpetrated by men against women" (p. 3190).

Federal legislation passed in 1994, entitled the Violence Against Women Act, demonstrates the conviction of the United States government that violence against women is the problem. We support the following claims of Dobash et al. (1992, p. 71):

> Violence against wives is often persistent and severe, occurs in the context of continuous intimidation and coercion and is inextricably linked to attempts to dominate and control women. . . . If violence is gendered, as it assuredly is, explicit characterizations of gender's relevance to violence is essential.

Once it is accepted that men deny or justify acts of violence towards women and children, the legal, medical, psychological, and social service fields will increasingly be required to reformulate their attitudes and behaviors.

The major intervention, when abuse occurs, must be the protection of the victims from further harm. It is imperative for judges, such as those hearing Kathy Germaine's request for an order of protection, to ask sufficient questions to understand the danger of the situation. Certain risk factors must be taken seriously. These include the escalating level and frequency of violence perpetrated, violence towards other family members, stalking behavior (now a punishable act in several states), and the presence of many guns in the house.

To gather knowledge about the abuse of women and children, simple questionnaires with *yes* or *no* answers never can be accepted as definitive sources of data. The voices of the abused must be heard in order to analyze the nature of abuse and its sequelae. When a policeman arrives at a home and finds a woman crying and screaming, and a man who calmly says, "Officer, you can see that she is hysterical/crazy," it is imperative that the officer recognize that the woman's "state" is almost certainly a function of her victimization. Redistributing the focus of attention from, "Why doesn't she leave" to "What gives him the *right* to batter" and "What must be done to stop him" will help address some of the errors made in the field.

Most of all, having addressed the fundamental fallacy of gender neutrality, it becomes imperative to consider the gender inequality that pervades social institutions in general and marriage in particular.

MYTH 3

The "helping systems" protect battered women and children from future acts of violence. Battered women who stay, remain because they choose to.

But:

Kathy Germaine sought assistance from the court by applying for an order of protection AND she had her husband served with divorce papers, immediately prior to her death.

Each year, thousands of deaths result from violence among family members and millions of women and children are seriously injured, demonstrating the failure of the existing systems. Violence, once begun, tends to escalate in frequency and severity. Appropriate intervention at several levels would diminish, although not end, violence. In the United States at this time, many laws were passed (National Center to Prevent the Abuse and Neglect of Children, 1974; the Violence Against Women Act, 1995), agencies established, and studies completed. However, epidemiological data indicate that on most measures, the number and severity of violent episodes is escalating, not diminishing.

Existing Interventions

Shelters. The most positive intervention to date are shelters for battered women and their children (Pagelow, 1984; Schecter, 1982). Change occurs in shelters where women are first of all provided with safety and secondly with the necessary supportive service to evaluate their options and the supports necessary to act upon them. Although many women do return to their homes before finally leaving or otherwise ending the violence, they receive support for their struggles and conflicts, gain knowledge about how to protect themselves, and gain some control of their lives.

Legal System. One failure of the legal system to protect women and children is clear in the case of Kathy Germaine, who appealed to the court and was denied a protective order and was murdered.

The police are frequently called to intervene when a woman or child is being abused. Because American law makes physical injury a felony, one might expect that beating or raping one's wife or child would be treated in the same way as beating or raping a stranger. This is often not the case, as illustrated by the following example.

Tracy Thurman, frequently beaten by her husband, called the police when he came at her with a knife. When the police arrived, Thurman had stabbed his wife repeatedly and almost murdered her. They confiscated his knife but did not restrain him. He continued to beat and stomp on her. Tracy sued the city of Torrington, which had to pay her two million dollars for failing to protect her (Jones, 1993). The lawsuit led to changes in police training throughout the country, not due to belief in social justice, but out of fear of cities facing further damages whenever police fail to adequately protect beaten women. Social change comes slowly and not necessarily for purely humane reasons.

Health Care. The system most committed to protecting human beings is health care. However, the medical profession has been extremely recalcitrant in dealing with battered women and children. Although stitching women's wounds and mending broken bones are activities common in emergency rooms, the source of injuries is rarely explored. Novello et al. (1992) reported that 35% of women visiting emergency rooms present with symptoms of abuse; only 5% are so recognized (McCleer & Anivar, 1989).

McFarlane et al. (1992) determined that 17% of pregnant women were beaten during their pregnancy. The majority were abused multiple times. Abused women were twice as unlikely to get prenatal care during the first two trimesters (McFarlane et al., 1992). Prior to the 1990s, abuse during pregnancy was not evaluated. Obstetricians rarely enquire about the bruises or injuries sustained by their patients (Jones, 1993). Jones has initiated a campaign to educate physicians and nurses in the detection of abuse in pregnant women and how to provide patients with appropriate resources.

Child Protection. The abuse of children was first raised as a social issue more than 100 years ago in the United States, and agencies were established to protect abused children. In 1974, the first federal legislation established the National Center on Child Abuse and Neglect. The center was established to study the extent of this national problem and to develop programs to protect abused and neglected children. Did the system protect Michael, Kathy's son? Was Michael, severely beaten, never seen with either physical injuries or behaviors indicative of being beaten? Did anybody report him to Child Protective Services? Did anyone, other than his mother, try to intervene on his behalf?

We show that the abuse of women and children frequently occurs in the same family at the hands of a husband or boyfriend. We have discussed some services established to diminish abuse and protect victims from continuous violence. In the 25 years of the movement to end violence against women some laws have changed, but the behavior of the relevant professionals changes slowly. Physicians, the police, and judges are often ineffective in their response to the needs of battered women. Although there is much in our culture that relegates women to second-class citizenship, we think our attitude and behavior toward victimized children is more supportive.

How are abused children faring? Although many states had child protective legislation in the 1800s, it is only in 1974, with the establishment of the National Center for the Prevention of Child Abuse and Neglect (NCCAN), that the federal government began to study the incidence of child abuse and neglect and to provide federal funds for research and services to abused and neglected children. Child Protective Services exist in every state, and there is a long list of persons required by law to report cases of abuse. The federal law mandates that children in immediate danger be removed from their homes. When the children are not judged to be in immediate danger, protective and preventive services must be put in place immediately. Two government studies of national statistics provide data on the systems in place.

According to the studies completed by NCCAN, less than half of the millions of cases of child abuse known to some members of the community are reported to the agency mandated to collect data and provide services (DHHS, 1988, 1996). Most distressing is that the situation has gotten worse and not better in the last 10 years. More cases are reported and fewer services are available. For instance, child sexual abuse was reported to be three times more frequent in 1986 than in 1980.

Of great importance is that in 1992, 60% of identified cases of child abuse received no services, a higher rate than the previous year (McCurdy & Daro, 1993). Each year we witness more abuse and fewer resources available to help abused children.

What, then, do we see as the necessary steps to diminish and ultimately eliminate the abuse of the vulnerable? We contend that violence within the family, like all violence, is gendered, and that ultimately reform depends on changing not only the laws, but the minds and hearts of individuals.

Some Recommended Solutions

Just as there is no single cause of violence against women and children, there is no single prevention effort that, by itself, would guarantee the eradication or even the diminution of the problem. To diminish the prevalence of male violence within the family, we must first recognize the magnitude of the problem and commit the resources necessary for its elimination. Public recognition requires training of teachers, physicians, nurses, social workers, judges, and the police. Trained personnel can identify the symptoms of abuse and recommend resources available to victims. Properly identified, victims will be more likely to receive treatment for sustained injuries and protection from further harm.

Recognition addresses treatment, but not prevention. Primary prevention efforts must be concentrated in the areas of: reduction of all forms of violence; support systems for families; education; economic independence for women; changes in the medical and legal systems; and changes in our fundamental attitudes and beliefs.

Health Care. Physicians and nurses must to be trained to ask appropriate questions of people with unexplained injuries: the pregnant woman with a bruised abdomen; the child who comes to school in the heat of summer wearing long sleeves; and the adolescent who runs away. Years before he murdered his wife Kathy, Thomas was known to have beaten her son Michael. Had Thomas' behavior been taken seriously then, Kathy Germaine might be alive today.

Routine health screening of children would facilitate the early identification and treatment of abuse. Inadequate nutrition and health care place children at greater risk for handicapping conditions and irritability, risk factors for abuse. Family planning services result in fewer unplanned pregnancies, thus preventing the conception of unwanted children. Women who receive adequate prenatal care, adequate food and health care during pregnancy are less likely to have children that are at risk for abuse (Birns, 1988).

Guaranteed health care for all women and children would ensure that all victims, regardless of socioeconomic class, would have access to medical treatment and prevention services. Studies indicate that 8% to 35% of all pregnant women are currently in abusive relationships (Jones, 1993; Helton & Snodgrass, 1987). Trained health care personnel can detect abuse and limit the threat to the fetus that comes from abuse. They might diminish the abuse of drugs and alcohol, as well as suicide attempts, all of which have negative effects on mother, fetus, and infants (Stark & Flitcraft, 1987).

Education and Economic Equality. Educational opportunities for women increase women's financial independence. For women without work skills, one answer to the question "Why don't they leave" is often that they cannot afford to. Without a job, and skills that enable them to earn a living, they cannot afford to pay rent, feed and clothe themselves and their children, and pay for child care and transportation.

Economic independence for women is a major prerequisite for violence-free families. Women who cannot support their own families remain at risk of entrapment in abusive relationships. American women still earn only $0.70 on the dollar earned by men. We need equal pay for equal and comparable work, reevaluation of the jobs in which women predominate and are low paid, the end of sexual harassment in the workplace, and welfare benefits that are above the poverty level.

Legal System. Changes in the legal system are essential. Divorce law and custody decisions should be revised to address the needs of battered women and their children. Top priority should be given to the protection of victims, rather than family preservation at all cost. Efforts to increase and enforce child support orders must continue to be strengthened so that women who leave abusive partners are not forced to live in poverty and in shelters for the homeless.

To reduce our societal sanctioning of violence, gun control legislation is essential. Incidents of family violence involving guns are 12 times more likely to result in death than incidents involving all other types of weapons. The expression of violence in the media, and corporal punishment in the schools should be controlled. Education efforts should include nonviolent conflict resolution as well as family life education.

While the changes noted above are imperative, experience teaches that they will not be adequate. Changes in statutes do not guarantee changes in practice, nor do they ensure concomitant change in attitudes and beliefs. The histories of the American civil rights movement and the Swedish battered women's movement are illustrative.

Changing Laws: Changing Attitudes

Brown vs. the Board of Education (1954), the landmark Supreme Court case mandating the desegregation of America's public schools, recently celebrated its 40th anniversary, yet racism in our schools remains a national disgrace. African American children remain clustered in poverty stricken neighborhoods with poorly funded schools. Although desegregation laws are on the books, implementation is grossly inadequate. In addition to changing laws we need to reeducate the public to bring about change in attitudes and behavior.

The plight of battered women in Sweden provides another instance of the inability of the legal system alone to enforce social change. The Swedish social welfare system is comprehensive, including many features (that) American battered women's advocates insist are necessary for the safety of women: universal health care coverage, availability and funding of excellent day care, subsidized housing with battered women accorded priority status, paid parental and sick child care leave, and a 10%, rather than 30%, gap in women's earning. Additionally, Sweden has more than 100 special programs for battered women. Nonetheless, the police are slow to respond, do not always arrest when women request it, and orders of protection are frequently refused.

Despite the array of services that decrease women's economic dependence on men, battered Swedish women report many of the same difficulties as their American counterparts including police reticence to interfere in "family disputes," and an insensitive legal system that prohibits women from obtaining orders of protection (Elman & Eduards, 1991). Despite a national commitment to sexual equality and a social welfare system envied in most of the world, Sweden fails to adequately protect battered women.

Both of the examples above document the fact that protective legislation is necessary but alone does not ensure social change. While statutes must be changed in the effort to curb intrafamilial violence, some of our fundamental attitudes and beliefs must be challenged in other arenas as well.

Moving Toward Sexual Equality

Some fundamental assumptions about the appropriate roles and behavior of men and women set the family up as a battlefield. Until we eliminate the sense of male entitlement, until we disperse the gender-based power and control found in all social institutions, until we reject violence as an acceptable conflict resolution strategy, we will continue to have violent families.

One of the most shocking findings in the research on woman battering is that over half of male batterers feel completely justified in their abusive behavior towards their partners (Rouse, 1983, as cited in Pagelow, 1984;

Stacey & Shupe, 1983). Self-justification is rooted in the sense of entitlement that boys acquire during their childhood socialization (Birns et al., 1994). When people believe that they are entitled to certain services or behaviors that are not forthcoming, they may believe that they have the right to obtain them by any means possible. Explanations offered by abusive men to support their behavior include, "I beat her because: the house isn't clean, she wouldn't have sex with me, she wasted my money, she couldn't keep the kids quiet." When boys are taught that their needs and wants should be provided for immediately, and girls are taught to please and defer to men, the stage is set for violent interactions. The use of violence may become the way to exert one's will.

The male sense of entitlement is closely tied to the gender-based locus of power and control of social institutions. The Supreme Court decides whether women may terminate unwanted pregnancies. It is Congress that legislates Americans' access to guns, and we are the "murder capital" of the world. It is legislators who decide how much free milk and eggs shall be available to very poor pregnant women. It is judges who determine how much financial support is provided to women who leave and whether women who are battered receive orders of protection. It is corporate chiefs who decide whether child care facilities shall be available to their workers' children. The list is long.

How do these decisions relate to violence within the family? Most directly, they determine what kind of resources are available to working women, whether they can feed their children, end unwanted pregnancies, as well as how safe women feel in their own homes.

We do not claim that all homes are authoritarian units. Indeed, women usually decide what kind of clothes are bought for the children, and what food is served. More egalitarian families also share decisions about where to live and how "family time" is spent. However, even today, women do most of the housework and men determine major family decisions (Birns et al., 1994). In homes where women are battered or children are physically abused, men exert dominant and controlling behavior (Schecter, 1982; Walker, 1984).

Violence in the family is promoted not only by male entitlement, power, and control, but by the fact that American males frequently resort to aggression to resolve conflict. This tendency plays a crucial role in understanding male violence against women and children (Birns et al., 1994). This is true in the United States and in many other cultures. In a rare anthropological study on violence in the family, Levinson (1989) examined data on 90 nonindustrial societies. The most prevalent form of intrafamilial violence was wife beating, found in 86% of the societies. A seminal factor associated with the wife abusing societies, absent in the nonabusive societies, was the cultural approval of male violence as a conflict resolution strategy (Levinson, 1989).

SUMMARY

We demonstrate here the extent and severity of violence against women and children in the United States. We explore some of the popular myths regarding abusers and victims; the role of gender in abuse and the lack of social support services for abused women and children. Our position is that men are the perpetrators of most of the serious abuse, that violence against women and children is a reflection of male power and entitlement and that services for women and children are currently inadequate. We recognize that the immediate need is for additional services and education of the community. We stress that whereas each act of violence is an individual act, the extent of this behavior poses a major health problem. We suggest that in order to end violence within the family structural changes are necessary to create greater equity between males and females.

REFERENCES

Adams, D. (1988). Treatment models of men who batter: A profeminist analysis. In K. Yllo & M. Bograd (Eds.), *Feminist perspectives on wife abuse* (pp. 176–199). Newbury Park, CA: Sage.

Alland, D., Kalkut, G. E., Moss, A. R., McAdam, R. A., Hahn, J. A., Bosworth, W., Drucker, E., & Bloom, B. R. (1994). Transmission of tuberculosis in New York City. *The New England Journal of Medicine, 330,* 1710.

Birns, B. (1988). The mother-infant tie: Of bonding and abuse. In M. B. Straus (Ed.), *Abuse and victimization across the life span* (pp. 9–31). Baltimore, MD: Johns Hopkins University Press.

Birns, B., Cascardi, M., & Meyer, S. (1994). Sex-role socialization: Developmental influences on wife abuse. *American Journal of Orthopsychiatry, 64,* 50–59.

Bowker, L. H., Arbitell, M., & McFerron, J. R. (1988). On the relationship between wife beating and child abuse. In K. Yllo & M. Bograd (Eds.), *Feminist perspectives on wife abuse* (pp. 158–174). Newbury Park, CA: Sage.

Browne, A. (1992). Violence against women: Relevance for medical practitioners. *Journal of the American Medical Association, 267,* 3184–3189.

Cascardi, M. A., Langhinrichsen, J., & Vivian, D. (1992). Marital aggression: Impact, injury, and health corelates for husbands and wives. *Archives of Internal Medicine, 152,* 1178–1184.

Council on Ethical and Judicial Affairs, American Medical Association. (1992). Physicians and domestic violence: Ethical considerations. *Journal of the American Medical Association, 267,* 3190–3193.

Department of Health and Human Services. (1988). *Study findings: Study of the national incidence and prevalence of child abuse.* Washington, DC: U.S. Government Printing Office.

Department of Health and Human Services. (1996). *Child maltreatment 1994: Reports from the states to the National Center on Child Abuse and Neglect.* Washington, DC: U.S. Government Printing Office.

Dobash, R. P., Dobash, R. E., Wilson, M., & Daly, M. (1992). The myth of sexual symmetry in marital violence. *Social Problems, 39,* 71–91.

Elman, R. A., & Eduards, M. L. (1991). Unprotected by the Swedish welfare state: A survey of battered women and the assistance they received. *Women's Studies International Forum, 14,* 413–421.

Finkelhor, D., Gelles, R. J., Hotaling, G. T., & Strauss, M. A. (1983). *The dark side of families: Current family violence research.* Beverly Hills, CA: Sage.

Goldstein, D., & Rosenbaum, A. (1985). An evaluation of the self-esteem of maritally violent men. *Family Relations: Journal of Applied Family & Child Studies, 34,* 425–428.

Helton, A. S., McFarlane, J., & Anderson, E. (1987). Battered and pregnant: A prevalance study. *American Journal of Public Health, 77,* 1337–1339.

Helton, A. S., & Snodgrass, F. G. (1987). Battering during pregnancy: Intervention strategies. *Birth, 14*(3), 142–147.

Jones, R. F. (1993). Domestic violence: Let our voices be heard. *Obstetrics and Gynecology, 81,* 1–4.

Koop, C. E. (1992). Violence in America, a public health emergency: Time to bite the bullet back. *Journal of the American Medical Association, 267,* 3075–3076.

Levinson, D. (1989). *Family violence in cross-cultural perspective.* Newbury Park, CA: Sage.

McCleer, S. V. (1989). Education is not enough: A systems failure to protect battered women. *Annals of Emergency Medicine,* 651–653.

McCleer, S. V., & Anivar, R. (1989). A study of battered women presenting in an emergency department. *American Journal of Public Health, 79,* 65–66.

McCurdy, K., & Daro, D. (1993). Current trends in child maltreatment. *Violence Update, 3,* 3–8.

McFarlane, J., Parker, B., Soeken, K., & Bullock, L. (1992). Assessing for abuse during pregnancy. *Journal of the American Medical Association, 267,* 3176–3183.

McKibben, L., DeVos E., & Newberger, E. H. (1989). Victimization of mothers of abused children: A controlled study. *Pediatrics, 84,* 531–535.

McNeely, R. L., & Robinson-Simpson, G. (1987). The truth about domestic violence: A falsely framed issue. *Social Work, 32,* 485–489.

National Center on Women and Family Law, Inc. (1993). *Couples counseling and couples therapy endanger battered women* (Item No. 63). New York: Author.

Novello, A. C., Rosenberg, M., Saltzman L., & Shosky, J. (1992). From the Surgeon General, U.S. Public Health Service. *The Journal of the American Medical Association, 267,* 3132.

Okun, L. (1986). *Woman abuse: Facts replacing myths.* Albany, NY: State University of New York Press.

Pagelow, M. D. (1984). *Family violence.* New York: Praeger.

Schecter, S. (1982). *Women and male violence: The visions and struggles of the battered women's movement.* Boston: South End Press.

Stacey, W. A., & Shupe, A. (1983). *The family secret: Domestic violence in America.* Boston: Beacon Press.

Stark, E., & Flitcraft, A. H. (1988). Women and children at risk: A feminist perspective on child abuse. *International Journal of Health Services, 18,* 97–117.

Stark, E., Flitcraft, A. H., & Frazier, W. (1979). Medicine and patriarchal violence: The social construction of a private event. *International Journal of Health Services, 9,* 461–493.

Steinmetz, S. K. (1977–1978). The battered husband syndrome. *Victimology, 2,* 499–509.

Straus, M. A., & Gelles, R. J. (1986). Societal change and change in family violence from 1975–1985 as revealed by two national surveys. *Journal of Marriage and the Family, 48,* 465–479.

Straus, M. A., Gelles, R. J., & Steinmetz, S. (1980). *Behind closed doors: Violence in American families.* Garden City, NY: Doubleday.

Taylor, L., & Gallagher, M. (1992, July 10). Wife's frantic call. *Newsday,* pp. 3, 37.

Tolman, R. M., & Bennett, L. W. (1990). A review of quantitative research on men who batter. *Journal of Interpersonal Violence, 5,* 87–118.

Violence Against Women Act of 1994, National Resource Center on Domestic Violence and the Battered Women's Justice Project (1994).

Vitello, P. (1993, June 17). Boy's grief for mom: If only. *Newsday,* pp. 8, 12.

Walker, L. E. (1984). *The battered woman syndrome.* New York: Springer.

Walker, L. E. (1989). Psychology and violence against women. *The American Psychologist, 44* 695–702.

Young, G. H., & Gerson, S. (1991). New psychoanalytical perspectives on masochism and spouse abuse. *Psychotherapy, 28,* 30–38.

9

DEVELOPING THE NEW LINKS WORKPLACE: THE FUTURE OF FAMILY, WORK, AND COMMUNITY RELATIONSHIPS[1]

Don Edgar
Centre for Workplace Culture Change
Melbourne, Australia

Australia, like most other western societies, has undergone profound changes in family structures and processes over the past two decades. From a post-War rush to almost universal marriage and child-bearing, which consolidated in actuality the ideal of the breadwinner–housewife model of marriage and the family, we moved toward a much more diverse and complex array of family formation and reformation. The next century will inevitably see a more balanced partnership, both within marriage and between the family and the workplace.

Neither work policies nor family policies can be based any longer on this so-called traditional concept of men as the sole breadwinners and women as the sole caretakers of the children. This formulation never applied to the everyday lives of working class families, small business, rural farm families or to many migrant and Aboriginal families, in which breadwinning and family care were handled by a variety of family members. It is even less applicable today, when the majority of adults with dependent children are employed.

I need to sketch the elements of family change only briefly here:

- Women are better educated, more career-oriented, and more independent.

---

[1]This chapter was originally presented at the international conference "The Family on the Threshold of the 21st Century: Trends and Implications," Ministry of Science and Technology, Jerusalem, Israel, May 29, 1994.

- Gender values have shifted, with women demanding, and men coming to see the value in, more equal and balanced lives.
- People marry later, have fewer children later, so the childbearing period is shorter and less of a restriction on opportunities.
- Young people are financially dependent on parents longer, have prolonged education, limited job opportunities in a declining youth labor market. But their casual and part-time wages are an important supplement to their family's household income.
- The aging of western populations (contrary to some alarmist talk about dependency ratios and the future costs of health care for an aging population) is based on the reduction of birthrates as much as on longer life expectancy, so is less of a problem than some might imagine. However, the economy will need to keep women in the workplace and keep older people working longer. The end of compulsory age retirement is only the start. We will have to develop phased retirement policies, job sharing, and permanent part-time work further in order to preserve the skills, experience, and wisdom of our aging workforce. Continual life education and retraining will also be essential (Edgar, 1988). We cannot assume today's work patterns will stay the same, especially when we face increasing levels of productivity per nondependent worker.
- The aging of our population also means that the brunt of family care will shift from child care to elder care. A 1992 Australian Bureau of Statistics (ABS) Survey of Families (1993) found 11% of all adults cared for at least one older family member in the previous 6 months. Our New Links Workplace (NLW) survey of Alcoa shows that 16% of employees already have elderly parents dependent on them, and another 50% expect to have elder care responsibilities within the next 15 years. This is typical of other survey findings and highlights the fact that elder care, unlike child care, cannot be handed over to wives so easily, not when husbands' parents need assistance. Cross-generational and interhousehold support is a vital part of family life that impacts on work and job performance.

What this adds up to is, in my view, a significant shift in the balance of work and family life. Roles are changing, the nature of care is changing, the stress related to juggling the balance is increasing.

Yet the workplace is still premised on an outmoded model of work–family links that reflects a profound ignorance on the part of most employers and policy analysts of both the changes themselves and a lack of awareness of the crucial importance of social policy to any nation's economy.

The future of work can no longer be based on economic demands that ignore social realities. Blindness to the way private needs and responsibilities affect morale, performance and productivity can no longer be accepted. We need a full-scale effort to help families achieve a better balance between work and family and a more equal partnership in family life itself.

To replace the disjunction between rigid work structures and these new family arrangements, new networks, new links across institutional boundaries, new community partnerships must become the 'best practice' way, so that the skills and resources of every sector operate for the good of all.

Despite unemployment (9% of two-parent families and 50% of one-parent families in Australia have no parent in the workforce), what we are seeing happen, and what will continue into the foreseeable future, is the development of a new partnership model of family life, one in which family members share paid work and family care responsibilities and where various family members move into and out of the labor force as the balance of those responsibilities changes through a changed family life course.

FAMILY AS PARTNERSHIP

The family sits at the center of civil society, affected by the nature of the balance between state and market but in turn actively affecting the way in which these interact (Fig. 9.1).

Overreliance on the state can lead to the excesses of communism; overreliance on the free market economy can damage the well-being of many in a society of dog-eat-dog. In Australia and many European social democratic societies, we try for a better partnership, some sort of accord between governments, unions, employers, and the people. The character of the society we aim for is thus very different from one in which individuals have no freedom, or another in which there is little concern for equity and social justice (Pusey, 1991).

The family itself is the key partnership which reproduces society by breeding, feeding, housing and educating the next generation. It may sound odd to speak of the family as a partnership, a system of cooperation. But it is in fact the first partnership of all social reproduction. Despite the ongoing media and research fascination with family conflict, violence, divorce, and child abuse, the family unit is first and foremost a unit of cooperation.

The *family* is a unit in which men, women, and children who care enough about one another to combine their various skills, property, and other resources, produce through work enough to meet their combined needs, consume and distribute the rewards and benefits of that labor, and care for one another as well. There are trade-offs and negotiations, and of course there are inequalities and inequities, usually in favor of males. But the family is essentially a mutually organized and beneficial partnership.

The point here is that, because the family partnership is changing, so too must change the work–family partnership and the nature of community links to both family and the workplace.

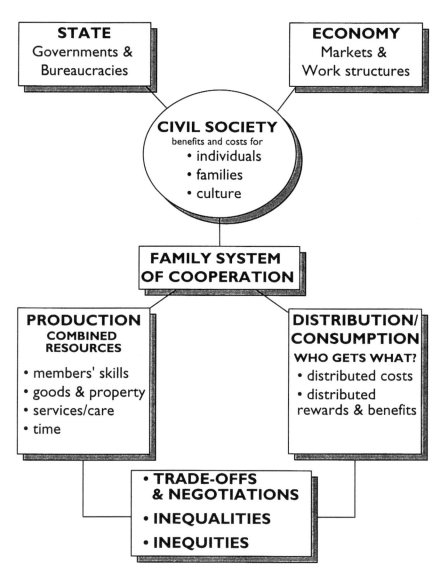

FIG. 9.1. Civil society and the family.

Because of economic and social change, strains and disjunctions are growing between family and work life. Those discrepancies are being noticed, cannot be ignored, so action is needed—in the workplace and within the community—whose support services must change too, perhaps even more drastically than current practices in the workplace.

Outlined here is the way in which those changes seem to be operating:

In the family context, there seems no doubt that a new partnership model is emerging. The old breadwinner–housewife model was relatively short-lived, historically, but still exercises a dominant place in employment practices. Many business leaders still assume that every male worker has a housewife at home to cope with private business.

For Australia, workforce participation figures are 86% for fathers and 56% for mothers in two-parent families, and 65% for male and 43% for female sole parents. In 1993, 53% of couples with dependent children were both employed (both full-time in 42% of cases). Forty-three percent of employed men and 40% of employed women have dependent children (ABS, 1993).

Women's earnings contribute an additional 40% to total family income (24% when working part-time) and a higher proportion in low income families. Structural change in the labor market seems to be displacing male full-time breadwinners and opening up new sectors of part-time work. Young people are structured out of the labor market into prolonged education, training, and dependence on parents.

On the other side of the ledger—the caring tasks of the family partnership traditionally left to women—there are signs of change also, despite gender-based socialization of children and male resistance to change. Time use studies are usually quoted as evidence of inequality (the double burden of the working mother), but I see the figures as a hopeful sign of a new balance emerging. The ABS Survey of Time Use in Australia (1993b) shows that partnered mothers, employed full time, still carry the biggest work load overall (including paid work, household duties, and child care), an average of 10 hours per day. But their husbands are not as far behind as they used to be. Men average 72% of their total working time on paid work, compared to women's 48%, reflecting the old gender division of labor and the preponderance of women in part-time employment. But men now do carry out more housework, more shopping, more of the child care. The discrepancy between what men say they should do and what they do in fact is now less marked (Figs. 9.2 and 9.3).

Even more to the point, both men (24%) and women (37%) say they have difficulty managing paid work and child care (ABS, 1993a). Thirty percent of both men and women report going home with little energy to be a good parent. Twenty percent have been absent, or late getting to and from work, for family reasons. Some 39% of mothers and 26% of fathers had taken days off work in the past 12 months to care for a sick child, and 35% of women, 21% of men, had taken time off to look after their aging parents or other family members. (ABS, 1993a; VandenHeuvel, 1993).

As already indicated, the aging of Australia's population will add a new dimension to the work–family debate—that of elder care—and employed men will find it more difficult to expect their employed wives to take responsibility for two sets of aging parents.

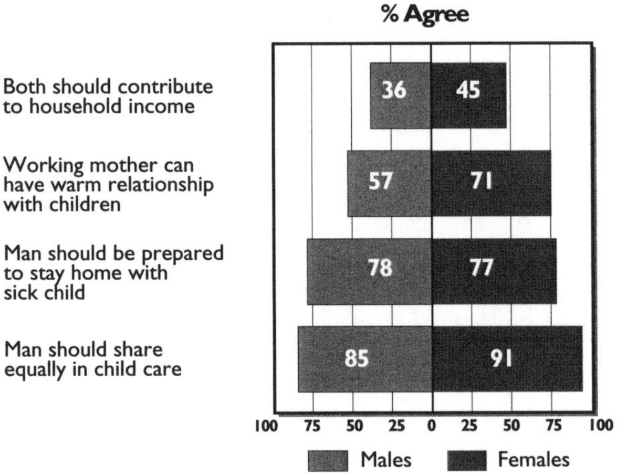

% Agree
Both should contribute to household income
Working mother can have warm relationship with children
Man should be prepared to stay home with sick child
Man should share equally in child care
36
45
57
71
78
77
85
91
100 75 50 25 0 25 50 75 100
Males
Females

FIG. 9.2. Family values.

%
Males
Females
70
60
50
40
30
20
10
0
56
53
41
43
3
4
Both do same amount
Wife does more
Husband does more

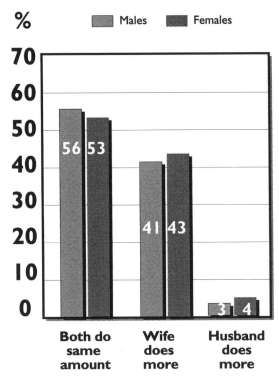

FIG. 9.3. Sharing of household tasks for married males and females.

What began as a women's issue is increasingly being regarded as a family partnership issue. Many men of course are being dragged reluctantly into such new arrangements, but the family is the crucible of change and it is a matter of "shape up, or ship out." The younger generation of men especially is saying they would like a balanced life, to see more of and share more in the raising of their children instead of being the workaholic, absent father.

Most government (and industrial) reform follows and codifies changes already taking place in society (as did the Family Law Act 1975, which replaced fault with irretrievable breakdown as the sole cause of divorce); it rarely sets the pace ahead of social values, though it can speed up change by legitimizing a new order.

The dilemma is evident in women's preference for part-time work following maternity leave (Glezer, 1988) and in the unmet need for places in formal child care services doubling from 242,000 in 1987 to 514,000 in 1990. The demand is not just for creches or long day care centers. There is a major gap in short-term day care, outside school hours care, emergency care, and school holiday programs for the children of parents who are employed. Costs are still a major problem despite government fee relief and rural areas suffer acute shortages of family support services.

Some of our leading-edge companies, interested in achieving best practice, are becoming aware of the need to change. The term *industrial relations* has given way to *employee relations*, though many of the old-guard IR managers are still locked into their confrontational mode and anxious about the new skills that might be required for effective team development in the seamless organization.

Some companies can see that private lives affect job performance and that better personal communication and home management might transfer productively to workplace relationships and systems. Moreover, there are obvious cost benefits to derive from reduced absenteeism, staff turnover, recruitment, and improved productivity if employees are less preoccupied with their private family problems while at work. As shown in Fig. 9.4, stress affects partner relationships and parenting for many employees.

As well as these dawnings of awareness, there are external pressures for companies to be more responsive to family needs. At the government level in Australia, we altered the links between work and family life in 1979 through unpaid maternity leave in Federal awards (Glezer, 1988) and through the 1990 Industrial Relations Commission test case which extended those standards to parental care and covered permanent part-time work during pregnancy and up to the child's second birthday (National Women's Consultative Council, 1993).

We also more recently legislated in accord with ILO (International Labour Organisation) Conventions to ensure equal pay for equal work value, unpaid parental leave and minimum award wages through use of a common rule

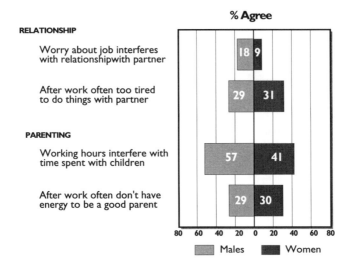

FIG. 9.4. Work and family stress among married men and women.

by which workers do not have access to compulsory arbitration (Australian Law Reform Commission, 1993; George, 1993). Ratification of ILO 156 on Workers With Family Responsibilities has led to something of a scramble on the part of major companies to understand what this is all about.

The government's Children's Services Program was also developed in the context of the union–business–government Accord partnership as part of a new order of wage fixation and the social wage approach to achieving better family standards. This provides fee relief for child care, additional child care center places, subsidies for employers and others who provide child care, and a national accreditation system to ensure high standards in child care centers, both public and private.

ILO Convention No. 156 (Workers with family responsibilities) will offer new opportunities for change, but Australia, which has not yet achieved Organization for Economic Cooperation and Development (OECD) best practice in providing a minimum of paid parental leave and enterprise agreements, will increasingly have to address the work–family trade-off.

Nevertheless, there is a major change in demand and expectations that the workplace must respond to. That response is as yet very patchy because many bosses and managers have wives who were (or still are) full-time homemakers, and they cannot see the wave coming in. This collective employer blindness requires a full-scale effort to achieve a more equal balance in the life of every employee.

How to do that requires a focus on the diverse needs of each employee, on the whole person trying to do a good job, and it will require new linkages, new partnerships across the social fabric rather than piecemeal and limited

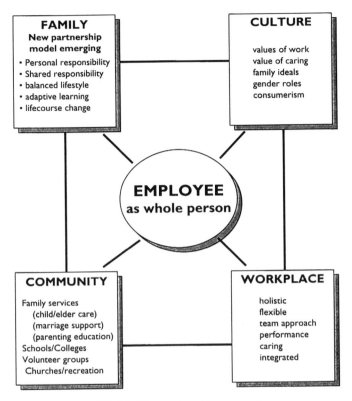

FAMILY
New partnership model emerging
- Personal responsibility
- Shared responsibility
- balanced lifestyle
- adaptive learning
- lifecourse change

CULTURE
values of work
value of caring
family ideals
gender roles
consumerism

EMPLOYEE
as whole person

COMMUNITY
Family services
  (child/elder care)
  (marriage support)
  (parenting education)
Schools/Colleges
Volunteer groups
Churches/recreation

WORKPLACE
holistic
flexible
team approach
performance
caring
integrated

FIG. 9.5. New partnership prospects.

change (Fig. 9.5). The employee must be seen as a whole person, in a changing family, community and cultural context, with the workplace as one (vital) partner in ensuring the quality of life.

THE NEW LINKS WORKPLACE

It is this philosophy that forms the New Links Workplace (NLW) Project. The project is funded by the Australia and New Zealand (ANZ) Trustees as a new approach to philanthropy, one which may prevent family and social problems and may entice employers into a broader view of their social responsibilities. It involves a few major Australian corporations (Alcoa, Australia Post, Pacific Power and Lend Lease) in testing out a model which combines best economic practice with an improved social consciousness at the highest corporate level.

There are two broad aspects to this approach. One is to integrate, to link more effectively, the variety of family-responsive practices and programs internal to the company. The second is to develop better links with those community services and resources that already exist outside the company and build on them rather than create costly and company-specific Employee Assistance Programs (EAPs) or services.

To illustrate, I have adapted the four stages of work–family corporate initiatives outlined by Galinsky, Friedman, and Hernandez (1991) in the United States and added three more stages (see Fig. 9.6). Their point was that most companies start with actions to solve a specific problem. For example, child care, or occupational health, or accident prevention, or Equal Opportunity/Affirmative Action programs. Companies at Stage 1 have few work–family policies and are barely aware of the broader issues. At Stage 2, there are some policies but not a packaged response; they are seen mainly as women's issues, with a focus on child care. A few U.S. companies integrate their programs to create a better work–family balance for employees (Stage 3), but even fewer reach Stage 4, which takes a holistic approach, addressing gender equity, life cycle and community intervention as a total package to enhance the quality of work and family life.

As part of the NLW, the Council for Equal Opportunity in Employment has been setting up a database on best practice in Australian companies on family-related measures. While it is too early to put too much reliance on the numbers of companies categorized, I identify seven stages rather than the four described by Galinsky, Friedman, and Hernandez.

This is like a Guttman scale, in which all the earlier stages are included in the later ones. Some 31 companies on the database are at what I call the *problem-specific* Stage 1. There is no holistic policy, no human resource approach that incorporates a work–family perspective. They have some child care provisions, or an employee assistance program on alcohol and drug abuse, or a separate health center for employees.

The next Stage 2 is *gender-specific*, in that child care, equal employment opportunity (EEO) policies and some affirmative action initiatives are set up to solve the "problems of women." Companies want to recruit and retain female employees, so they look closely at how that might be done more effectively.

ONE	Problem-specific (child care, etc.)	31
TWO	Gender-specific (EEO, harassment, etc.)	22
THREE	Internal flexibility (work times/PT)	19
FOUR	Wider flexibility (leave arrangements)	19
FIVE	Employee needs focus (surveys/information/education programs) (family contacts)	13
SIX	Community links	10
SEVEN	Corporate culture (holistic approach)	8

Numbers refer to companies listed on the NLW Database that fit into each stage of Partnership.

FIG. 9.6. Seven stages to partnership.

Stages 3 and 4 are not always separate, but *internal flexibility*, such as flexitime or part-time work, or job share arrangements, usually come first in response to family needs, with the more difficult issues of *family leave* being left to a later stage.

Only a dozen or so have reached what I call Stage 5—*employee needs focus*—where a real effort is made to understand employees' family circumstances through Work/Family Surveys or Focus Groups to discuss actual needs and to understand how family and work responsibilities actually affect one another. For example, Caltex, Pacific Power, Alcoa, and Australia Post have conducted detailed surveys of employees' family responsibilities so that responses can be designed more appropriately for their diverse character.

Stage 6—*community links*—is what we are aiming for in the NLW Project, and Stage 7 is the ultimate in which the whole *corporate culture* is permeated with a holistic approach to employee–community relations. The only Australian companies that yet come close to these stages of thinking are Unisys, Alcoa, Kemcor, Melbourne Water, Caltex, National Road & Motor Association (NRMA), the Body Shop, Esso, and the Sydney Water Board.

Most companies have some community programs. These are usually public relations efforts, sponsorships of various kinds, corporate image-building exercises. Most are donations or scholarships, or school work experience opportunities, and are not seen as part of the overall work–family policy of the company. They are also very "thing"-oriented: They frequently give gifts of new playground equipment, for example, rather than address the human service people-oriented needs of a community.

Our vision for the future of work is one where community links go well beyond this sort of thing. This second, externally focused edge to the NLW concept cuts across current approaches to welfare service delivery.

We have been rightly critical of a top-down, hierarchical business management approach which ignores the first-hand experience and knowledge of employees. We will never do without professional expertise or without someone at the top with whom the buck finally stops, but a participatory, team approach which relies on shared skills, mutual respect and cooperative effort is clearly superior to a do-as-I-say approach.

Yet that approach still permeates most community and family support services as well. We have to seek help as they provide it, when they are available, whether that suits our particular needs or not. The worst example perhaps is the medical practitioner who rejects the patient's description of his or her own symptoms, who fails to explain the prescribed treatment, and who ignores the emotional side of traumatic illness or surgery. Other agencies at the community interface can be almost as bad. Social workers, counselors, those who control access to and delivery of services have given themselves a bad press and suffer from it still. The very language used illustrates the top-down mentality: *professional* versus *client; services* not *resources; delivered to,* compared with *available for use by; needs* rather than *strengths; treatment of problems, correcting weaknesses,* and *curing deficiencies,* not *building of strengths and competencies,* which would help prevent difficulties arising in the first place.

Our whole welfare and social support system is based on targeting, on categorizing problems and deficiencies, on ensuring that only the "needy" get help, whether income support or other services. There is little emphasis on prevention, on enhancing and building on the skills people already have, on open access to resources which people might draw on if and when they need them, in contrast to when some bureaucrat decides they are eligible.

In my view, we have to create links between personal and work needs very early, in a new social work ethic that shows every young person their value to others, not just their value to the market or to themselves alone. Given the family and social changes outlined previously, and the massive strains currently being felt in our systems of social–community support, we should capitalize on the already clear shift towards human service and communication industries.

In the action implementation phase of the NLW Project, we are modeling new policies of training, preparation for the world of work and for harmonious community. This is based on my belief that we must prepare young people for future work in a way that highlights sharing, cooperation, and care of human resources as the key to quality, rather than pure self-interest or competition.

The value of effort and the value of work are denied to many of our youth because of our myopic focus on producing "widgets" and a too narrow definition of *vocational training.* We have employers suggesting schemes of tree planting, rubbish removal, and building "things" needed as part of the physical infrastructure. We also hear them complain about poor work attitudes, lack of responsibility, poor motivation, and so on. And we hear our social youth workers complaining about the same difficulties. They bleat about self-esteem, with no comprehension that self-esteem derives from positive interaction with others and producing desired effects on our environment through focused effort. Self-esteem cannot be taught and is not an entity that floats free of real effort, impact on, and feedback from others.

Thus, the future demands much more social awareness, more cooperation and mutual respect, a greater feeling of usefulness to other people and of each individual's value to the rest of society. Without that sense of real contribution, people have no place, no stake in society and will sit apart from it in apathy or in alienated rebellion.

There is a vast range of "people work" that is needed now and in the future. It is the human services, the human relationships that make the wheels of the economy turn effectively. Good managers recognize that team efforts and a sense of joint contribution to an achieved goal will enhance morale, and improve productivity. But we do not start early enough.

People work could be done by our unemployed and by those youth not yet employed. Companies could assist by developing NLWs with community organizations, encourage voluntary work, mentor relationships, and school-business partnerships. Managerial skills could be applied to family and community organization needs, and we should see the end of "payments for doing nothing" via a more imaginative creation of meaningful work in the human services that would give these people a renewed sense of pride and a stake in the community as a whole. The society of the future will spend more time, not less, on personal, interpersonal, and community relationships. The world of work would benefit by getting on this wave and riding it.

We are looking for a new approach to family support which integrates the "new partnership family" with the NLW. This was well described in the literature on family resource programs overseas (Dunst, 1990); it had scant impact in Australia, though some worthy attempts have been made (Wolcott, 1991; Wolcott & Glezer, 1995). However, we are trying to encourage the four major corporations involved in the NLW Project to influence family support services along these lines.

COMMUNITY SCANNING

Just as the employer needs more direct, firsthand knowledge of employees' skills, family responsibilities and needs, so too we need to know more about the community resources that could be drawn on that affect the lives of workers and the areas of strengths or needs that could be built upon.

This involves what we call a *community scan*, a process of surveying and consulting key services and other groups within the company's employee encatchment area. So far, we have completed this for the Mandurah community in Western Australia which houses 70% of Alcoa's employees. The results are very revealing, for they show that the area has problems Alcoa itself can only indirectly address, but which can be addressed via new partnerships with groups in the community. For example, the schools and welfare groups report enormous problems with parenting; there is a lack of emergency rather than full-time child care; a high degree of family violence and breakdown is affecting the behavior of children at school; and there is a growing problem of access to services for the elderly. The Alcoa Employee Survey shows the same problems in a different way, but the two sets of evidence complement one another.

Agencies and schools in the district are very keen to work in and through the workplace of the major employer of the area to address such problems. Alcoa's Work/Family Committee has developed a set of proposals that may begin to establish some innovative approaches to the problems. As well, location-based NLW Teams are being set up to ensure local differences and priorities are being addressed.

The point is that Alcoa, as a company itself, cannot and does not have to set up programs of their own to address these issues. Instead, they can add to and assist the efforts of local agencies who have the expertise to do so. Alcoa can help improve the quality of community life as well as reduce the impact of such problems on employee morale, performance and productivity.

The solution thus lies in partnership, developing new family resource programs that will build a better community, a better human environment that will reduce the impact family stresses have on the workplace. This is the reciprocal side to the company's internal attempts to reduce the impact of work structures and work practices on family life. This is an integrated, systems approach to balancing the partnership, one that does not assume that families alone, or employers alone, or even both together, will solve the dilemma of the balance between work and family life. The individual who sits at the fulcrum of the work–family scales must be seen in context. That context is cultural (the dominant and competing values which guide social attitudes, choices and behavior), and it is community-based, location-specific, and immediate in its impact on which way the scales will tip.

It makes sense for companies to work with the communities from which their employees come, not apart from them. It makes sense to locate what resources exist already and build on them rather than develop costly new Employee Assistance Programs exclusive to the workplace. It makes sense to extend the notion of a holistic workplace to helping improve the whole community context in which employees live. And it makes sense to ginger up the services and agencies which affect family lives because that way improvement in functioning and performance is available for everyone.

CORPORATE MODELS

Some examples may help illustrate how different working life can be if employers recognize that employee morale and performance are affected by their 'private' concerns, like it or not.

UNISYS was one of the winners in the 1994 Corporate Work and Family Awards sponsored by the Business Council of Australia and the federal Department of Industrial Relations. Its workers often work off site, so ethics, teamwork, self-help networks, and quality control have always been important to the company. But UNISYS sees paying attention to family issues as the key to all of this, not just as benevolence or a passing human resources management fashion.

Apart from moving to develop more flexible working arrangements that will fit better with varied family responsibilities (such as job sharing, tele-commuting, part-time work, and extended leaves of absence for family reasons) they have tried to involve the whole family through running Family Days so children and partners can see the workplace and meet colleagues. They publish a monthly *Health Yourself* newsletter addressed to the whole family; and they encourage schools to request work experience for 12th-grade students of UNISYS employees.

They also see the links between more flexible leave and work time arrangements, an active Equal Employment Opportunity program for women and a systematic staff development and training plan. Their Human Assets and Resources Information (HARI) database contains a skills inventory for each employee, used to design training plans and careers paths for individuals. Women on maternity leave are kept informed through electronic mailboxes and regular workplace visits.

An alliance was formed with Quality Children's Services in Sydney to secure child care places and to help staff coordinate school holiday classes. Spouses are invited to attend conferences which combine a business review with personal and professional development. Staff executives have developed school links through the "Business Alive" program which offers secondary students a practical introduction to best Australian business practice.

The road vehicle insurer and service giant NRMA also has an active community program which meets some of the criteria of the NLW. Some of this is the usual sponsorship of community activities typical of the PR efforts of most big companies. NRMA spends over $1.2 million per annum on such things as Care Flight, an emergency helicopter rescue service, the Festival of Sydney Motorfest, and donations to groups such as the Ted Noffs Foundation. But other donations create valuable links with community-based organizations and assist preventative community action. For example, NRMA gives $250,000 a year to the NSW Police for administrative support; runs a pilot project (Residents in Safer Environments; RISE) to work with the community to reduce local crime levels; and supports staff volunteer involvement in the community, matching dollar for dollar amounts raised up to $1,500.

NRMA also provides staff with an Information Kit on School Holiday Activities for the Kids, a listing of Vacation Centers by local council and information on child care centers in staff priority areas. The Body Shop's staff teams devote time and materials each week to help groups such as Homes for the Aged, Homes for the Blind, Women's Refuges, and others. Their business objectives include the following statement: "We care about humanizing the business community: We will continue to show that success and profits can go hand in hand with ideals and values." Their new Moorabbin work-based child care center was designed for Body Shop employees' children, but spare places will be open to others in the local community.

Some companies buy time with counseling agencies instead of setting up their own internal employee assistance programs (EAPs), which would be both more costly and less confidential. For example Ericsson Australia addresses job performance problems by offering self-referral counseling on family breakdown, bereavement, drug and alcohol problems, psychological disorders, and other health crises. Westpac's EAP has operated in Victoria for 6 years, recognizing that it is unrealistic to expect staff to leave their personal problems at home each morning. It offers a professional counseling and referral service and is open not just to employees but also to other immediate family members. Education packages and talks are offered on topics such as financial budgeting, marital and relationship problems, diet, exercise, and stress.

Caltex is another company moving towards an approach close to the NLW concept. They specifically aim at developing a family-friendly work culture; are planning an EAP that is not internal but draws on outside agencies for confidential personal and family counseling; are using the Lady Gowrie Child Care Information and Referral Service; and are pressing for a national data base on child care. They also developed a new Relocation (Transfer) Policy which provides better support services to help find a new home, new schools, spouse job search, and counseling services, and try to ensure that all work and family initiatives are integrated into Caltex business objectives.

Kemcor is a relative latecomer to this field but has moved further than most companies since formal Family Friendly Policies were approved in August 1993. These include flexible start and finishing times to fit in with family needs; part-time work on return from maternity leave; job sharing; special emergency leave with no salary loss; paternity leave up to 51 weeks; retirement planning seminars; paid education assistance for employees; reserved child care places in the Altona community; ITIM (chaplaincy) care search and marital and parenting advice; an integrated Employee Care Program built into their Enterprise Agreement; Women's Forums to offer peer support; Family Days and work experience for employees' children; and a wide range of community initiatives. These include a Resource Kit for Schools; a link with regional groups to develop a Female Apprentice Program; and efforts to encourage girls to enter nontraditional occupations. An annual survey will monitor Kemcor's progress towards a quality work life which "minimizes the disruption to employees' home and family lives."

The *H-P Way* is the way Hewlett-Packard describes its attempt to create a caring organizational culture around the linked themes of *work, life,* and *diversity*. They see this as a series of partnerships between their own people, shareholders, customers, and the environment, the goal being for H-P to be seen as an "Employer of Choice." This involves very flexible work practices, including telecommuting and salary packages, careful needs assessments (both current and future needs) and a systematic process of women's net-working to ensure valued employees are not lost through insensitivity or lack of support.

Esso, winner of last year's Corporate Work and Family Award, continues to advance on its core values of concern for people, teamwork, excellence, safety and managing diversity. They moved from seeing Equal Opportunity as treating everyone as "the same," to treating each person as an individual, with a focus on work results and performance. Whereas in the past it cost over $80,000 to replace a female accountant who did not return from maternity leave, their family-friendly work culture now means Esso gets close to a 100% return rate at minimal cost to the company. Two main obstacles they identified to further reforms are the resistant Australian taxation regime and the residual resistance to family-related change by the "clay layer" of middle management. If the method of slow infusion does not work, one gets the impression that Esso may be prepared to flush out such obstacles to improve work–family relationships.

Such companies deserve high praise for treating their employees as whole people, not just automatons who bring their skills to work each day. It is not that they are necessarily being soft and cuddly; rather, they recognize the hard economic reality behind losses through absenteeism, turnover, accidents, and poor morale and performance.

In summary, the NLW is one that integrates its internal work practices with changing family needs and draws cost-effectively on family support resources, services, and expertise in the community of which it is an integral part. This philosophy is outlined in the following principles (Fig. 9.7).

A sense of community is necessary both within and outside the workplace. Employees are not separate from others, and enhanced well-being for all will include them. This requires the development of linkage skills, the

1. Enhancing a Sense of Community
    *   well-being of all people
    *   community-based efforts
    *   local needs and resources
    *   part of a caring unit

2. Mobilizing Resources and Supports
    *   build on and strengthen existing networks
    *   flexible, individualized and responsive
    *   decrease dependency on professionals

3. Shard Responsibility and collaboration
    *   exchange ideas, skills
    *   partnership in community-building
    *   service-providers as partners

4. Protect Family Integrity
    *   family rights and responsibilities
    *   diversity of family beliefs and practice

5. Strengthen Family Functioning
    *   build on strengths, not correct deficits
    *   enable and empower
    *   help master wide range of tasks

6. Proactive Human Services Approach
    *   prevention and promotion models
    *   intervene prior to poor functioning
    *   resource-based and consumer-driven

FIG. 9.7. New links family support principles.

capacity to draw on supports that already exist (the *family-as-maker* concept of Elise Boulding, 1983), to exploit their interdependency with formal and professional services. Service-providers should be placed in a partner relationship, exchanging ideas and skills collaboratively. Respect for family and individual differences is essential to ensure resources are available in varied and flexible ways. The whole social context should promote healthy, stable relationships in families and extend their capacities to cope so that work-intrusive problems are prevented in the first place and costly professional intrusion is minimized. Services should be resource-based and consumer-driven, aimed at promoting well-being and prevention rather than toward intrusive remedial intervention by formal services.

If we apply this approach to family support instead of the usual damage control policy, we may start to get some truly innovative, productive solutions. It is my hope that we will see major changes in corporate culture, in government policies affecting families and family support services and in the value the whole community places on the important work of families themselves. Only in this integrated way will we see an expansion of social capital in a caring civil society. Regardless, the pressures faced by families trying to balance their two major tasks—earning a living and caring for their members—necessitate a more integrated, "New Links" workplace in the 21st century.

REFERENCES

Australian Bureau of Statistics. (1993a). *Australia's families: Selected findings from the Survey of Families 1992* (ABS Cat. No. 6224.0). Canberra, Australia.

Australian Bureau of Statistics. (1993b). *How Australians use their time* (ABS Cat. No. 4153.0). Canberra, Australia.

ALRC. (1993). *Child Care Discussion* (Paper No. 55). Sydney: Australian Law Reform Commission.

Boulding, E. (1983). Familia Faber, the family as maker of the future. *Journal of Marriage and the Family, May,* 257–266.

Dunst, C. J. (1990). *Family Support Principles* (Monograph No. 5, Vol. 2). Morgantown, NC: Western Carolina Center, Family, Infant and Preschool Program.

Edgar, D. (1987). *Focus on adults: Towards a productive learning culture (The Edgar report).* Ministry of Education, Victoria, Australia.

George, J. (1993). *Equity in Enterprise Bargaining.* Paper presented at the Women in Leadership Public Lecture Series, Edith Cowan University, Perth, Australia.

Galinsky, E., Friedman, D. E., & Hernandez, C. A. (1991). *The Corporate Reference.* New York: Families and Work Institute.

Glezer, H. (1988). *Maternity leave in Australia* (Australian Institute of Family Studies Monograph No. 7). Melbourne: AIFS.

NWCC. (1993). *Paid Maternity Leave.* Canberra, Australia: National Women's Consultative Council, AGPS.

Pusey, M. (1991). *Economic rationalism in Canberra.* Cambridge, England: Cambridge University Press.

VandenHeuvel, A. (1993). *When roles overlap: Workers with family responsibilities,* Australian Institute of Family Studies, Monograph No. 14, Melbourne.

Wolcott, I. (1991). *Work and family: Employers' views* (Australian Institute of Family Studies Monograph No. 11). Melbourne: AIFS.

Wolcott, I., & Glezer, H. (1995). *Work and family life: Achieving integration.* Australian Institute of Family Studies, Melbourne.

10

THE TRIPLE REVOLUTION: SOCIAL SOURCES OF FAMILY CHANGE

Arlene Skolnick
University of California, Berkeley

Over the past three decades, family life in the industrialized nations changed dramatically. The trends are remarkably similar across North America and Western Europe: a divorce revolution, a sexual revolution, couples' marrying later, a drop in fertility rates, an increase in single-parent families, an increase in the number of women working outside the home, and an increase in the diversity of family forms. As a result of these and other changes, there is also increasing uncertainty about how to define the family, and widespread concern over whether the institution will continue.

To be sure, countries differ in current and past rates of various demographic indicators. The United States has higher divorce rates than most other countries; Sweden has higher rates of unmarried cohabitation; Italy has the lowest birth rates. But regardless of national variations, the broad dimensions of family change are similar across the Western world and even beyond. It does not seem too farfetched to suggest that we are witnessing another world revolution in family patterns (Goode, 1963)

Although it is obvious that a major transformation occurred, there is no consensus as to what it means. Is the family a disappearing institution? Have individuals in recent years become more self-centered, less willing to make commitments or to invest in family ties? Whereas scholars debate whether or not the family is in decline, or merely changing, the general public, particularly in the United States, assume the disintegration of the family to be a simple social fact, part of a general breakdown of morals and values. These anxieties have made family issues a major battleground in American politics.

There have been relatively few efforts to make sociological sense of the recent upheavals in family life, or to place them in historical context. Social analysis often consists merely of noting demographic trends, such as rising divorce rates or rates of unwed motherhood, and making attributions about the individual motives and values that might account for them. In fact, however, as the burgeoning field of social history shows, family life has always been in flux. At periods of societal transition, change is especially rapid and dislocating.

In this chapter, I argue that recent family trends must be understood as responses to long term changes in the larger society. The trends are most pronounced in the industrialized world but reflect global forces. Each country's response to family change, however, is shaped by its own cultural and political traditions.

The era we are living through today bears many resemblances to two earlier periods of family crisis and transformation in Western history. The first is the time of transition when the preindustrial family-based economy began to give way to the urban, industrial way of life, with its separation of work and family. In the United States, this shift began in the early decades of the 19th century.

Briefly, the movement of fathers and work out of the home disrupted existing patterns of daily family life as well as cultural blueprints for gender and generational roles (Ryan, 1981) These dislocations in the functions and meaning of family life unleashed a wrenching era of personal stress, social disorder, cultural confusion, and political ferment. The crisis was eventually resolved when a new paradigm of family emerged that rationalized and sanctified the new patterns and practices.

No longer a workplace, the home as an emotional and spiritual refuge, a "haven in a heartless world," was at the center of the new model of family. And at the center of the home was the wife and mother, who would nurture both children and the father who had to enter the heartless world each day.

The "new domesticity," with its doctrine of separate spheres for men and women, was a middle class creation, but it became the dominant cultural definition of *family* as well as a blueprint for the good and proper way to live. Few families could live up to the ideal in all its particulars; working class, Black, and ethnic families, for example, could not get by without the economic contributions of wives, mothers, and daughters. And even for middle class families, the sentimentalized Victorian image of family life prescribed a standard of perfection that was virtually impossible to fulfill (Demos, 1986). Nevertheless, the new model supplied the cultural coherence that had been sorely lacking; at last people had a definition of family not based on the household as an economic enterprise in which the family worked together.

Eventually, however, social change overtook the new domesticity. Around the turn of the 20th century, another period of rapid economic, social, and cultural change destabilized Victorian family patterns, especially its gender arrangements. Several generations of "new women" challenged the constraints imposed on women by Victorian domesticity. This ferment culminated in the victory of woman's suffrage movement, the first wave of women's liberation. It was followed by the 1920s jazz age era of flappers and flaming youth, the first, and probably the major sexual revolution of the 20th century.

To many observers at the time, it appeared that the family and morality had broken down. Another cultural crisis ensued, until a new cultural blueprint emerged—the companionate model of marriage and the family. The new model reconciled older Victorian ideals with a more informal and sexualized version of the marriage bond.

This highly abbreviated history of family and cultural change forms the necessary backdrop for understanding the family upheavals of the late 20th century. As in early times, a set of major changes in economy and society destabilized an existing paradigm of family life, and the everyday patterns and practices that sustained them. Three distinct but related structural shifts seem to have set the current cycle of family change in motion: first, the move towards a postindustrial service and information economy; second, reductions in mortality and fertility that reshaped the individual and family life course; and third, a psychological transformation rooted mainly in rising educational levels.

Although these shifts have profound implications for everyone in contemporary society, women have been the pacesetters of change. Most women's lives and expectations inside and outside the family over the past three decades have departed drastically from those of their own mothers; today's men also are different from their fathers' generation, but to a much lesser extent.

THE POSTINDUSTRIAL FAMILY

In historical perspective, the breadwinner–housewife type of family most people in the West define as *traditional* is actually an uncommon arrangement. It is associated with the early stages of the industrial revolution, when, as noted earlier, work first moved out of the home and the family ceased to be an economic unit. According to sociologist Kingsley Davis (1988), the breadwinner family develops slowly in the early stages of industrialization, characterizing the growing but still small middle class. Then, after reaching a peak in which very few married women are employed, it declines. More and more women find work in a growing service sector—in offices, schools, hospitals, stores. Davis found this pattern recurring in countries now undergoing development.

As Jesse Bernard (1972) once observed, the transformation of a housewife into a paid worker outside the home sends tremors through every family relationship. It creates a more symmetrical family, undoing the sharp dichotomy between roles that characterizes the breadwinner–housewife pattern. It also increases the opportunity costs of pregnancy and childrearing and reduces women's economic dependence on men, thereby making it easier for women to leave unhappy marriages.

Beyond drawing women into the workplace, shifts in the nature of work and a rapidly changing globalized economy have unsettled the lives of individuals and families at all class levels. The well-paying industrial jobs that once enabled a blue collar worker to own a home and support a family are no longer available to the sons. The once secure jobs that sustained the "organization men" and their families in the 1950s and 1960s were made shaky by downsizing, an unstable economy, corporate takeovers, and a rapid pace of technological change.

The new economic climate has also made the transition to adulthood increasingly problematic. The reduction in opportunity is in part responsible for changes in family behavior on the part of young adults—later marriage, lower fertility, and women flooding into the workplace. Further, the increased educational demands of postindustrial society are incompatible with the family formation patterns of the 1950s. In those years, particularly in the United States, young people entered adulthood in one giant step—going to work and marrying young, having children quickly, moving to households separate from parents. Today, few young adults can afford to marry and have children early. In an economy in which a college degree is necessary to earn a living wage, such a family formation pattern impedes education for both men and women. Those who do not go on to college do not have access to jobs that can sustain a family.

Particularly in the inner cities of the United States, growing numbers of young people have come to see no future for themselves at all in the ordinary world of work. In middle class families, economic constriction and a narrowing opportunity structure increased anxieties about downward mobility for offspring as well as the parents. Another problem is the Hamlet syndrome or the incompletely launched young adult syndrome—referring to young adults who deviate from their parents' expectations by failing to launch careers and become successfully independent adults, and may even come home to crowd their parents' empty nests (Schnaiberg & Goldenberg, 1989).

THE LIFE COURSE REVOLUTION

The demographic transformations of Western society over the last century are no less significant than the economic. We cannot understand current predicaments of family life without understanding how radically different are the demographic and social circumstances facing 20th-century Americans. The widespread myth of a golden past of family stability is in large part a product of public unawareness of the feature of family life, and daily life in general in the past that most sets it off from our own era—the omni-presence and visibility of death.

In earlier times, most mortality took place in infancy, but death remained an ever-present possibility at any age. It was not unusual for young and middle aged adults to die of tuberculous, pneumonia, or other infectious diseases. Before the turn of this century, only 40% of women lived through all the stages of a "normal" life course—growing up, marrying, having children, and surviving with a spouse to the age of 50 (Uhlenberg, 1980).

Today, by contrast, despite accidents, disease, crime, environmental pollution, and stress, most people in modern societies go about their business on the assumption they will live out a full life. Today, death at any time before old age has become a rare event; about 75% of all deaths occur after the age of 65.

These simple changes in mortality rates had a profound effect on family life. Peter Uhlenberg (1980) examined the impact of mortality change on various aspects of family life by contrasting mortality rates in 1900 with those of 1976. He found that under 1900 conditions, half of all parents experienced the death of a child. By 1976, only 6% did. In the conditions of the early 20th century, more than half of all children who lived to the age of 15 experienced a death in the immediate family—either a parent or a sibling.

When death could strike adults at any age, large numbers of children experienced orphanhood. In 1900, about 1 out of 14 children lost a parent before the age of 15, 1 out of 62 lost both. In 1976, only 1 out of 20 lost one parent by age 15, 1 out of 1,800 lost both. Because so many children were orphaned in the early 20th century, the chances that a child was not living with either parent was greater than it is now. Indeed, some of the current growth in single-parent families is offset by a decline in the number of children raised in institutions, foster homes, or by relatives.

One psychological result of our escape from living with death on a daily basis is that we are ill-prepared for it when it does occur. The confrontation with one's own mortality now comes for most people in their later 30s and 40s, when the time already lived comes to exceed the time left.

Another effect of shifting mortality rates is that the death of a child is no longer a sad but normal hazard of parenthood. Rather, it has become a devastating, life-shattering loss from which the parents may never fully recover (Knapp, 1887). The intense emotional bonding between parents and infants we take for granted today, and see as a sociobiological given, became the norm only in the 18th and 19th centuries. The privileged classes created the modern "emotionally priceless" child, a powerful ideal which gradually filtered down through the rest of society (Zelizer, 1985).

Another major result of falling death rates is a decline in fertility rates. By granting parents confidence that they did not have to have "extra" children to ensure that some would survive to adulthood, lowered mortality rates in early childhood encouraged careful planning of births and smaller families. The combination of longer lives and fewer, closely spaced children created a still-lengthening "empty nest" stage of the family. This in turn encouraged the companionate style of marriage, which focuses on the relationship between husband and wife; this shift in the meaning and function of marriages may have a good deal to do with the increase in divorce.

In sum, reductions in mortality have encouraged stronger emotional bonds between parents and children, lengthened the duration of marriage and parent–child relationships, made grandparenthood an expectable stage of the life course, and increased the number of grandparents children actually know. More and more families have 4 and even 5 generations alive at the same time, creating what has been called the *bean pole family*.

At the same time, lengthened life spans have increased the number of frail elderly and made chronic rather than infectious disease the leading causes of death. Contrary to the myth of the "abandoned" elderly, adult children (mostly daughters) remain the primary caregivers to the elderly. The big change is that people in the past were far less likely to be called upon to care for an aging parent, because few people lived to be old and frail.

We have no cultural precedents for the mass of the population living long enough to be old. The traditional shape of a country's population is like a Christmas tree: a broad base of the very young, smaller and smaller bands at older ages, rising to a point at the top. In modern times, the shape is roughly a rectangle until the oldest ages.

In his influential book *The Culture of Narcissism* (1976), Christopher Lasch pointed to the fear of aging as one of the chief symptoms of our alleged psychological impairment. But earlier generations never had the opportunity to experience old age on a mass scale. Anthropologist David Plath argued that "the gift of mass longevity" was so recent, dramatic and rapid that it has become profoundly unsettling in all postindustrial societies: "If the essential cultural nightmare of the nineteenth century was to be in poverty, perhaps ours is to be old and alone or afflicted with terminal disease" (Plath, 1980, p. 1).

As a result of the new longevity, many people find themselves in life stages for which cultural scripts have not yet been written; family members face one another in relationships for which tradition provides little guidance. A study of 5-generation families in Germany reveals the confusion and strain that result when people and their parents are both in advanced old age. Who has the right to be old? Who is to take care of whom? (Hagestad, 1986). Similarly Plath, who has studied the problems of mass longevity in Japan, found that even in that familistic society, the traditional meaning of family roles has been put into question by the stretching out of the life span.

Mass longevity, however, has produced the happier but also problematic phenomenon of what Peter Laslett (1989) called *the third age*—a new stage of life created by the extension of the life course in the advanced economies and their systems of retirement. Recent decades witnessed the first generations of people to live past age 65 as healthy, vigorous, alert, financially self-supporting individuals. These people are "pioneers on the frontier of age" (Fitzgerald, 1987).

PSYCHOLOGICAL GENTRIFICATION

The third major transformation is a set of psychocultural changes that might be described as "psychological gentrification" (Skolnick, 1991). That is, cultural advantages once enjoyed only by the upper classes, in particular, education, are extended to those lower down the socioeconomic scale. Psychological gentrification also involves increased leisure, travel, and exposure to information, as well as a general rise in the standard of living. Despite the persistence of poverty, unemployment, and economic insecurity in the industrialized world, far less of the population than in the historical past is living at the level of sheer subsistence.

Throughout Western society, rising levels of education and related changes have been linked to a complex set of shifts in personal and political attitudes. One of these is a more psychological approach to life—greater introspectiveness, a yearning for warmth and intimacy in family and other relationships (Veroff, Douvan, & Kulka, 1981). There is also evidence of an increasing preference on the part of both men and women for a more companionate ideal of marriage and a more democratic family. More broadly, these changes in attitude have been described as a shift to postmaterialist values emphasizing self-expression, tolerance, equality, and a concern for the quality of life (Inglehart, 1990). The concern with environment is one aspect of this approach to life, but it also includes the desire for a friendlier, less impersonal society, greater equality, and a tendency to challenge rather than accept society.

The demographic changes of recent times have also had psychological effects. The long-lived citizens of an advanced society in the last decades of the 20th century are obliged to have a more elaborated sense of self than their ancestors. In modern industrial societies, the movement of a person through life has become more individualized, more self-conscious, and at the same time more institutionalized (Kohli, 1986). The life course is the framework around which a person makes life choices and weaves a sense of self, but it has at the same time become part of the structure of modern social institutions—schools, the workplace, pension plans.

There is also a political dimension to psychological change. The United States and Western Europe experienced what is called a *rights revolution* or the "democratization of personhood" (Clecak, 1983). At the center of this shift is the claiming of political and cultural rights by disadvantaged groups of all kinds—from racial minorities, individuals living with physical disabilities, gay males and lesbians, older adults, as well as women and children.

A similar rights revolution is taking place in many countries around the world. The growth of state power has accompanied social and economic development and tended to expand the citizenship rights of both women and children. For example, public laws preventing child labor and compelling school attendance have a profound effect on parent–child relations; compulsory education, as John Caldwell (1982) showed, has a rapid and dramatic effect on fertility rates wherever it is introduced. In response to these changes, children shifted from being economic assets to their parents to being "economically useless" but "emotionally priceless" (Zelizer, 1985).

Psychological democratization applies to the family as well. Despite the persistence of gender inequality in marriage, there has been a normative shift towards more egalitarian relations between spouses. And parents are increasingly regarding children as unique individuals, if not equals. More broadly, we have witnessed a transition from what has been called the "positional" family to the "personal" or person-centered family.

The terms stem from British sociologist Basil Bernstein's research on childrearing, language, and social class (1970). The *positional* family emphasizes roles, status, hierarchy. The emphasis is on conforming to rules, respecting authority. The *personal* family emphasizes the individuality of each family member, feelings and motives, the reasons for rules.

The positional family is not necessarily authoritarian or cold, but there are clear boundaries between age and sex roles, and the authority structure of the family is clear-cut and, in a sense, impersonal. Thus, a child in a positional family will by controlled by statements such as the following: *Little boys don't cry* or *Children don't talk to their fathers like that.*

In the more democratic, personal family, the child is controlled by appeals to feelings, motives, and reasons. In the 1950s and 1960s, Bernstein and others discovered that although the positional family could be found in both the working and middle class, the personal family was a largely middle class phenomenon, linked to the educational level of the parents and or their educational aspirations for the child. Bernstein found it especially prevalent among the new postwar middle class employed by universities, large corporations, and government bureaucracies.

Since Bernstein's original research, there has been a societal shift towards the personal family. Reviewing survey data over the past several decades, Alwin observed a marked turn in childrearing attitudes away from an emphasis on obedience, towards an emphasis on autonomy, which he linked to increasing levels of education in the population (Alwin, 1988). Also, to the extent that television can be used as a guide to popular norms of childrearing, the personal mode of family interaction seems to dominate in the leading situation comedies, even those depicting working class families.

Each family mode has its own costs and benefits. In positional families, the roles and rules are clear; the central concern for parents is whether or not the child behaves, not what he or she feels or thinks. In personal families, the parents are concerned with both outer behavior and inner feeling. There is a paradox here. The personal family celebrates the autonomy and unique value of the child, yet more of the child's self is subject to the parent's scrutiny and control.

The messages in middle class childrearing are complex and demanding: "The child is to act appropriately, not because his parents tell him to, but because he wants to. Not conformity to authority, but inner control; not because you're told to, but because you take the other person into consideration" (Kohn, 1959).

For parents, the positional style of family may also be a mixed blessing; the more education parents have, the more stress they experience in parenting. Also, the more education the children have, the less happy are their evaluations, as adults, of their own childhoods (Veroff et al., 1981).

The rise of personal family can be seen as part of a wider shift in interpersonal relations. Much of what Lasch and others condemned as narcissism may reflect a shift from "management by command" to "management by negotiation" (de Swann, 1981). The new, less formal, more democratic mode of managing interpersonal relationships applies not only to parents and children, but to men and women inside and outside the family, as well as in the workplace and in government.

Parents, bosses, managers, bureaucrats, or police chiefs are no longer expected to rule by simply issuing commands or threats. Rather, they must operate with at least some consent from the managed or governed. The higher-ups must give at least the appearance of taking the wishes and desires of the lower-downs into consideration. The latter, in turn, have an enlarged sense of their own rights and entitlements.

The shift from "commanding" to "negotiation" was also grounded by a change in the nature of work. In the large factories and mills that dominated in the earlier stages of industrial society, most jobs required relatively low levels of skill. The whole factories could be managed from the top down. The shift to postindustrial society, with its more complex organization and demands for a more highly trained and educated workhorse, necessitates a different kind of manager, one more skilled in human relations. Even at the lower levels of the work force, most jobs are service jobs that also call for interpersonal skills on the part of worker and employer.

In many ways, the new style of interpersonal relations is actually a new morality, more stringent than the old. "The restraint on violent behavior has not lessened," de Swaan (1981) observed, "the inhibition upon self-aggrandizement has probably increased, and the discipline in the handling of time, money, goods and the body has grown" (p. 376). Similarly, it is a mistake to believe restraints on behavior and emotional expression were abandoned and that anything goes. Instead, certain socially disruptive emotions such as anger and jealousy have come to be disapproved of and more suppressed than they were in the past.

Despite the widespread impression that family violence has increased, there is little clear evidence that this is so. In fact, statistics on child abuse and wife-battering may reflect shifting definitions of acceptable behavior in the family, increasing rights granted to women and children, and a growing intolerance for hitting and slapping for any reason.

And despite the relaxation of traditional sexual rules, such as the prohibition of sex before marriage, there are new rules for taking into account the wishes and consent of the other person. For example, men now have less permission to be mindlessly hedonistic than in the past; they can now take fewer of what used to be called *liberties* with women. "Rape, roughness, scorn and degradation, so common and acceptable for employers to inflict upon servants and factory girls, or customers upon prostitutes only a few generations ago, have become more distasteful to the general public" (de Swann, 1981, p. 373).

Changes in the law reflect the new, more stringent standards for consent in sexual matters. Consider the new concept of *sexual harassment*. Once simply taken for granted as part of the vicissitudes of everyday life in the workplace, sexual harassment has become not just unacceptable but unlawful.

The negotiating style of management and the new morality of dignity and personhood have not made life easier. It has certainly become harder for men, especially if they are White. But more generally, no matter what their gender, race, age, they have to navigate through life without the old rules and dogmas that guided interpersonal relationships in the past. Further, although the new relational styles promote greater equality and mutual respect, the negotiated consent can mask and mystify real inequalities of power. Despite the new rules, negotiations between parents and children, husbands and wives, and employers and employees, are enacted in a world in which one party generally has more advantages and options than the other.

The new styles also make increasing demands on personality. In the workplace, as well as at home, simply following orders or giving them is no longer enough. New and different forms of self-control are necessary; managers must display concern for the desires of those they manage, employees must develop the skills of assertiveness. Both must be sensitive to a wide range of interpersonal signals and have a degree of skill in responding to them. Temperamental quirks of personality, such as shyness or a hot temper, may now be greater liabilities than they were in the past. It is little wonder, under these circumstances, that people scrutinize themselves, become introspective, consult with therapists, and frame their problems in psychological terms.

THE PSYCHOLOGICAL SOCIETY

For most cultural critics, the current spread of an interest in psychology is symptomatic of two seemingly different things: on the one hand, a pathological weakness of character preoccupation with self, on the other, a refined instrument of manipulation on the part of capitalist society—its service bureaucracies, the mass media and the capitalist state. Thus, the increasing concern with the inner life, with motivations, and above all, with sexuality, is not just symptomatic of moral decline, but is also a deep form of social control.

But new kinds of interpersonal relations at home and work suggest an alternative explanation of the rise of a psychological idiom. Modernity liberated people from inherited identities, statuses, employments, and family links, they argue, but the cost has been a sense of "disorientation and insecurity" (Gellner, 1985) The realm of human relationships replaced the natural world as the focus of anxiety, particularly for the typical middle class citizen of the modern world. Comfortable, but not especially rich or powerful, his or her happiness, fulfillment, and self-esteem are dependent on other people—on spouses, children, other close kin, coworkers, and bosses.

The best as well as the worst emotional experiences of modern (and postmodern) life are found in personal relationships. It was this state of emotional affairs that psychoanalysis and other brands of psychology addressed. The new psychology filled a vacuum; it offered a set of insights into the new forms of malaise, a language for speaking about experiences that were widespread but had not been named, and what's more, the promise of a cure.

IMPLICATIONS OF CHANGE

The multiple social transformations of this era have brought both costs and benefits: Family relations became more fragile and more emotionally rich; mass longevity has brought us a host of problems as well as the gift of extended life. Change brought greater opportunities for women, but because of persisting gender inequality, women bore a large share of the costs. But we cannot turn the clock back to the family models of the past. Furthermore, despite nostalgia for the world we have lost, few of us would actually want to return to conditions of life endured by most people in generations past.

Paradoxically, after all the upheavals of the recent decades, the emotional and cultural significance of the family persists. Family remains the center of most people's lives, and as numerous surveys show, a cherished value. Although marriage has become more fragile, the parent–child relationship—especially the mother–child relationship—remains a core attachment across the life course (Rossi & Rossi, 1990).

The family, however, can be both permanent and beset with difficulties. There is widespread recognition that the massive social and economic changes we lived through call for public and private sector policies in support of families. Most European countries have recognized for some time that governments have a role in supplying an array of supports to families—health care, children's allowances, housing subsidies, support for working parents and children, such as child care, parental leave, shorter work days for parents, as well as an array of services for old people.

Each country's response to these changes, as I noted earlier, is shaped by its own political and cultural traditions. The United States remains embroiled in a cultural war over the family; many social commentators and political leaders have promised to reverse the recent trends and restore the traditional family. In contrast, other Western countries, including Canada and the other Anglo countries, adapted to family change by policies aimed at mitigating the problems brought about by change. As a result of these policies, these countries have been spared much of the poverty and social disintegration that has plagued the United States in the last decade.

LOOKING AHEAD

The world at the end of the 20th century is vastly different from what it was at the beginning, or even in the middle. Families are struggling to adapt to new realities. The countries that have been at the leading edge of family change still find themselves caught midway between yesterday's norms, today's new realities, and an uncertain future.

As we have seen, changes in women's lives are pivotal factors in recent family trends. In many countries there is a considerable gap between men's and women's attitudes and expectations of one another. Even when both partners accept a more equal division of labor in the home, there is often a gap between attitudes and behavior. In no country have employers, the government, or men fully caught up to the changes in women's lives.

The ferment in women's roles is now global, prompted not just by education and economic development, but women's participation in independence and other grass roots movements. The United Nations legitimized the global discussion of women's lives and rights through a number of world conferences on women as well as the vision of the family articulated for the Year of the Family—"The Smallest Democracy at the Heart of the Society."

Family patterns, however, do not necessarily change quickly, nor all in the same direction. Tradition can and does coexist with modernity. Indeed, a forceful reassertion of patriarchy is a feature of various fundamentalisms around the world. In Eastern Europe, the collapse of Communist regimes led to a resurgence of "traditional" notions of women's roles. Diversity is likely to be a continuing feature of family life, not just because of traditional differences in terms of race, class, ethnicity, but because so many family matters are now based on individual choice.

To be effective, government policies must recognize the pluralism of family forms, as well as diversity within families. The needs of individuals and families vary across the life course; infancy and early childhood, adolescence, and old age pose particular challenges in modern societies that need to be addressed. More broadly, the interests and perspectives of different family members do not always coincide. A focus on *family* never should obscure the fact that "his" marriage is not necessarily the same as "hers," or that the parents' family is not necessarily the children's.

The family around the world is likely to be in transition well into the 21st century. Anthropological and historical studies of cultural change suggest that it is a long and often painful process (Wallace, 1970), marked by individual and family stress and political and cultural conflict. There are no quick, inexpensive solutions to solving the problems besetting family life today. Yet any government in an advanced industrial society that ignores the well being of its children and families does so at its peril.

REFERENCES

Alwin, D. F. (1988). From obedience to autonomy: Changes in traits desired in children, 1924–1978. *Public Opinion Quarterly, 52*, 33–52.

Bernard, J. (1972). *The Future of Marriage.* New York: World.

Bernstein, B. (1970). A socio-linguistic approach to socialization. In J. Gumperz & D. Hymes (Eds.), *Directions in sociolinguistics.* New York: Holt, Rinehart & Winston.

Caldwell, J. (1982). *Theory of Fertility Decline.* New York: Academic Press.

Clecak, P. (1983). *America's quest for the ideal self.* New York: Oxford University Press.

Demos, J. (1970). *Past, present, and personal.* New York: Oxford University Press.

Davis, K. (1988). Wives and work: A theory of the sex role revolution and its consequences. In S. M. Dornbusch & M. H. Strober (Eds.), *Feminism, children, and the new families.* New York: Guilford Press.

de Swann. A. (1981). The politics of agoraphobia: On changes in emotional and relational management. *Theory and Society, 10*, 337–358.

Fitzgerald, F. (1987). *Cities on a hill.* New York: Simon and Schuster.

Gellner, E. (1985). *The psychoanalytic movement.* London: Paladin Books.

Goode, W. J. (1963). *World Revolution and Family Patterns.* New York: Free Press.

Hagestand, G. O. (1986). The aging society as a context for family life. *Daedalus, 115*(1) 119–139.

Inglehart, R. (1990). *Culture shift.* Princeton, NJ: Princeton University Press.

Knapp, R. (1987). *Beyond endurance: When a child dies.* New York: Schocken Books.

Kohli, M. (1986). The world we forgot: A historical review of the life course. In V. M. Marshall (Ed.), *Later life: The social psychology of aging.* Beverly Hills, CA: Sage.

Kohn, M. M. (1959). Social class and parental values. *American Journal of Sociology, 64*, 337–351.

Lasch, C. (1976). *The culture of narcissism.* New York: Norton.

Laslett, P. (1989). *A fresh map of life: The emergence of the third age.* London: Weidenfeld and Nicolson.

Plath, D. (1980). *Long engagements: Maturity in modern Japan.* Stanford: Stanford University Press.

Rossi, A. S., & Rossi, P. H. (1990). *Of human bonding: Parent–child relations across the life course.* Hawthorne, NY: Aldine de Gruyter.

Ryan, M. (1981). *The cradle of the middle class.* New York: Cambridge University Press.

Skolnick, A. (1991). *Embattled paradise: The American family in an age of uncertainty.* New York: Basic Books.

Uhlenberg, P. (1980). Death and the family. *Journal of Family History, 5,* 313–320.

Veroff, J., Douvan, G., & Kulka, R. A. (1981). *The inner American: A self portrait from 1957–1976.* New York: Basic Books.

Wallace, A. F. C. (1970). *The death and rebirth of the Seneca.* New York: Knopf.

Zelizer, V. (1985). *Pricing the priceless child.* New York: Basic Books.

11

THE SITUATION OF FAMILIES
IN WESTERN EUROPE:
A SOCIOLOGICAL PERSPECTIVE

Wilfried Dumon
Catholic University Leuven, Belgium

I begin with two preliminary remarks.

DEFINITION OF *FAMILY*

Addressing the issue of family, more particularly *changing* families, immediately invokes the following question: What is family? It is not by accident that in scholarly work as well as in social and political action, including the organization of the International Year of the Family, the definition of *family* has been at the center of attention (United Nations, 1992). Indeed, the dramatic changes occurring over the last decades, have put the notion of *family* itself into question. Out of the discussion, two new elements have emerged:

1. Recognition of the plurality of family forms, to the effect that many would address the issue in plural form and rather would refer to *families* than to *family*. The diversity was a focus of attention far more than the unifying denominator. Yet, a common characteristic basic to all family forms, ranging from the traditional family to cohabitation to so-called *LAT-relations* (living apart together), can be identified: They all serve as person-supporting networks.

2. Recognition of subsystems within the family and of the disparity between family and household. More important is the recognition that there is even a plurality of families within the family, that is, the different family

members are likely to perceive the composition of their family, who belongs to it, in differentiated ways. ! 1 · Thus from a methodological point of view, one can make a distinction between subjective and objective definitions of the family. From a theoretical point of view the delineation of the family boundaries has become an issue. From a practical, even political point of view, the growing autonomy of subsystems, the growing disparity between family and household, the growing autonomy of each individual to define his or her family boundaries, including rights and obligations, confronts society with new problems, new challenges.

WESTERN EUROPE

Ever since October 1991 the definition of Western Europe no longer is very clear. The sharp demarcation between East and West has disappeared and some countries have explicitly proclaimed their affiliation to the Western European system as expressed for example by their application for joining the Common Market. Yet, from a demographic or sociologic perspective, Western Europe in itself by no means represents a monolith. The often applied divide: Northern versus Mediterranean is not applicable either. Some demographic indicators are seemingly analogous in countries so different as Ireland and Turkey, other features are quite differentiated between a Scandinavian country such as Sweden and a Mediterranean country such as Italy, and, for some aspects, in reversed order of what one might expect (e.g., fertility rate). One can stress the differentiation between the different European countries and even indicate that similar demographic parameters hide strongly differentiated situations and come to the conclusion that Europe represents a patchwork or a *manteau d'Arlequin*, or one can take an opposite stand and stress the common features, the similarity.

As a matter of fact it is not surprising that there are divergences and convergences. Yet, it is not a question of personal preference or of cultural mood, fads and modes, it rather represents a methodological issue: the differentiation between a static and dynamic perspective. As Roussel (1992) demonstrated, the demographic variables related to family features, such as fertility (birth rates), nuptiality (marriage rates), cohabitation, and divorciality (divorce rates) across Europe show great disparity and hardly cluster at all. Yet, if one looks at the dynamic perspective, they all tend to evolve in a similar direction and moreover they show a remarkable simultaneity in magnitude: dramatic changes. More remarkable even is that the laggers-

---

[1]Lately, from two independent sources techniques were developed that could be used to measure who belongs to a family and to identify family boundaries (see Bien, Marbach, & Neyer, 1991; Levin, 1990).

behind tend to experience more rapid and more dramatic change (e.g., fertility levels in Ireland) than the forerunners of new tendencies and developments, to the effect that trends and developments are remarkably similar and even that some laggers behind may overtake forerunners (as is the case in fertility levels between Italy and Sweden).!2·

CHANGES IN THE THE FAMILY LIFE CYCLE

The most important changes of the last three decades relate to alterations or even mutations, in the family life cycle. More particularly the dramatic changes occurred in the stages of family formation and family dissolution: the beginning and the end.

Family formation

Until the 1950s in Europe there was a sharp and marked, that is, ritualized transition, especially for women, from the so-called family of orientation into the so-called family of procreation. This change was heavily ritualized by the wedding, giving new rights and new obligations, in terms of role (including sexuality) and new positions as expressed by name change, in terms of status. This sharp transition gradually is being replaced by the insertion of a new phase in between the family of orientation and "family" of "procreation." The latter terms both have to be put into quotation marks. Two quite different relatively new features were emerging: independent living of youth and juvenile cohabitation.

Independence and Autonomy of Youth. The independence and the autonomy of youth culture of the 1960s, 1968 having become a symbol, did not only mark the importance of youth culture (as expressed in clothing, music, sexual behavior, etc.) but also in social and political influence, ranging from the political dreams of the so-called movements of 1968 to the ecological movement, heavily supported and carried by the younger generation. In terms of "family" life the autonomy has to be taken almost literally as shown in the growing number of persons living away from home or, put more accurately, living independently, establishing a one-person household. This trend was even more pronounced for females than for males, which does not imply that females outnumbered males but that the increase was far more marked for females than for males.

---

[2]Total fertility rate 1937–1941: Italy: 3.08, Sweden: 1.82. In 1990: Italy: 1.29 (provisional figure for 1989), Sweden: 2.10. For further analysis of the demographic situation in Europe see Rallu and Blum (1991, 1993).

The most important feature however lies in the ambiguity of the situation (i.e., in many instances this autonomy is partial or fragmented, reflecting the essential characteristics of the postmodern society). A sharp discrepancy and even inconsistency between social and economic dependence can be observed. Many youngsters remain economically dependent on their parents,[3] but socially gaining independence. The statistical apparatus has even become inadequate in revealing an accurate situation. In quite a few European countries, as census data demonstrates, youngsters are reported to be living at home whereas, in reality, they have their own living arrangements, either as a standard arrangement or on a part-time basis. This development was heavily facilitated by the growing participation in higher education in Western Europe. For families it implied that this period is not well delineated and vague. For many families it is not very easy to give a clear-cut answer to the question "How many of your (adolescents/adult) children are still living at home?" The family boundaries have become flexible or, put more accurately, not very clearly defined. This does not imply that youngsters do leave home at an earlier age; an opposite trend is documented. Youngsters tend to stay longer at home although the notion of "staying at home" remains very ambivalent indeed.

Juvenile Cohabitation.   The second and even more spectacular development concerns juvenile cohabitation. Cohabitation was contrasted with marriage and in many Western countries the question was put in terms of cohabitation as a substitute for or a replacement of marriage, versus cohabitation as a phenomenon delaying marriage. Unmarried cohabitation in itself was not so new in Europe but acquired totally new features. In this respect there is a qualitative difference between the old *union libre*, or common-law marriage, and cohabitation.

First of all, as to social stratification, the situation has been almost reversed. Cohabitation, not exclusively but predominantly, is occurring in highly educated groups. If the latter are overrepresented, it does not imply that others would be excluded. On the contrary, unmarried cohabitation has become a common feature in all social layers. Yet, the overrepresentation of higher educated groups sharply contrasts with the old situation whereby common-law marriage predominantly was to be found in groups and even regions that could be characterized as economically disadvantaged.

A second marked difference is located in the ideological or cultural component. Certainly in the 1970s and even early 1980s, some qualified family and marriage as oppressing institutions. This can be situated on two levels: internal (hierarchical situation resulting in the oppression of women)

---

[3]In some Western European countries this system was even reinforced by the system of allocation of scholarships for higher (university and nonuniversity) education.

and external (entailing control by state and church[es]). In a more recent period these ideological overtones are fading away and one can even observe an increase in nuptiality rates all over Western Europe (Roussel, 1992). Yet, from a sociological point of view, *cohabitation* rates can be considered to be an indicator of deinstitutionalization, that is, of privatization of family. Also the nature of marriage has changed, as has been recognized for some time now, from a ritual of initiation to a ritual of confirmation (Trost, 1978).

Unmarried cohabitation not only is important from a theoretical point of view but also a factual one. It has remarkably changed basic features of the fabric of society, such as fertility patterns and inheritance patterns, that is, the passing on or continuation of generations and the passing on or continuation of property. The Scandinavian model, in which the distinction between legitimate and illegitimate children has become totally irrelevant and in which the number of children born to unmarried parents dramatically increased ever since the 1950s, now is an emerging model for other European countries such as France and the United Kingdom where, respectively, over and just under 30% of all children are born out of wedlock.[4] Although the disparity in Western Europe is quite considerable, the tendency unequivocally goes in the same direction, even to the effect that the total birth rate and the replacement level in Europe has become partly dependent on the increasing proportion of the birth of these children. Some explained the low fertility rates, for instance in Italy, by the low frequency of illegitimate children, which, in turn, relates to the low level of cohabitation. Thus the label *illegitimate* can be qualified as outdated on demographic, social, and cultural grounds. Consequently, legal systems and discrimination gradually are disappearing and eventually the distinction is likely to become socially irrelevant.

Lately concerns are not related to the social status of the mother, but to her age at parity, more particularly at first parity. Although there is some variation, the average age at first parity in European countries has risen sharply. For example in the Netherlands, it has risen to a level of about 27.6 years. This tendency has raised public concern,[5] and the phenomenon of late transition to motherhood has been identified in Europe, for some time now, as an issue for research (Engstler & Lüscher, 1991).

Dissociation of Partnership and Parenthood. The changing demographic parameters, fertility rates, marriage rates, and cohabitation figures reflect structural changes or, as already indicated above, mutations in our society.

---

[4]See Council of Europe (1990). Crude birth rate and extra-marital births (%). 1970: Sweden: 18.4 (high figure). France: 6.8, U.K.: 8.0, Netherlands: 2.1. 1988: Sweden: 51.0, France: 26.3, United Kingdom: 25.1, Netherlands: 10.2.

[5]For an analysis of the European situation see De Graaf (1992). Average age at first birth: Some figures 1970: Denmark 23.7 (low figure); Switzerland: 25.1 (high figure). 1989: Denmark: 26.2; Switzerland: 27.6 (from Europstat/Council of Europe).

Three processes can be identified: (a) the dissociation between marriage and fertility, which actually reflects the dissociation between the institutions of marriage and family; (b) the decision to get married and the decision to have children; these are not only quite separate decisions, taken on differentiated rationale (Nave-Herz, 1992), but the order in which these decisions have to be taken can be reversed; (c) the *internal* subsystems in the family; the spousal- or partner-relationship and the parental relationship tend to become dissociated and are acquiring their own autonomy. This represents not only an intrafamily process but a real dissociation, to the effect that lone parenthood has been recognized as an institutionalized form. The pluriformity actually is not a situation but a process as clearly indicated in German: *Ausdifferenzierung der pluralen Familienformen* [The ongoing differentiation of the plurality of family forms].

As noted, dissociation of parenthood and partnership by definition implies that both have become autonomous processes. Thus, partner formation has become an autonomous process too. The clear expression of its dissociation from fertility is the growing recognition of same sex marriage-like formations or, more accurately, same-sex family formation. Although the latter has not yet received full recognition and although acceptance of gay male, lesbian, or same-sex relationship is quite differentiated across European countries, yet, in some European states it is gaining so much recognition that it has become semi-institutionalized, as is the case in Denmark and, to some extent, though on a much lower level of recognition, in the Netherlands.[6]

Parenthood and eventually marriage not only tend to become independent as to sequence, they also cross-cut each other. This implies that transition to parenthood no longer exclusively is related to marriage, cohabitation or singlehood, but also is claimed as a right for same-sex couples, and is occurring more frequently, particularly in lesbian relationships. An essential feature here is that not only access to natural offspring is involved, but also eligibility for adoptive and foster-parenthood is claimed under the style of nondiscrimination. The same applies to access to medical assisted fertility regulations.

High-tech babies and medical assisted fertility crosscut the status of the parents and mothers and are the result of an achievement of the last decades in which the total mastery to control and organize one's own fertility pattern has become a realistic prospect due to modern chemical

---

[6]Denmark: In 1989 the Act on Registered Partnership enabled two persons of the same sex to have their partnership registered. With certain exceptions this registration has the same legal effect as a marriage contract. The Netherlands: Some municipalities offered to homosexuals the possibility to register as partners in the municipal registry. This represents a symbolic gesture and bears no legal or other consequences (Communications by P. Schultz-Jorgensen respectively by C. de Hoog/CEC European Observatory on National Family Policies).

and medical techniques. Fertility control is not only put in negative terms of avoiding unwanted pregnancies but reversely, also put in positive terms of having a baby if one wants and at the time at which one wants. If the former has resulted in demographic effects all over Western Europe, then the latter form has had, until now, hardly any demographic effect. Yet it has raised a totally new awareness of changes to come. Governments have felt the need to establish so-called biomedical or bioethical commissions. The claim for total control of one's own fertility is almost absolute, to the effect that also the question of abortion tends to surface as a societal concern and a political issue in Western Europe. The way in which both problems of negative and positive fertility control, respectively, are presented, however, is technically differentiated, but, as to value orientation, they tend to mark existing divisions in society.

From a sociological point of view, techniques such as donor insemination and in-vitro fertility among others, not only allow one to notice divisions in society on ethical, social, and other grounds on a macrolevel, but to relate to sharp and new forms of organization on a microlevel, that is, family and kinship structures. More particularly, the role of the father, and the distinction between genetic and social fatherhood and parenthood become visible. The symbolic meaning of the new techniques has bearing on far larger a scale than the actual (demographic) prevalence would suggest. The high technical developments have been paralleled, not in numbers but in feasibility and even practice, by low technical devices of self-insemination and, for instance, surrogate motherhood. In the latter case, not the role of the father, but the mother's role is being put to test and the dissociation between biological and social motherhood is virtually complete.

In general, society, as expressed by governmental action, tends to be far more repressive and negative toward (artificial) methods that do not imply medical assistance than toward highly sophisticated technological procedures. Some sociologists have explained this by the concept of *control* (Bruynooghe, 1986; Humphrey, Humphrey, & Ainsworth-Smith, 1991). According to that theory, the medical profession exerts control by selection and thus controlling numbers, and, far more important, controlling the effects by (professional) assessment of the situation in which the service is to be rendered. The problem is then put in terms of *a request* to be granted "on certain grounds." The medical profession is being bestowed with a new function (or at least with a more explicit recognition of a function they already have virtually), of assessing situations in which so-called artificial parenthood can be allowed. The analogy between beginning and ending of life is here obvious. Yet, there might be a conflict of interest between societal demands and requirements (as expressed by the medical profession) and the request to parenthood (motherhood or fatherhood) by individuals, couples, persons living in a relationship. The requests of parents tend to increase and become more specific according to the advancement of medical technology ranging, on the positive side, from acquiring gender-specific babies (which is possible, at least on theoretical grounds) and, on the negative side, to avoiding any physical deficiency in a child to be born.

Conclusions. Compared with the 1950s, marriage no longer serves as an initiation ritual toward sexuality. Neither does it serve as granting permission for procreation (the problem of premarital conceptions, popular research topic of the 1960s, has become obsolete). Yet, marriage is still popular and marriage rates are rising again in many European countries. Since they reflect two quite different phenomena, first *le calendrier*, or timing, and second prevalence, one hardly can offer adequate interpretation. Yet, it might be safe to state that marriage and cohabitation do not represent two totally different lifestyles; one tends to evolve into the other, involving the same persons, on the microlevel; on the macrolevel they tend to influence each other. If cohabitation has been characterized as marriagelike, conversely, marriage has become, to some extent, cohabitationlike, as is expressed in the latter phase of the family life cycle.

Family Dissolution

A mirror image of the dramatic changes in family formation is to be observed in the process of family dissolution. In contrast to the 1950s, increasingly marriages tend to be dissolved not by death but by divorce. The middle of the 1970s can be identified as a divide; in most Western European countries, at that time, divorce figures rose dramatically, the increase tending to level off in the late 1980s.[7] From the late 1960s until early 1970s, the institutionalization aspect of divorce changed from a fault to a no-fault divorce procedure, the main basis becoming the irreconcilable disruption of the marital bound (Commaille, 1983).

Divorce. The earlier studies focused on causes for divorce. The problem was identifying what lead to divorce. The underlying implicit factor was how to avoid divorces. The focus of attention gradually changed to effects of divorce, more particularly economic effects on women and psychological effects on children, the implicit issue being how to cope with divorce. Lately, the attention has been directed, not so much to divorce as family disorganization but to divorce as family reorganization. New terms were coined such as *fusion families*, *merged families*, *reconstituted families*, and, more and more, the expression *"new" stepfamilies* is gaining recognition.

---

[7]See Council of Europe (1990). Total divorce rate: Greece: .05 (low figure), Denmark: .25 (high figure). 1988: Greece: .13 (1987), Denmark: .47.

The divorce process results in differentiated and usually sequential family or household formations. Generally divorce is preceded by separation and results in either one-person households, actually involving one-parent families, or cohabitation situations. All of these forms may constitute either an interim or a permanent situation. They can evolve from one into the other, sequentially but in either direction. This process not only can be differentiated according to the order of phases or itineraries, but also as to duration of each of the phases and the reorganization process as a whole. This results in pluriformity of family forms but, most important, it reveals that the plurality of family forms cannot be understood in static terms as a patchwork, but only can be understood in dynamic terms, with the sequence of forms not occurring according to a fixed pattern but representing a dynamic process of its own.

The high divorce levels partially result in and, conversely, are a result of the changing *nature* of divorce. The no-fault divorce has led to notions such as *friendly divorce*, referring to civilized forms in which partners or divorcees-to-be, divorcees or ex- or former partners, are relating, or are expected to relate, to each other. A new term had to be coined, indicating new professional ways of dealing with family dissolution: the so-called *family*—or *divorce—mediation*. This term refers to a process in which not a judge, a public instance, but a private person, a professional, helps the divorcing individuals either to settle their differences—leading to reconciliation—or, more frequently, to agree to the terms of their separation and settle the allocation of goods and provisions for future exchange of material and nonmaterial goods and services.[8] Currently, the technique of divorce mediation is spreading rapidly all over Western Europe and is complementing and supplementing the existing services for marriage and family counseling which did emerge in the late 1950s and 1960s.

The notion of friendly divorce actually points to the need for making a clear distinction between the individual, and the societal level of analysis. On the individual level, although the belief-system is to the effect that one should make it possible to have a civilized procedure in divorce, this does not necessarily imply that one expects it to happen and it certainly does not imply that one would expect it to happen in all cases. More important, it certainly does not imply that divorce should not create problems (e.g., tensions, stress, pain) for persons. It simply means that divorce is being deproblematized on the societal level. It has become an accepted phenomenon and even can be identified as a turnover of partners. Paradoxically, the societal deproblematization of divorce has been instrumental in having the

---

[8]Council of Europe (1992), more particularly, Hogett, B., Law Commissioner (England and Wales) on: "Legal provisions to prevent and reduce dispute in divorce cases"; Danielsen, S., High Court Judge (Denmark) on "Alternative methods of dispute resolution in family matters."

public authorities set up the instrumentarium dealing with persons in distress or facing problems in their relationship, for example, centers for marital and family counseling. Most crucial is that personal problems have become a societally relevant issue. This applies to adults, for instance as to their capacity to function adequately in their professional life. It applies to children about whom we have conflicting research evidence on the impact of divorce. Yet, it certainly has become a societal problem since family traditionally was the institution guaranteeing the socialization of children.

Reconstituted Families.   Also in this respect reconstituted families often have been regarded as a solution. Reconstituted families represent a growing phenomenon on which we have reliable research data but on which we lack accurate statistical data. Even the latest censuses in Europe, dating from 1990 to 1991, hardly supply the necessary information. The architecture of the questionnaires was designed long before this type of family formation was common. Moreover, the information requested to secure adequate data, might be regarded as being too personal and even constituting an intrusion into the private sphere and a violation of privacy. Reconstituted families do represent a rather complex structure indeed.

One can even take issue with the label *new stepfamilies* because, unlike in traditional steprelationships, the parents (mother or father) are not dead but alive. From the point of view of the child, there is not only the new partner (of the father or mother) in its reconstituted family, there also can be a new partner for the other parent. While one can take issue with the labels *stepmother* or *stepfather*, it at least represents a position one can refer to. However, for the new spouse or partner of the biological parent, one does not even have accepted terms of reference yet. This can be the expression of anomie or it could be the indication of a far-reaching privatization of family life.

From the point of view of children, the reconstituted family can involve dramatic changes, not only in the parental relationship but also in the sibling relationship. Two elements are here at stake. A first is the rank order of children. The oldest child, for instance, can lose that position and become second in rank. Similarly, a youngest child can even become the oldest (in case of splitting). The same applies to only children and so on. More fundamental is the differentiation among the siblings—half-brothers and half-sisters—who, in case of new procreation in the family, even might belong to different generations. In order to understand what reconstituted families do represent, it is very important to take the perspective of the child. Taking that perspective provides quite a different picture than the one resulting from the perspective of the parents.

From the perspective of the adults (spouses or cohabitees) the reconstituted family also presents a complex situation in respect to children and partner relationship. As to children, there can be *mine*, *hers* or *his*, and *ours*.

For the former, one has to take into consideration the relation with the ex-spouse, with whom one increasingly is expected to make joint decisions. The process of maintaining or breaking away from the former in-law networks and joining the new in-law networks, hardly has been studied. However, the question of relationship with grandparents has become an issue for which legislative measures had to be taken, for instance re visiting rights for grandparents.

Reconstituted families imply that we are confronted with new stepfatherhood and new stepmotherhood, in which the identity (position) and contents (role) do not imply substituting for the actual father or mother, but does imply the creation of a totally new and somewhat ambivalent role, involving caretaking and support-giving functions. Stepmothering and stepfathering are not only replacing failing support from an ex-spouse but also involve giving additional support from an ambivalent position towards the new partner's children, as contrasted to having a stated, explicit position with respect to the partner. For the latter indeed it is replacement of support.

Bereavement and Widowhood. Next to divorce, the last phases in the family life cycle are marked by bereavement. It is a paradox that increasing longevity dramatically has changed the latter phases in the life cycle after death of the spouse. The emphasis on the status and problems of old age has been supplemented by and, to some extent, even altered into focusing on the process of aging. Retirement from work, or pensioning, no longer can be simply equated with entering the phase of old age. The retirees tend to constitute an active, also sexually active, population, strongly involved in maintaining and acquiring new relationships. As to age structure, the no longer active population can no longer be equated with the aged. The aged population no longer constitute one group but, due to increasing life expectancy, differentiated layers (subgroups), according to age, are to be clearly distinguished and are getting differentiated connotations such as *very old* (80 years old and older). In demographic terms the centenarians constitute the group marked by the sharpest increase, in relative numbers.[9]

In family terms, the younger old aged (persons in their 50s and 60s, even some in their 70s) tend to represent able-bodied and economically prosperous grandparents. They, however, cannot be reduced to the sole role and position of grandparents. They are involved in their own partner-relationship, many also after bereavement. Actually this group has been greatly contributing to the development of unmarried cohabitation and living apart together (LAT)-relationships. In some countries and in some period of the development, they tended to be overrepresented in the former forms, as

---

[9]Council of Europe (1992). Life expectancy. 1970. Sweden, M: 72.12, F: 77.66 (high figure), Turkey, M: 53.4, F: 56.5 (low figure). 1988. Sweden: M: 74.15, F: 79.86, Turkey (1989), M: 63.4, F: 68.6.

was documented for Belgium. Unlike forms of juvenile cohabitation, unmarried cohabitation in latter phases of life does not represent ideological stands against marriage, on the contrary, it represents an opposite symbolic meaning. From an institutional point of view unmarried cohabitation and LAT-relations can represent typical forms of personal relationships, that is, not involving existing kinship and parental relationships with the new union. Thus the adult children are not faced with new stepparents but with a mere companion for their mother or father. This holds true for the effects of marriage such as the transfer of property, inheritance rights, and so on. This offers one more example of the growing dissociation of the partner relationship and the parental relationship. The LAT relationship moreover is based on, as well as guarantees, economic independence. It enables individuals to enjoy simultaneously maintaining of a close-knit network with one's offspring and family and to establish a private relationship and companionship with a partner. The compartmentalization of the result of the former marriage and cohabitation and the new relationship formation endanger neither the former nor the latter situation.

The problems married couples face by bereavement, of course apply to unmarried couples as well. The latter however find themselves in a more precarious situation, more particularly in Western Europe, in which marriage in itself is a contract regulating to a large extent inheritance and usufruct. In contrast to marriage, in unmarried cohabitation death of the partner immediately brings one into an unprotected situation regarding those material provisions and also nonmaterial provisions such as the automatic continuing of the lease of the home one lives in and so on.[10]

Conclusions. The plurality of family forms on one hand and the differentiated European legal systems (more particularly family law) actually have contributed to growing complexity in the lineage structure, as was amply documented (Meulders-Klein, 1989).

The analysis of the last phases in the family life cycle confirm the conclusion reached from the analysis of the first phases, that is, the growing disparity and even dissociation between the partner–spousal relationship and the parent–child relationship. As to the latter, it should be added that it is imperative to put the child in the focus of attention and analyze the situation from his or her perspective, because this yields additional information and, more important, insight.

The developments as described relating to the first phase, family formation, have bearing on the developments occurring in the latter phase, family

---

[10]These problems are recognized to the effect that the Council of Europe made a Recommendation (No. R[88]3) on the validity of contract between persons living together as an unmarried couple and their testamentary dispositions (Adopted by the Committee of Ministers on March 7, 1988).

dissolution (e.g., cohabitation, LAT-relations, etc.). The family indeed has become a complex system, a network of complicated and virtually ambivalent relationships. In developmental terms, there is a dissociation between the sequence of personal events, the life cycle and the family life cycle.

What we are observing does not only reflect changes but also a profound mutation of the family life cycle. The nature of the family life cycle has evolved from a linear development over time, with one phase sequentially developing into another, to a complex matrix, a system in which the order of the phases is to be reconstructed (in French, *bricolé*) by the partners—who might experience turnover themselves. Not only has the family become a complex structure (static), but the family life cycle (dynamic) too has become very complex indeed.

CHANGES IN FAMILY ORGANIZATION: INSIDE THE FAMILY

As the family life cycle has changed dramatically, so has family organization. Family organization refers to the way in which a family operates, the processes occurring *inside the family*.

Allocation of Power and Division of Labor

The issues at stake relate to the way in which family members deal with each other. Authority (power structure) decision making, task allocation (division of labor) are here at stake.

Power. As a general characteristic, one can qualify change in power relations in the family, having occurred since the 1950s, as a transition from a system of command to a system of negotiation. Authority is not taken for granted, but decisions taken have to be explained. More important even, is the decision making process in itself. Decisions have to be reached through negotiation. This applies not only to the spousal relationship but also to the parental relationship. Children tend to be gradually involved in the decision making process. Children are gradually accepted to participate in power sharing. The erosion process of the prescribed roles and power structure has resulted in a family organization being qualified as *la famille incertaine*, or the uncertain family (Roussel, 1989).

Labor. The negotiation process not only relates to power structure but also to division of labor. Task allocation which, in the 1950s, tended to be gender-specific and even could be qualified as *gender-apartheid* (instrumental vs. expressive roles), now has turned into the idea of interchangeability of tasks and roles. Three issues are here at stake that have received successive attention: (a) the defamilization of women (the disappearance of the house-

wife-homemaker); (b) the emergence of the new father; and (c) the emancipation of the child. The introduction of women, more particularly wives or
mothers, into the labor market brought an inner familial issue to a societal
level and turned it into a political issue. Currently, all over Europe, the
reconciliation of family and work is getting key priority on the political
agenda (Commission of the European Communities, 1992). Lately, it has been
recognized that balancing work and family schedules provides an insufficient
solution, since provisions should be made to secure for women (and men)
the opportunity to participate fully in the sociopolitical and cultural and
family life. Citizenship in its full meaning is being recognized. The full participation of wives or mothers in all aspects of public life secures economic
independence and increases their bargaining power inside the family. This
has become so much an integral part of our societal life that it is essential
for the economic well-being of family and household to the effect that, in
many European countries, one-earner families are regarded as being threatened by social insecurity. The one-earner family, once a model, has become
a virtually deprived family.

As for task allocation of domestic work, the picture is far more nuanced.
The allocation of household tasks remains extremely gender biased in terms
of number of tasks to be performed as in terms of time to be invested, as
well as in overall responsibility of household management. Yet, ever since
the late 1980s a new cry is heard under the style of the new fathers (Danish
Ministry of Social Affairs, 1993). *New fathers* are men who are allowed by
society to reveal human traits such as emotions, tenderness, and to perform
formerly typical "female" tasks such as nurturance and caregiving. The term
new fathers refers to the relationship between male parents and children,
and, indeed, young fathers tend to play roles for which their fathers hardly
can serve as role models. Although the expression *new fathers* does not
refer to the spousal or partner relationship—the term *new husbands* has not
yet been coined—yet in modern sociological literature there is a renewed
and heavy emphasis on romance and romantic relationships.

Conclusions. In the early 1970s some still proclaimed "the death of the
family" (Cooper, 1971). Yet, at present, the family tends to be very much alive.
The family organization however has dramatically changed from a hierarchical into a more democratic organization. Although one cannot characterize
the family as symmetrical in task allocation, yet men have gained access to
expressive and women to instrumental roles.

Social Support for Family Tasks

Next to the allocation of power and the division of labor inside the family,
the issue of social support for household work and domestic tasks, as well
as for the care of dependent family members is at the focus of attention.

Domestic Tasks. According to some, contemporary times can be characterized as the postmodern society. Postmodern society actually refers to dissociation, deconstruction, or what sociologists have identified as processes of differentiation which, to some extent, imply ambiguity. These characteristics actually do apply to household work and domestic tasks. On one hand there is some claim to recognize informal work, domestic work in particular, as an economic activity, that should be taken out of the informal sphere and be integrated in the formal economy, or, at least, that this informal added value should be recognized as constituting a part of the gross national product (GNP; Goldschmith-Clermont, 1982). This stand can be identified as controversial and, currently, as a matter of fact, in none of the European countries, until now, have governments granted any recognition to that type of work. Yet, also in this domain, a dissociation process has taken place, to the effect that caring is being dissociated from household tasks, is gradually being recognized as valuable and thus being assigned material and non-material rewards. More particularly the care for dependent family members, children, aged, or impaired (ill or disabled) are in the focus of attention.

A New Phase Added in the Life Cycle. The increasing life expectancy has led to the recognition of, not only added years to life but to added phases to the life cycle, implying new types of relationships between the generations. Moreover it urges the organization of care for the elderly as a social group, as a social category. As a consequence, a new political issue is emerging: the allocation of funds, the investments in a zero-gain situation, either to the older or the younger generation.[11] On the microlevel this implies re-evaluation of family functions. On the mesolevel this implies the involvement of nongovernmental but community organizations under the style of moving from welfare state to a caregiving society. The Vienna Center coined this development as *mixed welfare* (Evers & Wintersberger, 1988), which is programmed under differentiated styles in different countries, that is, *social renewal* in the Netherlands. On the macrolevel it implies the re-discovery of the family as the caregiving institution.

Two striking features are to be mentioned. First is the gender bias. The caregivers predominantly are women as daughters or daughters-in-law. Men in their position of fathers and husbands tend to be (all other elements kept constant) overrepresented as care-receivers. The group of at-home caregivers is fast growing in sheer numbers, but their needs hardly are recognized, thus, in some countries, they are organizing themselves into almost militant groups.

A second morphological characteristic relates to age. Although there are caregivers of any age, children not excluded, a new feature is the importance

---

[11]For the original formulation of this problem, see Preston (1984).

of the emerging group of caregivers age 50 and beyond. Persons in their 50s tend to remain not only physically fit but to have mature social skills. On the family level this implies that persons in their 50s and even in their 60s increasingly are faced with caregiving tasks for their elder relatives in their 80s and 90s, and, simultaneously can have caregiving obligations toward adolescent or even adult children and their offspring, grandchildren. They represent a sandwiched generation.

Conclusions. The term *generation* marks the new importance given to the intergenerational relations. We are witnessing the emergence of new four- or even five-generation interrelational networks and family is being conceptualized as *la famille: affaire de générations* [the family: a generational issue] (Godard, 1992). From a sociological point of view this serves as one more indicator of the process of dissociation of household and family. *Family* increasingly is to be conceptualized in terms of *person-supporting network*. The kinship tie, the intergenerational rights and obligations, consist of ties that bind.

Empowering Families

The added phases to the life cycle, as already being stated above, bring the process of aging into the focus of attention, recognizing a generalized risk for being in need of care. Care is gradually being recognized as a need differentiated from illness, thus care for the aged gradually becomes the mirror image of care for the young, who also need permanent attention without being ill or disabled.

Elderly. This led in some countries (e.g., Germany[12]) to the idea of establishing a system of generalized insurance for old age care. The debate is on whether this type of social security should be governmental sponsored or based on private investment. An analogous controversy is reflected on the microlevel: collective versus private (family) responsibility for care of the elderly. The controversy, family versus institutional care, is being eased by the emergence of a third strategy, which can be labeled as *self-reliance.* Next to the huge apparatus of care-giving institutions and next to the yet not fully documented system of informal (family) care, there is a third solution becoming operational. It consists of giving incentives for self-reliance, which not only include a vast supply of ambulant services, providing at-home help, and so forth, but consists of giving financial and other support to the care-receivers, rather than to the care-givers. This means giving financial

---

[12]For this and other policy measures, see Commission of the European Communities (1991, 1993).

support to the elderly in order that they can afford paid services, or of giving subvention or tax reduction to families employing professional persons for taking care of children, as is the case in France and other countries.

Children. This empowerment of families is a phenomenon reaching far wider than simple at-home care. It also relates to institutional care in which increasingly parents are given material and nonmaterial incentives to use their power, for example, in Denmark the representation of parents on the boards of child-care facilities. In most other European countries the increased power parents have in the educational system, ranging from representation in school management, to the idea of vouchers for schooling, which would give a mandate to parents to have the school they select financed.

Conclusions. Families indeed are recognized as person-supporting groups, to the effect that, if the emotional support fails, the spousal relationship can be dissolved. In contrast incentives are provided to have the parental relationship maintained and *child support* and *child maintenance* are indicative of this approach. Next to this change in the nuclear family, we are witnessing the emergence of a new type of extended family, dually located and united by support relationships. Because this type hardly can be identified as constituting a total unity, it offers one more example of the ambivalent situation characterizing modern family life. Another problem is the tension between the growing demand for care versus the bearing capacity of family. In this respect, the family can be considered to be only one of the elements constituting a mixed welfare system.

Societal Intervention in the Family

It is a paradox that the privatization process of the family—cohabitation, easy divorce, turnover of partners—is parallelled by growing societal intervention and involvement in the family when it becomes an oppressive or coercive system.

For example, integrity and the self-determination of spouses is at least minimally guaranteed since the gradual introduction in the 1980s, in Western European countries, of the notion of marital rape, parallelled by the notion of sexual harassment in the workplace and related situations.

Another example is that of violence in the family. Child abuse and neglect, wife abuse, and elder abuse, all relate to intrafamily violence that is no longer tolerated by society. In this respect it is noteworthy that new functions are being bestowed on the medical profession rather than relying solely on the profession of social work. The medical profession, for example, was very instrumental regarding child abuse by bringing it to the public forum and turning a private family problem into a problem of social concern, which called for appropriate social response (Smet, Van Veldhoven, & Evers, 1991). By now, in most European countries, systems of detection and surveillance are established and, more particularly, preventive actions are taken.

Conclusions

The growing support for families as person-supporting networks is parallelled by monitoring family functions and societal intervention in the family when it becomes coercive or oppressive. It is not the social status of the family which is at stake here, but rather the status one is delegated within the family, particularly in the case of more vulnerable women and children.

The problem of child abuse offers only one element of the growing recognition of the child as a person with their own rights and is illustrative of the growing recognition of children as a distinct social entity and of childhood as a unique social phenomenon (Qvortrup, 1992–1993).

GENERAL CONCLUSIONS

The changes in the family life cycle, namely, the dissolution and reconstruction of the family and life cycle on the one hand and the changes in the family organization, with emphasis on negotiation processes on the other hand, cannot be identified as mere personal issues. Paradoxically, the so-called individuation and individualization processes, have profound societal impact and call for specified family policies, geared at avoiding discrimination on the personal and on the societal levels, as well as providing for personal and interrelational development.

The plurality of family forms and structures cannot be understood in terms of juxtaposition but rather as a dynamic process in which a person evolves through her or his life cycle. All of these forms represent person-supporting networks, with double functions: The family provides internal support and comfort, expected by society at large and increasingly being sanctioned (positively or negatively); and also acts as a transfer mechanism between its members and society. In the latter respect, families increasingly can be seen as actors and reactors toward society, rather than as mere receptors of change. Thus the growing importance of family organizations can be identified as offering comfort to its members and bringing their claims to society at large (Donati, 1990).

This chapter focuses on internal developments within the family. Yet, it tries to demonstrate the societal relevance of these developments and hence this analysis should be parallelled by focusing on societal developments and their impact on families. Second, this chapter addresses the situation of the families in transition. In Western Europe we are experiencing not only tendencies towards unity and uniformity in behavior, but also a tendency towards pluriformity, or *multiculturalism*, even in nation states. Family issues are crucial in the process of integration of cultural minorities (European and non-European) in Europe and to promoting stability in the face of change. It should be noted, in this respect, that in our highly modern and even postmodern society, we still observe some family forms which seemingly appear as traditional, with unity between the family and work spheres, for example, in some agricultural families. Yet, there may still be complementarity between the past and present. The so-called old forms have adapted to contemporary times and, vice versa, with many new forms taking on features of the older types, such as the new emphasis on home-based business and home-based services (including the area of child care).

Third, there is also a dual social categorization in terms of sex and age: gender divisions, male versus female, with emphasis on equity, equal rights, and the emancipation movement as well as horizontal stratification accord-ing to age—for example, the *aging adult* or the *child*—all of these categories, claiming to be and obtaining the status of both object and subject of gov-ernmental policies, greatly influencing the shape and functioning of families.

Although this chapter was started by addressing internal family develop-ments, it also focuses on societal developments which influence family life. Family policy can be understood on two levels: specific policy addressing families directly, and, secondly, the impact other policies, such as economi-cal policies, have on families. The latter indirect policies might exert (often unintentionally) greater impact on the family than the former. Essentially this points to the value of studying families as a strategic instrument to monitor changes occurring in our society. Therefore, the International Year of the Family may prove to be not just another special year but also may be instrumental in understanding the profound transitions our so-called postmodern society is experiencing.

REFERENCES

Bien, W., Marbach, J., & Neyer, F. (1991). Using egocentered networks in survey research. A methodological preview on an application of social network analysis in the area of family research. *Social Networks, 13*(1), 75–95.

Bruynooghe, R. (1986). One-parent families in the context of variations in parenthood: Between deviance and commitment. In F. Deven & R. L. Cliquet (Eds.), *One-parent families in Europe* (pp. 29–45). The Hague: NIDI.

Commaille, J. E. A. (1983). *Le divorce en Europe Occidentale. La Loi et le Nombre* [Divorce in Western Europe. The law on the figures]. Paris: INED.

Commission of the European Communities. (1991). *Families and policies. Evolutions and trends in 1990.* Brussels: Author.

Commission of the European Communities. (1992). *Europe '93—Business and the family: What strategies do bring them together?* Brussels: Author.

Commission of the European Communities. (1993). *National family policies in EC-countries in 1991* (Vol. 1 & 2). Brussels: Author.

Cooper, D. (1971). *The death of the family.* London: Allen.

Council of Europe. (1990). *Recent demographic developments in the member states of the Council of Europe and in Yugoslavia.* Strasbourg: Author.

Danish Ministry of Social Affairs. (1993, June). *Fathers in the Families of Tomorrow. Conference Proceedings.* Copenhagen.

De Graaf, A. (1992). Women in the Netherlands start a family at an older age. *Maandstatistiek van de Bevolking, 40*(4), 16–18.

Donati, P. P. (1990). Social policy formulation and implementation: The case of the family. *The Annals of the International Institute of Sociology, 1,* 167–196.

Engstler, H., & Lüscher, K. (1991). Späte erste Mutterschaft. Ein neues biographischer Muster der Familiengründung? [Delayed motherhood. A new biographic mold of family formation]. *Zeitschrift für Bevölkerungswissenschaft, 17*(4), 433–460.

Evers, A., & Wintersberger, H. (Eds.). (1988). *Shifts in the welfare mix. Their impact on work, social services and welfare policies.* Vienna: Eurosocial.

Godard, F. (1992). *La famille affaire de générations* [The family: A generational issue]. Paris: PUF.

Goldschmith-Clermont, L. (1982). *Unpaid work in the household.* Geneva: ILO.

Humphrey, M., Humphrey, H., & Ainsworth-Smith, I. (1991). Screening couples for parenthood by donor insemination. *Social Science and Medicine, 32*(3), 273–278.

Levin, I. (1990). How to define family. *Familje Rapporter, 17,* 7–19.

Meulders-Klein, M. T. (1989). Vers la co-responsabilité paternale dans la famille Européenne [Toward joint parental responsibility in the Western European family]. In (Ed.), *Les Actes, Familles d'Europe sans Frontières* (pp. 125–144). Paris: INED.

Nave-Herz, R. (1992). Ledige Mutterschaft: eine alternative Lebensform [Single motherhood: An alternative lifestyle]? *Zeitschrift für Sozialisationsforschung und Erziehungssoziologie, 12*(3), 218–232.

Preston, S. H. (1984). Children and the elderly: Divergent paths for America's dependents. *Demography, 21*(4), 435–457.

Qvortrup, J. (1992–1993). *Childhood as a social phenomenon. An introduction to a series of national reports and 13 countries' reports.* Vienna: European Centre.

Rallu, J.-L., & Blum, A. (1991). *European population. I. Country analysis.* Paris: INED.

Rallu, J.-L., & Blum, A. (1993). *European population. II. Demographic dynamics.* Paris: INED.

Roussel, L. (1989). *La Famille incertaine* [The insecure family]. Paris: Jacob.

Roussel, L. (1992). La famille en Europe occidentale: divergences et convergences [The family in Western Europe: Divergencies and convergencies]. *Population, 47,* 133–152.

Smet, M., Van Veldhoven, I., & Evers, D. (Eds.). (1991). *Physical and sexual violence against women. Situation in Europe 1991 (First conference of European Ministers on physical and sexual violence against women).* Brussels: Cabinet of the Secretary of State for the Environment and Social Emancipation.

Trost, J. (1978). *Unmarried cohabitation.* Västeras: International Library.

United Nations. (1992). *International year of the family. Family: forms and functions* (Occasional Paper Series, No. 2). Vienna: Author.

FAMILY CHANGE, FATHERS, AND CHILDREN IN WESTERN EUROPE: A DEMOGRAPHIC AND PSYCHOSOCIAL PERSPECTIVE

Antonio Golini
Angela Silvestrini
IRP-National Institute for Population Research

FAMILY AND HOUSEHOLD

The concept of *family* has changed in the course of history, as has its value, the sentiment that bonds members of the family and its importance for the individual. At the beginning of the 1960s Ariès wrote:

> It was long held that the family constituted the ancient foundation of our society, and that beginning with the 18th century the progress of liberal individualism had loosened and weakened it. Its history in the course of the 19th and 20th centuries was taken to be the history of deterioration: the proliferation of divorces and the loss of the authority of the husband and father were taken to be indications of its decline. In considering modern demographic phenomena, however, I have been led to the exact opposite conclusion. It seems to me . . . that in our industrial societies the family plays a critical role, and that perhaps it has never influenced the human condition in so decisive a manner. (Ariès, 1986, p. 6)

The dynamic nature of the family was thoroughly demonstrated by historical studies, which show that it is not a constant and immutable cell, but it evolves together with the evolution of the entire social structure. Several family models have been dominant in different countries at different times, but the crisis of each model did not involve a crisis in the family per se, only a change brought about by the loss or gain of new characters, functions, and specializations.

It seems to us that today the family still constitutes a great value for the life of every individual, even though it has lost some of its stability. Perhaps, paradoxically, the strong idealization of interpersonal relations in the family is itself the cause of the phenomena that are helping to weaken the family group. In particular, love, which becomes all-important at the time of the establishment of the couple and in the life of the couple, is often too idealized. When it falls short of expectations it may lead to separation or the search for new relationships. *Sentiment*, the affective link, increasingly appears to be the central bond that keeps the various members of the family united. This agrees with a recent schematization (Roussel, 1980), in which four marriage models are identified in contemporary society. The two prevailing ones are deeply founded on affective factors.

The life of every individual appears ever more fragmented and marked by its passing through various family situations. At one time, not very long ago, one's entire life was passed in two different family groups: the one into which one was born and the one formed after marriage. Often the extended family and the rural environment engendered great family stability, so that it was not rare for one to live in the same house and in the same household for one's entire life, with one's parents first, then with wife or husband and children, and finally with one's children and grandchildren.

At present considerable family "mobility" is becoming more common. Let us take an example: An individual is born into a family composed of mother and father (nuclear family of origin). Following a divorce, he or she is entrusted to the mother alone (single-parent family) with whom he or she lives for a certain length of time until the mother remarries; the individual thus joins a new nucleus (stepfamily), in which he or she probably acquires stepbrothers and -sisters, children of the mother and of her new husband or children of the new husband from a previous marriage; he or she may at the time of becoming independent leave the family and live alone (one-person household), then marry and have children (own family), divorce and remarry (own stepfamily) and end life as a widower or widow not living with his or her children (one-person household). The person in the example will have lived in 7 kinds of families or households, an example that in any case does not constitute the most egregious instance of family mobility.

This variety and number of possible kinds of family in which one person may find himself or herself living is certainly profoundly modifying family relationships and hence the place of the person in an affective network that may change substantially in time and space. There is a danger that this new reality in the life of the person may fuel an excessive individualism, which in any event may become a necessary form of defense with respect to the instability of one's "journey through family life" and of the great mutability of one's "system of family relationships." Conversely, It may be that both the process of modernization of Western societies (especially as regards the general rise in the level of education and women's work in nonagricultural sectors) and the loss of the family's function as an economic support system and as an economic enterprise (especially important in a rural economy) has led to greater individualism and hence to more frequent conjugal instability.

FAMILY CHANGES IN THE PAST 30 YEARS

For more than a century we have witnessed in Europe not just a decline in mortality and fertility rates—a well-known and well-studied phenomenon that goes by the name of *demographic transition*—but a transition as well from a three-generation household to a one- or two-generation household or family.

These great changes had their beginnings in the past, but as with many other aspects of contemporary society, from the demographic point of view it seems that they have picked up speed, so that great and rapid change of the family has been clearly evident the last 30 to 40 years.

The changes have been so swift and of such scope that neither legislation nor the statistics have managed to keep pace with them. In fact, it is precisely in the area of marriage and the family that there are legal categories that largely determine the statistical and demographic categories for the collection, classification and interpretation of data. But in recent years we have witnessed the most varied forms of *union between two partners*, and hence of families, along side the official and legal ones—unions that are free, private, secret, trial, irregular, illegitimate, semilegal, not definite, and "part-time" (Fresel-Losey, 1992). The system for gathering data is thus to some extent inadequate for studying marriage and the family, which are increasingly characterized by a considerable increase in matrimonial mobility and the emergence and spread of new forms of conjugal life. In many countries consequently (France and Italy, for example), new forms of inquiry on the family are being readied, sampling surveys that begins with one particular person make it possible to identify all the persons who with him or her constitute a family or a household; that make it possible, that is, to identify "the tree of linkages." At the moment, however, we must necessarily refer to the current statistics and to the legal categories from which originate the majority of statistical data.

At the beginning of the past 30-year period, we were looking at a society that presented a well-established model of the nuclear family (family nucleus) and a reduced number of children. But the basic rules that governed society, in the social sense, and often also in the legal one, were very different from the current ones. Many events and attitudes regarding the formation of the family and family life, which 30 years ago were impossible because prohibited by law, or untenable because of strong social disapproval, or looked upon as a negative example because they were not acceptable under governing moral and social rules, are now not only legitimate, but widely accepted and increasingly common. This is true even in those societies traditionally most conservative and predominantly linked to Catholic morality, such as those in southern Europe.

The principal demographic indicators and the legislative framework show this. In the whole of western Europe the main changes began at the beginning of the 1970s, first in the countries of the north, and then spreading and becoming progressively established in the other countries as well. In Italy, for example, the greatest legislative changes took place at the end of the 1960s and in the course of the 1970s (new family law, institution of divorce, liberalization of birth control advertising, legalization of abortion), a period when we also began to see the greatest changes in demographic indicators relative to the formation, growth, survival and dissolution of the family.

The data in Table 12.1 clearly show how great a transformation there has been in all phases of the life of the family and to what extent the situation is diversified in the main European countries, a situation that presents itself as relatively homogeneous in the groups constituting the countries of the North, the Center and the South of Europe. Ireland remains a completely separate case, and for that reason, we are omitting any reference to it.

Going from the North to the South of Europe, almost all the indicators concerning the level of growth through fertility and of dissolution of the family decline. In the Scandinavian countries divorces and marriages subsequent to the first one are higher, as are births, outside of marriage. Consensual unions are much more common in the North than in the South, and they are on the rise in the countries of central Europe (young people 25 to 29 years of age who were living in cohabitation around the middle of the 1980s amounted, for example, to 31% in Sweden, 11% in France, and near 0% in Italy). Thus in many cases marriage no longer constitutes the sole way to establish families. Similarly, the death of one of the spouses no longer represents the sole cause of dissolution of marriages: Divorce is more common, and even here the primacy goes to the North, and it progressively decreases toward the South. A great difference is not noted, however, when we look at the gross marriage rate (GMR); this index in fact counts all marriages, including those subsequent to the first one. Thus in the Scandinavian countries and in central Europe the GMR is declining less, because it is buoyed by the marriages of divorced persons (in the UK almost 1 marriage in every 4).

In essence the structure of family attitudes brings to light the following:

- Southern Europe is characterized by the "traditional" family, accompanied, however, by a low marriage rate and a very low fertility rate. The fact is that young people want to unite in a family through marriage

TABLE 12.1
Change in Some Demographic Indicators Related to the Family in Western Europe Around 1960 and 1990

Countries	Gross Marriage Rate*		Total Fertility Rate		Extramarital Births**		Marriages of Divorced				Divorce Rate	
							1960		1990			
	1960	1990	1960	1990	1960	1990	M	F	M	F	1960	1990
Denmark	7.8	6.1	2.54	1.67	78	464	12.2	11.2	22.0	22.2	18.5	44.0
Finland	7.4	4.8	2.71	1.78	40	252	6.8	5.4	14.5	15.0	13.7	41.0
Norway	7.4	5.2	2.94	1.93	38	409	5.7[b]	4.9[b]	16.2	14.8	8.5	42.9
Sweden	7.1	4.7	2.13	2.14	113	482	8.3[b]	7.7[b]	20.3	19.8	16.0	44.1
Belgium	7.1	6.5	2.54	1.62	21	113	4.8	4.9	26.2	26.5	6.5	31.0
France	7.0	5.1	2.73	1.78	61	300	6.5	6.0	15.2	14.4	9.6	31.5
Germany	9.5	6.5	2.37	1.45	76	153	7.7	6.2	16.5	17.0	12.0	29.2
Switzerland	7.8	6.9	2.44	1.59	40	6.5	5.2	1.3	15.9	14.0	12.4	33.0
United Kingdom	7.5	6.5	2.71	1.84	52	279	5.0	4.8	23.5	22.8	6.7	1.7
Greece	7.0	5.9	2.28	1.42	12	24	2.7	2.0	8.9	7.2	3.7	12.0
Italy	7.7	5.4	2.41	1.26	24	63	--	--	4.0	2.9	5.0[a]	8.0
Portugal	7.8	7.3	3.10	1.51	95	147	0.7	0.5	5.9	4.1	1.4[a]	11.6
Spain	7.8	5.6	2.86	1.31	23	96	--	--	3.5	2.4	--	--

Note. *per 1,000 pop. ** per 1,000 births. [a]1970, [b]1967, [c]England and Wales. Sources: Council of Europe [CE] (1993), Eurostat (1993), Monnier and Guilbert-Lantoin (1993), Nordic Statistic Secretariat [NSS] (1994).

(with the possibility of divorce in the event things go wrong) and to have children in marriage. Because various factors and real difficulties—above all the very high rate of unemployment among the young—tend to delay marriage, it is precisely the rate of marriages and of fertility (because children are only to a very small extent conceived outside of marriage) that suffer the consequences. This is thus characterized by low marriage mobility.

- Northern Europe is more "avant-garde" and characterized by a medium to high rate of conjugal unions (the result of a low marriage rate counterbalanced by a high proportion of cohabitation) and by medium to high fertility (the result of births both within and outside of marriage). It is characterized by high marriage mobility (divorces and remarriages of divorced).
- Central–western Europe is in an intermediate position.

Taking into consideration some of the parameters of Table 12.1 and other parameters, Roussel (1992) reached a typology of European families that is a little different. Beginning with Group A ("Mediterranean model"), in which he placed the countries of the south (Greece, Italy, Portugal and Spain) with very low fertility, divorce rates, cohabitation, and births outside of marriage, he ends with Group D ("liberal model") of western Europe (France, Great Britain, Norway, Low Countries) with relative high values in these four parameters; the Group B ("temperate model") countries of eastern Europe (Austria, Belgium, Germany, Luxembourg, Switzerland) and the Group C ("Scandinavian model") countries of northern Europe (Sweden, Denmark) are located in an intermediate position.

THE FORMATION OF THE FAMILY NUCLEUS

Marriage is no longer the sole way to establish a family, at least in many European countries. The period indices relative to marriage show a very strong decline. This does not necessarily imply that a lower number of unions of a conjugal kind are being established, but only the fact that the union is being legalized less often.

If we take the 1960s as the starting point of our analysis, we note that in those years, in Europe, there were record numbers of marriages. Nearly 90% of people of marriageable age married. The economic boom after the war caused an increase in marriages and births, aided by the parallel decrease in the average age at marriage and at the birth of a child.

The decline in marriage began in Sweden in the second half of the 1960s and spread gradually from north to south in the course of the 1970s. The

TABLE 12.2
Period Total Female First Marriage Rates,[1] Selected European Countries, 1965-1991

Years	Denmark	Sweden	France	Germany	Italy	Spain
1965	984	957	993	1102	1024	982
1970	799	624	919	974	1007	1003
1975	661	628	858	764	931	1024
1980	532	525	706	656	765	735
1985	572	525	540	598	709	630
1990	596	557	563	593	670	650
1991	587	503	548	518	na	na

Note. Source: Monnier and Guibert-Lantoin (1993).
na = not applicable.
[1]These rates represent the number of first marriages of a hypothetical cohort of 1,000 women, assuming the constancy of the period of first marriage rates.

progressive decrease in marriages ended in northern Europe at the beginning of the eighties, and it was followed by a slow recovery which is still under way. Overall, in the past 6 to 8 years the trend has stabilized in all countries. If this very reduced propensity for marrying continues for some time, then from 40% to 50% of nubile women in western Europe would end up by not marrying (see Table 12.2).

This reduced number of marriages is complemented, as is noted, by a large number of cohabitations. It is in the northern countries that cohabitations are most numerous: In Denmark they constitute 22% of all unions. Many unions are legitimized only after a certain number of years, or only after the birth of a child. They are very frequent, especially among the young. In Sweden they constitute 75% of all unions of young people of between 20 and 24 years of age and 46% of those between 25 and 29 years of age, and they diminish progressively to only 10% of those between 45 and 49 years of age (Näsman, 1991).

In Great Britain, in the 1980s, a large proportion of consensual unions consisted of persons who had already experienced one marriage, and often one of the two persons involved was temporarily unable to remarry (separated while awaiting divorce). Thus, also in Italy (1988), in 72% of the consensual unions one or both partners were already married; overall, however, the phenomenon of cohabitation was of slight proportions because the percentage of consensual unions did not exceed 1% to 1.5% of all unions.

In Great Britain at the end of the 1960s, 3% of the women who married had previously lived with their husbands for a certain length of time; in only 10 years the percentage reached 20%, and today half of all couples live together before marriage. Overall, even today the great majority of persons unite in marriage, to the extent that in several countries of the north the proportion of women of between 30 and 39 years of age who have never been married has actually declined.

   Cohabitation before marriage, together with the increase in the level of education and the rise in the number of people who join the work world, is one of the factors that contributed to the increase in the average age at the first marriage. This increased from 22.9 years (1960) to 27.9 years (1991) for women in Denmark; there was an analogous increase in Sweden (27.7 years in 1989). In central European countries the increase was on the average of 2.5 years for France and Germany and was very small in Great Britain (23.3 to 23.9 years of age). For the countries of Mediterranean Europe the entire period from 1960 to 1990 must be considered; we may thus note that the average age declined in the period from 1960 to 1980, but then increased rapidly in the last decade, to the point of canceling, and in many cases widely exceeding, the decline of the preceding 20 years (Fig. 12.1). In any case the mean age is much lower than is it the nordic countries as a consequence of lower rates of cohabitation before marriage.

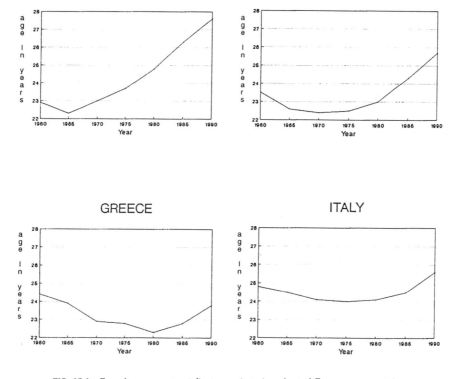

FIG. 12.1. Female mean age at first marriage in selected European countries (1960–1990). Source of basic data from Eurostat (1993).

THE DISSOLUTION OF THE FAMILY

The great increase in longevity (the average life span has reached about 73.5 years for men and over 80 for women in almost all the countries of western Europe) has increased the longevity of a couple markedly. Under current mortality conditions, 90% of all couples would be able to celebrate their 25th wedding anniversary; hence death has in many countries taken an absolutely secondary place to divorce in the dissolution of marriages.

In all of Europe divorce is legal, except in Ireland and Malta, and an increasing number of couples are resorting to legalized divorce, to such an extent that it is estimated that almost half of the marriages of the Swedes, British, and Danes will end in divorce; in the other countries of central Europe we can expect that 30% to 40% of marriages will end in divorce (CE, 1993). Lower percentages are found in the Mediterranean countries, among them Italy and Spain, which introduced the institution of divorce in 1971 and 1980, respectively (see Table 12.3).

Important changes with respect to greater liberalization of divorce have involved almost all the European countries in the course of the last 30 years. Toward the end of the sixties, partial or total reforms were effected in Denmark, Great Britain, Norway, Finland and Holland, and in the course of the 1970s and 1980s in Sweden, Belgium, France, and Italy.

THE GROWTH OF THE FAMILY NUCLEUS: FERTILITY WITHIN AND OUTSIDE OF MARRIAGE

As a consequence of the marriage peak of the first half of the 1960s, there was a baby boom in virtually all European countries in the same period, followed almost everywhere by a net and continuous decline in births. Currently, fertility has a diversified aspect as regards level, kind (within and

TABLE 12.3
Divorce Rate in Some European Countries: 1965-1990 (per 100 Marriages)

Years	SW	FIN	DK	NOR	GB*	D	F	B	I	GR	P
1965	17.8	13.7	18.2	10.2	10.7	---	10.7	8.2	---	---	---
1970	23.4	17.1	25.1	13.4	16.2	12.2	12.0	9.6	5.0	5.0	1.4
1975	49.9	25.8	36.7	20.7	32.2	23.4	15.6	16.1	3.1	5.0	6.4
1980	42.2	27.3	39.3	25.1	39.3	22.7	22.2	20.8	3.2	10.0	---
1985	45.5	28.0	45.2	32.6	43.8	30.2	30.4	27.0	4.1	11.0	---
1990	44.1	41.0	44.0	42.9	41.7	29.2	31.5	31.0	8.0	12.0	11.6[a]

Note. * [a]England and Wales (1989)
Source: Monnier and Guibert-Lantoin (1993).

outside of marriage), and the way it combines with different and new family models (one-parent families, stepfamilies).

The decline in the years following the baby boom could be viewed as a transitional period of rebalancing. But the consolidation and propagation of the decline cannot be explained by this factor alone. Yet it is impossible to identify a single theory to explain the decline in fertility in Europe, as it is to create a single descriptive model beyond the general one of demographic transition. Theories on the decline in fertility are intrinsically linked to changes in the family institution (Bumpass, 1990).

In the period under consideration, three phases may be identified. The first includes the first 5 years of the 1960s, which is marked by an increase in fertility rates associated with an increase in marriages and to a more youthful average age at marriage and age at the birth of the first child. The second phase, which in general begins after 1965 (10 years later in Greece), lasted until the beginning of the 1980s and was characterized by a strong and generalized decline in fertility. The last phase, from 1980–1985 to the present, is accompanied by a heightened differentiation between the countries of the center-north of Europe and those of the Mediterranean. In the former we witness a moderate recovery or a substantial stabilizing, while in the latter, which began their decline later, beginning in general from higher TFR, the decline is continuing and is reaching low levels never before touched in Europe. The primacy in low birth rates is held by Italy (1992) with a little more than 1 child per woman, but fertility is also very low in Portugal, Spain, and Greece.

It may be noted that the decrease in the period fertility index declines at a rate that in a certain measure keeps pace with the rise in the average age of parents at the birth of the first child (see Fig. 12.2). The shift in the timing of births is thus a cause both of a heightened period variation and, in all probability, of a diminution in the number of children per woman calculated by generation. We may in fact hypothesize that women may lack the time to make up the "delay" involved in giving birth to the firstborn.

With regard to the number of children born outside of marriage, this has increased to a considerable extent in the northern countries, where as early as the 1960s it had reached high levels. In the countries of southern Europe, however, fertility remains essentially an intramatrimonial matter. In Italy and in Greece, the percentage of children born of unmarried parents varies between 2% and 7%, while in Denmark and in Sweden it varies between 46% and 52% of children.

THE DIFFERENT KINDS OF HOUSEHOLDS AND FAMILIES

In the past 30 years the average number of members per household has been in strong decline in all the European countries and, except in Spain, the mean never exceeds 3 persons. The countries of southern Europe have

DENMARK

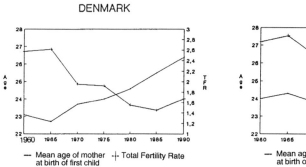

FRANCE

GREECE

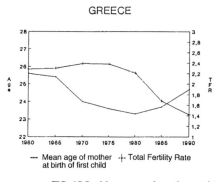

ITALY

FIG. 12.2. Mean age of mother at birth of first child and total fertility rate in selected European countries (1960–1990). Source of basic data from Eurostat (1993).

the highest averages, not only because low fertility and higher longevity came later for them than it did in central-northern Europe, but also because of the higher average age at which children leave the family.

The total number of households has increased more than that of families, because the percentage of nonfamily households, a preponderant part of which are constituted by a single person, have greatly increased. In the 1982 census in Denmark, nonfamily households already constituted 38.4% of the total, but the variability from country to country was still very marked; in a pilot study of 1990 they constituted 23% of the total in Italy.

The strong increase in one-person households is primarily a consequence of the aging of the population. In particular, more and more women, for the most part widows, live alone. During 30 years in Great Britain, the percentage of one-person households has doubled, and similar relative increases have been recorded in almost all the European countries. Around 1990 the maximum was reached in Sweden with 39.6%. In this Scandinavian country such a high percentage was due, however, also to the great number of young persons living alone (Table 12.4).

The extraordinary change we are seeing in households in Europe is of course also reflected in the distribution by number of members. In Sweden and in Germany, for example, in 1960 the modal value consisted of households of 4 and more persons, whereas more than 50% of the population lived in households having more than 3 persons; today this percentage reaches only to 30% to 35%, and the greatest frequency consists of households with a single person. In Italy too, at the beginning of the 1960s, the most common household consisted of a group of 4 or more persons, but structural changes in the country have been slower than in the other two countries cited, to the extent that in 1990 the proportion of households with 4 or more persons was still the most common despite the strong increase in those consisting of a single person (Table 12.5).

Although they began from different levels, demographic tendencies in Europe in recent decades have been rather similar, and it is only very recently that they have begun to diversify again. The impact on the structure of households and families has therefore been similar in all the countries. Considering the possible projections that may be made regarding marriage (first and successive marriages), fertility and divorce, it may reasonably be expected that in the near future there will be:

- a further decline in the average size of households;
- a strong increase in the small households, particularly with regard to one-person households, which may even reach proportions of 40% to 50% of the total;
- a more than proportional increase in households in which the reference person is of middle age or older;
- a less than proportional increase in traditional family households;
- an increase in the number of new and heterodox "conjugal unions."

THE RAREFACTION OF CHILDREN

In considering the demographic impact of the great decline in fertility, a subject that has been neglected is the rarefaction of children. We look at the psychological and social atmosphere that the aged will find themselves in, but we neglect that of those few children who may be living. We look at the need for an intergenerational balance between the aged and adults (above all for purposes of the social security system), but not at the need for intergenerational balance between the children and aged or intragenerational balance between children and children.

TABLE 12.4
Indicators of Families and Households in Europe Around 1960 and 1990

European Countries	Number of Household (X 1000) Around		Average Size of Household Around		One-Person Households (%)		One-Parent Families (%)	Nonfamily Household (%)
	1960	1990	1960	1990	1960	1990	1990	1990-1991
Denmark	1.544	2.325	2.9	1.8	19.8	34.4	5.8	38.1
Finland	--	2.605	--	2.4	--	31.7	4.1	38.0
Norway	1.077	1.936	3.3	2.2	14.2	--	5.6	--
Sweden	2.582	3.830	2.8	2.2	20.2	39.6	3.9	44.0
Belgium	1.393	3.806	3.0	2.6	16.8	28.4	9.2	31.4
France	14.589	21.850	3.1	2.6	19.6	27.1	7.2	29.2
Germany	19.460	32.256	2.9	2.3	20.6	33.6	6.3	37.7
Switzerland	1.581	2.541	3.3	2.6	14.2	--	5.1	35.8
United Kingdom	16.623	22.698	3.2	2.4	13.4	26.7	9.0	30.0
Greece	2.143	3.369	3.8	2.9	10.1	16.2	6.0	21.1
Italy	13.747	20.284	3.6	2.8	10.7	20.6	8.5	23.7
Portugal	2.357	3.267	3.7	2.9	10.8	13.8	6.8	16.6
Spain	8.854	11.261	3.8	3.4	7.5	13.4	8.2	16.9

Note. Source: Council of Europe (1993), Eurostat (1993).

TABLE 12.5
Size of Household in Some European Countries (%)

Number of persons	Sweden			Germany			Italy		
	1960	1990	Var	1961	1991	Var	1961	1991	Var
1 Person	20.1	39.6	19.5	20.6	33.6	13.0	10.7	20.6	9.9
2 Persons	27.0	31.1	4.1	26.5	30.8	4.3	19.6	24.7	5.1
3 Persons	22.5	12.3	-10.2	22.5	17.1	-5.4	22.4	22.2	- .2
4+ Persons	30.4	17.0	-13.4	30.3	18.5	-11.8	47.3	32.5	14.8

Note. Source: Istat (1995), Linke (1988), Statistiches Bundesamt [SB] (1993).

Looking at Fig. 12.3, it is possible to perceive how intense and rapid is the rarefaction of children in many European countries. In Italy today there are about 2.8 million children under the age of 5 and 1.3 million elderly people 80 years of age or older. One scenario envisages that 50 years from now, there will be 1.5 million children and 4.3 million aged persons, with a ratio of about 1 to 3 (for those older than 60 years the ratio will be on the order of 1 to 12) and in the Emilia Romagna region it could reach 44,000 children to 297,000 aged persons, with a ratio of about 1 to 7 (1 to 25 for those over 60). Each child would be surrounded by all his or her grandparents, various great-grandparents and a very large number of elderly and aged persons ready to smother the child with care and attention and to satisfy promptly each and every physical and psychological need. Hence, we must ask ourselves what kind of emotional and psychological atmosphere these children will grow up in and what psychological structure they might have. These considerations become all the more poignant when we consider the fact that in the overwhelming majority of cases we will be dealing with only children, and hence children to a great extent deprived of the company of brothers and sisters, as well as of that of aunts, uncles, and cousins.

It is not easy to establish whether only children, in such numbers and increasing at such a rapid rate, find themselves facing difficulties with individual growth and socialization, since there are of course advantages and disadvantages to their being only children, both for the child and for the parents. Studies in psychology and psychotherapy that are particularly concerned with only children, with children as regards the order of birth, and with the sibling relationship, beginning with those of Alfred Adler (1954), are not unanimous in their conclusions, partly because there exists, along with the realities, a great number of presuppositions and prejudices.

ITALY

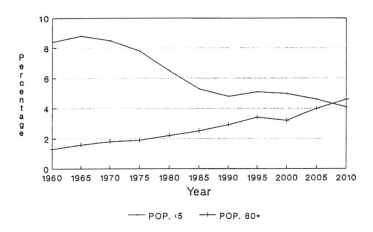

SWEDEN

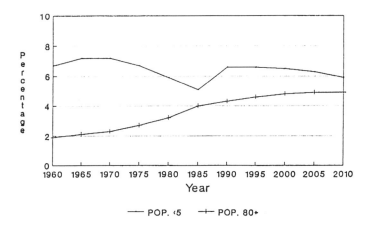

FIG. 12.3. Proportion of children 0–4 and people 80+ in Italy and Sweden (1960–2010). Source of basic data from United Nations (1993).

Only children certainly receive more attention from their parents, but this very fact can be positive or negative. If attention is given in a reasonable amount, it can lead to self-confidence, a sense of security, curiosity, and deep affection between child and parents; however, if the attention is excessive it can oppress the child and lead him or her to become too dependent or to reject the parents entirely. Fully one-third of only children, when interviewed about the advantages of being only children, state that the greatest advantage consists precisely in "greater attention from their parents." But when they are then asked to articulate what the disadvantages are, they again, in about the same percentages, indicate "greater attention from their parents" as disadvantageous; the parents are characterized as "too protective," "too strict," and as "expect[ing] too much"; and *too much* is the term repeated most often (Hawke & Knox, 1977, p. 34). The prevalent educative attitude of the modern mother is in fact overprotective, and her concerns regard every aspect of the child's life. In the modern Western family mothers have to a great extent focused their attention on their children, who are led to reciprocate, thus creating in many cases a strong and exclusive bond (Oliverio Ferraris, 1990).

At the same time, many believe that children are losing some of their rights, their freedoms and their living space, including physical space, which are increasingly occupied in an invasive way by adults and by the elderly. Not only—as was observed in the United States (Packard, 1985)—is the space at their disposal being reduced, but dependence on television, drugs, and violence in the schools increased. Furthermore, many children are prematurely involved in the marital problems of their parents and in separations and losses in the family, a fact which is thought to be at the root of anxieties, disturbances, and other problems. In fact, as Bowlby (1982) wrote, it was found that some psychiatric syndromes, such as psychopathy and depression, are often preceded by ruptures in emotional ties in childhood. Not just psychological disturbances and psychiatric syndromes, but physical problems as well are rooted in childhood emotional trauma in the family, as a very interesting French study demonstrates (Menahem, 1992). This may have a negative effect on a broad stratum of those belonging to the next generation when they themselves reach adulthood and when they become parents. There is also evidence that in many cases the life of the children of separated parents is conditioned either by a lack of educative resources or by the excessive burden of responsibilities that a custodial parent may impose on a child to substitute for the absent partner, leading the child to become what is known as the *parental child* (Winn, 1984, p. 146). A number of psychotherapists pointed out that this function involves a premature assumption of responsibilities which, paradoxically, may lead to difficulties in fulfilling, or even in undertaking, the parenting role when these children become adults because of a saturation effect.

An American study also reported that only children are diagnosed more often than others as psychologically disturbed (Belmont, 1977). The presence of so many adults and elderly people around them often translates into the prompt and complete satisfaction of all their needs and desires, which may lead to a lowering of the threshold of independence and tolerance for frustration. This may result in problems of socialization in adulthood with abuses or inhibitions engendered by a basic insecurity. In a Chinese study, aimed at evaluating the manifestations and processes of socialization of only children and of those with siblings, it was found that only children are more selfish, whereas children with siblings possess more positive qualities of perseverance, cooperation, and a sense of equality. Habits of cooperation, reciprocity, and confrontation—taken up at any early age and promoted essentially by play activity and by learning the dynamics of sibling interaction—lead to the acquisition and development of *habitus*, that is, group mentality and better communicative and interactive capabilities that are particularly important for greater productivity in teamwork, at school age, and in adulthood.

The fact is that when there are intense "horizontal" family relationships such as those among siblings or cousins, one is in a "playground" of life that is of great importance and that often leads to positive results. The sibling relationship, rarely considered in demographic-social studies, is indeed one of the principal relationships in the life of every individual. It is first of all the relationship of longest duration, even longer than the relationship between parents and children, which is generally considered as the only one that is determinant in the socialization and development of the child. In fact when there are intense horizontal relationships such as those between brothers and sisters, and also cousins, we witness positive results on children's adjustment differentials.

As adults, only children frequently may find themselves subject to anxieties and concerns due to the fact of their being alone in managing the increasing physical, psychological, cognitive, and health problems (and perhaps *financial* ones) of the parents as they gradually become elderly and very aged. Indeed, one of the reasons why it is thought that having brothers and sisters leads to a greater sense of emotional security derives from the fact that in a family with more than one child, no one feels completely alone, and there is less fear of facing and resolving family difficulties. We should also bear in mind that in the changing scenario of the modern family, brothers and sisters very often give one another that reciprocal help that they do not receive from their parents. In a study on children of divorce it was brought out that during conjugal crises, siblings constitute a very important system of reciprocal support; older siblings frequently assume a parenting role relative to their younger brothers and sisters (Winn, 1984).

FATHERS AND CHILDREN

"Where are the men in children's lives?" (Gianini Belotti, 1985). This question ended the book *Non di sola madre* ("Not of the Mother Alone"), which was published in Italy in 1985, fewer than 10 years ago. There was a perceived need at that time to emphasize the lack of the presence of men, but above all of fathers, in the lives of children. This, beyond being a problem for the psychological–physical development of the child, was a problem for the mothers, who, ever more present in the labor market, found themselves covering the dual role of worker and mother, without any support on the part of their partners. Ten years ago, especially in southern Europe, fathers who took care of children in the first years of their lives were the exceptions.

After World War II the maternal figure was indeed identified as the person principally responsible for the development and growth of the child. The concept of "lack of maternal care" maintained by John Bowlby (1951) found support in the overwhelming majority of experts in child development. The tie to the mother, and in particular to the biological mother, was overemphasized to such a degree as to identify in it the root of every pathology, as well as the hope for recovery, whereas at the same time the importance of the father figure in the first years of the lives of children was negated (Gianini Belotti, 1985).

From this also derives the fact that the educative attitude of the modern mother is overprotective and that her concerns involve every aspect of the life of the child. In the modern Western family mothers focused their attention on their children, who reciprocate it, creating in many cases a strong and exclusive bond (Oliverio Ferraris, 1990).

At present there exists a greater awareness of the joint responsibility of parents toward their children, but still too often—in terms of time, organization, and responsibility—the care of children, especially when they are very little, is left almost exclusively to mothers.

There still remain in Italy attitudes similar to those described by two studies, among others, which were done in 1971 and in 1978 (cited in Federici, 1984), from which we deduce that male participation in domestic activities and the care of children was occasional and in 50% of the cases nonexistent. Analysis of data obtained in a study on the use of time in Italy, conducted by Istat in 1988 (cited in Palomba & Sabbadini, 1992), demonstrates that lone mothers do not suffer as a result of the way they spend their time in the absence of a partner: "Indeed men's contribution to housework and childcare is so small that the absence of a husband means an overall reduction in housework rather than an increase. In fact, if she is married a woman must also take care of her husband" (Palomba & Sabbadini, 1992).

In other European countries the situation is not much different. In Norway, for example, the time actually spent by fathers with their children is scanty: only an hour per day on average. Comparing the time spent by mothers and fathers with children under 7 years of age, we see a difference of about 4 hours per day (Jensen, 1992).

For some time now, however, we have been witnessing some changes, a symptom of a reality that has only just begun to take its first steps: a greater and widespread awareness and consciousness of the father–child relationship. In Italy, for example, there exists an Association of Separated Fathers that sent a complaint to the Commission on the Rights of Man at Strasbourg to denounce the fact that in Italy in 93.7% of the cases the children of separated parents are entrusted to the mother (Balbo, 1993).

With increasing frequency films, articles, books and organized meetings are being produced on the father figure; even advertising now often associates little children with the father rather than with the mother.

It should be noted, however, that it is only in the last few decades that women in Europe have attained equal rights relative to their children. In Sweden, an avant-garde country in family changes and in the promotion of rights based on equality, women reached equality with regard to the custody of children only in 1950. In Italy, the reform of family law replaced *patria potestà* (the authority of the father) with *parental authority* in 1975. In France unmarried women enjoy greater rights than fathers: Legal supremacy belongs for the first time to women. The same thing is happening in Norway, although the legislative provisions make possible, on request of the father, the recognition of his rights relative to the children, which can be enforced in the event of dissolution of cohabitation (Jensen, 1992).

Thus after years of letting women raise their children alone, while maintaining over them the so-called *patria potestà*, today fathers are finding themselves the victims of a system they themselves created through the creation of a mystique of maternity that gives precedence, to the role of mother over that of father. In a world view in which the rights of women in general, and hence also with regard to children, are inferior to those of men, the European situation must be considered as unique.

The overwhelming majority of children who live with a single parent live with the mother, who is, for the most part, separated or divorced. In Germany over 2,000,000 children (under 18 years of age) live in families with a single parent and are hence separated from one of the two parents, most frequently the father. The number of fathers is, however, doubtlessly higher than that shown by the census, because the cases in which the children live with a couple of which only one is the biological parent are ever more frequent (see Table 12.6).

In France too, as in Germany, stepfamilies are an increasing phenomenon. The percentage of divorces and of marriages of divorced persons is in fact almost equal for the two countries. For France, the 1990 study on families of the National Statistical Institute (Desplanques, 1994) showed that about

TABLE 12.6
Germany (1991): Children and Teenagers Aged 0-17 Years Living in Different Types of
Households and Sibling Structures

Total number of children	15,339,000
Percentage of children living with:	
two parents	86.9
mother	11.4
father	1.7
Only children	31.4
Children with one brother or sister	46.2
Children with two brothers or sisters	15.8
Children with three brothers or sisters or more	6.6

Note. Source: SB (1993).

18% of children 0 to 18 years of age live with just one biological parent, and 5.5% live in stepfamilies. That is, about 750,000 children, or a total of more than 2,000,000 children live separated from one of the two natural parents. Breaking this down by age groups, we may note that 1 child in 10 aged 0 to 4 years does not live with the natural parents, whereas there is fully 1 child in 5 aged 15 to 18 living in this situation (Table 12.7).

In Italy we do not as yet have complete results regarding this issue from the 1991 census. However, looking at two provinces in the north of Italy for which results are already available (Bologna, 907,000 inhabitants; Trieste, 262,000), the data is similar to that found in Germany and France. The proportion of children under 18 years of age who live with both parents is 86% to 87%, and of children who live with the mother is 8% to 11% (Table 12.8).

In Germany 31.4% of the children do not have brothers or sisters, whereas the number of nuclei composed of 1 or 2 parents and 1 child constitutes 51.3% of families with children—more than half. Almost half of the children, on the other hand, can count a brother or a sister among their relatives, whereas those with more than 1 brother or sister are even less numerous. Of course we cannot say how many of these children will remain only children. The data from the two Italian provinces is more discrete and permits, among other things, more exact evaluations; in looking at children of between 14 and 18 years of age, relative to whom we might assume that the probability of a brother or sister arriving is very low, we find that in 37% (Trieste) to 40% (Bologna) of families we are dealing with have only children.

But if the number of brothers and sisters is decreasing, the number of stepbrothers or -sisters is, instead, increasing. In the 660,000 recomposed French families, in fact, one million children and boys and girls of under 25 years of age are living with children who are the sons and daughters of another union.

TABLE 12.7
France (1990): Children and Young People Aged 0-24* Living in Different Types of Households

	0-4	*0-18*	*0-24*
Total number of children (x 1000)	3,151	14,096	19,274
Percentage of children living with:			
Mother and father	91.	87.8	78.
married	76.	79.5	71.3
not married	15.	8.3	6.7
Lone mother	6.6	8.7	8.6
Single	3.7	2.1	1.7
Married	1.1	1.5	1.4
Widowed	.3	1.2	1.7
Divorced	1.5	3.9	3.8
Lone father	.3	1.1	1.3
Widowed	.0	.3	.4
Divorced	.1	.5	.5
Recomposed families (One is the new spouse of the mother or father)	2.3	5.5	5.6

Note. *The total % is not 100, because out of family are living the 2.1, 2.4, and 12.2 of children. Source: cited in Desplanques (1994).

It has been estimated that in Great Britain in the year 2000 only half of the children will have lived their whole life in a family of the conventional kind, constituted by both natural parents (Kirnan & Wicks, 1990).

In the countries of southern Europe the great number of children who were growing up 30 years ago without the continuous presence of the paternal figure was due to intense male emigration (which brought about the so-called phenomenon of the *white widows*) or to the death of the father. It dealt in any case with a high number of children, in part because of the larger number of children per woman. Today the number of children who live without their father is due to the increasing number of separations and divorces, but the situation is very different in the European panorama.

According to several polls done in Sweden, many of the children of divorced parents lose contact with the parent not living with them. Almost half the children see the parent not living with them once every 15 days. Twenty percent have no contact, and 7% see the parent from time to time. It has been noted furthermore that one third of the children who have acquired a stepfather or a stepmother lose all contact with the parent not living with them (Näsman, 1991). From a Danish study in 1980, it emerged

TABLE 12.8
Provinces of Bologna and Trieste (1991): Children and Teenagers Aged 0-17 Living in Different Types of Households and Sibling Structures

	Bologna				Trieste			
	0-5	6-13	14-17	10-17	0-5	6-13	14-17	10-17
Number of children (× 100)	33.5	49.4	37.3	120.2	9.5	13.1	10.0	32.7
Percentage of children living with:								
Mother and father	88.7	88.2	84.0	87.0	89.5	85.6	82.7	85.9
Lone mother	7.2	7.9	9.2	8.1	8.3	11.2	12.6	10.8
Lone father	2.7	2.5	3.1	2.7	1.5	2.0	2.8	2.1
Out of family	1.4	.4	3.7	2.1	0.7	1.1	1.9	1.2
Only children	53.3	38.6	39.6	43.0	49.0	35.6	37.3	40.0
Children with one brother or sister	38.2	48.5	46.3	44.9	40.9	51.7	50.1	48.0
Children with two brothers or sisters	8.5	12.9	14.1	12.1	10.1	12.7	12.6	12.0

Note. Source: Istat (1994a, 1994b).

that 56% of the fathers saw their children at least every 15 days, 22% less frequently, and 20% very rarely or not at all (cited in Sullerot, 1992). A survey conducted in Germany for 5 successive years yielded results similar to the foregoing: 60% of the children had more or less regular contact with the father not living with them, but the frequency decreased with the passage of time following a divorce. It also emerged that for 40% of the children the relations were completely interrupted (cited in Sullerot, 1992). Were these situations the result of cruel mothers or disinterested fathers? Beyond the faults of the parents the fact remains that many children today find themselves living far from one of their parents and do not always find a suitable figure able to substitute for the missing parent with authority and affection.

In conclusion, we should ask ourselves, as E. Sullerot did (1992, p. 351): "Will our children and our grandchildren, who are today adolescents and who will be parents at the dawn of the 21st century, want to follow their fathers without recriminations on the path of being uncommitted and agree to be second-class parents?"

In some countries an unmarried father has no rights over a child recognized by him, but must contribute financially all the same; a father divorced from his child's mother, even without fault, has few rights but must still contribute financially; in England and Belgium the right of the single father to recognize his child is subject to the authorization of the mother, so the mother has also become the arbiter of paternity. Between 1965 and 1985 Europe experienced—justly and necessarily—a significant period of sexual liberation, of liberation of women and of liberation of the individual, by changing customs and laws: It eliminated patriarchy juridically and with it the *paterfamilias*, creating in the conjugal couple a just symmetry and a desired balance. But then, particularly when the conjugal couple does not exist or no longer exists, paternal rights are expropriated from the father, so that now the problem that presents itself is that of assuring to the single father, the separated father, and the divorced father the right to paternity with responsibility and joy. This is a right that becomes a duty when it is desired—as it ought to be—to assure their children their right not to have a single exclusive parent but to have both mother and father.

The role of tomorrow's fathers will be defined, on the one hand, by the social environment (determined, among other things, by the results of analyses of the psychological balance and the processes of socialization of boys and girls; by a necessary awareness of the new situation; by new responsibilities of men relative to their own wife or partner and their own children; and by the thrusts and counterthrusts of the feminist movements) and, on the other hand, by the nature and the strength of the aspirations of the persons who as children lived separated from their parents. All this, together with other factors, will contribute to give direction and shape to political action and to change the legal framework. The next ten or twenty years may be for the European family just as important as those between 1965 and 1985.

REFERENCES

Adler, A. (1954). *Conoscenza dell'uomo* [Man's knowledge]. Milano: Mondadori. (Original work published 1927)

Ariès, P. (1986). *Padri e figli nell'Europa medievale e moderna* [Children and family life during the ancien régime]. Roma: Laterza. (Original work published 1960)

Balbo, L. (1993). *Almanacco della società italiana* [Almanac of Italian society]. Milano: Anabasi.

Belmont, L. (1977). Birth order, intellectual competence and psychiatric status. *Journal of Individual Psychology, 33*, 94–104.

Bowlby, J. (1951). *Maternal care and mental health.* Geneva: World Health Organization.

Bowlby, J. (1982). *Costruzione e rottura dei legami affettivi* [Construction and break of affective links]. Milano: Raffaello Cortina. (Original work published 1979)

Bumpass, L. L. (1990). What's happening to the family? Interactions between demographic and institutional change. *Demography, 27*, 483–498.

Council of Europe. (1993). *Recent demographic developments in Europe and North America 1992.* Strasbourg: Author.

Desplanques, G. (1994, January). Les familles «recomposées» en 1990 [Recomposed families in 1990]. *Population et Société, 286*, 1–4.

Dunn, J. (1984). *Sisters and brothers.* London: Fontana Paperbacks.

Eurostat. (1992). *Europe in figure* (3rd ed.). Luxembourg: Author.

Eurostat. (1993). *Demographic Statistics.* Luxembourg: Author.

Federici, N. (1984). *Procreazione, famiglia, lavoro della donna* [Procreation, family, women's employment]. Torino: Loescher.

Fresel-Lozey, M. (1992). Les nouvelles formes de conjugalité: problèmes méthodologiques [New forms of marriage: methodological problems]. *Population, 47*, 737–744.

Gianini Belotti, E. (1985). *Non di sola madre* [Not of the mother alone]. Milano: Rizzoli.

Hawke, S., & Knox, D. (1977). *One child by choice.* Englewood Cliffs, NJ: Prentice-Hall.

Istat. (1994a). *Popolazione e abitazioni, fascicolo provinciale. Bologna. 13° Censimento Generale della Popolazione e delle abitazioni* [Population and housing. Province of Bologna. 13th Census of population and housing]. Roma: Author.

Istat. (1994b). *Popolazione e abitazioni, fascicolo provinciale. Trieste. 13° Censimento Generale della Popolazione e delle abitazioni* [Population and housing. Province of Trieste. 13th Census of population and housing]. Roma: Author.

Istat. (1995). *Popolazione e abitazioni. Italia. 13° Censimento generale della popolazione e delle abitazioni* [Population and housing. Italy. 13th Census of population and housing]. Roma: Author.

Jensen, A. M. (1992, January). Changing gender roles as reflected in children's families. Paper presented at the *Seminar on Gender and family change in Industrialized countries*, organized by the International Union for the Scientific Study of Population, Rome.

Kirnan, K., & Wicks, M. (1990). *Family change and future policy.* London: Family Policy Studies Centre.

Linke, W. (1988). *Changes in household structures in Europe.* Strasbourg: Council of Europe.

Menahem, G. (1992). Troubles de santé à l'age adulte et difficultés familiales durant l'enfance [Adults' health problems and family difficulties during childhood]. *Population, 47*, 893–932.

Monnier, A., & Guibert-Lantoine, C. (1993). La conjoncture démographique: l'Europe et les pays développés d'Outre-Mer [Demographic trend: Europe and overseas developed countries]. *Population, 48*, 1043–1067.

Näsman, E. (1991). Il caso svedese [The Swedish case]. In A. Golini, A. Monnier, O. Ekert-Jaffé, R. Andorka, J. Hecht, E. Näsman, R. Cagiano de Azevedo, G. Blangiardo, R. Lesthaeghe, G. Moors, S. Koesoebjono, R. Palomba, G. Calot, & M. Livi Bacci (Eds.), *Famiglia figli e società in Europa. Crisi della natalità e politiche per la popolazione* (pp. 169–208). Torino: Fondazione Giovanni Agnelli.

Nordic Statistic Secretariat. (1994). *Yearbook of Nordic Statistics*. Å Rhus: Author.

Oliverio Ferraris, A. (1990). *Determinanti storico-sociali dell'individuo* [Individual social-historical daterminants]. Milano: Libreria Cortina.

Packard, V. (1985). *I bambini in pericolo* [Our endangered children]. Roma: Editori Riuniti. (Original work published 1983)

Palomba, R., & Sabbadini, L. L. (1992, January). Fertility, family structure and time use in Italy. Paper presented at the *Seminar on Gender and family change in industrialized countries*, organized by the International union for the scientific study of population, Rome.

Roussel, L. (1980). Mariages et divorces. Contribution à une analyse systématique des modèles matrimoniaux [Marriages and divorces. Contribution to a systematic analysis of the matrimonial models]. *Population, 35,* 1025–1040.

Roussel, L. (1992). Le futur de la famille [Family's future]. In *Proceedings of the conference human resources in Europe at the dawn of the 21st century* (pp. 185–208). Luxembourg: Eurostat.

Statistisches Bundesamt. (1993). *Statistisches Jahrbuch für die Bundesrepublik Deutschland* [Statistical yearbook of the Republic of Germany]. Wiesbaden: Author.

Sullerot, E. (1992). *Quels pères? Quels fils?* [What fathers? What sons?]. Paris: Fayard.

United Nations. (1993). *The sex and age distribution of population. The 1992 revision*. New York: Author.

Winn, M. (1984). *Bambini senza infanzia* [Children without childhood] Roma: Armando. (Original work published 1983)

SITUATIONAL INFLUENCES AND FAMILY LIFE

13

Parental Attitudes of Soviets in Israel to the Immigration Process and Their Impact on Parental Stress and Tension

Shlomo Sharlin
Irina Elshanskaya
University of Haifa

BACKGROUND

The 20th century has been an era of migration. A considerable amount of research has been done on family and children's adjustment in a new country, but as revealed in Aronowitz's (1984) analysis, research findings contradict one another and "there has been very little work done toward constructing a conceptual paradigm within which to understand the process of migration as it affects children" (p. 240). Because the vast majority of research efforts were devoted to parenting problems of economic migrants from Asian or Latin American countries to Western European countries and the United States, they do not reflect the experience of Soviet immigrants, who have a qualitatively different set of problems. Although some studies have already been conducted on Soviet immigrants, especially in the United States, it is clear that a great deal more research is needed with this population. According to Chiswick (1993), studies of Soviet Jews in the United States indicate that they had a high level occupational status prior to emigration, are older at emigration than economic migrants, emigrate in the family context, and have a smaller number of children per family.

Brodsky found in his study on Soviet immigrants (1988) that in the absence of authentic information on Western countries, many people in the former Soviet Union created a utopian image of the United States. In addition to their expectations of American freedom and prosperity, they had misguided assumptions that the social benefits of the Soviet system, such as free medical care and education, inexpensive public transportation, subsidized housing and cultural events, and job security, would also be available in the United States. Faced with the reality of their new country, the Soviet immigrants' sense of security and vision of utopia were often quickly and painfully shattered.

The research on Soviet Jewish children is sparse. One study presents its case under very specific conditions of immigration to the United States in 1990 (Castex, 1992), whereas another (Aronowitz, 1992) points to the relationship between parental attitudes toward social change and new experiences with their children's school adjustment in the United States. Pearlin and Lieberman (1979) argued that although the family provides its members a support system during times of stress and tension, the family itself creates stress and tension, arising mainly from the demands of the roles played by providers and parents. In spite of the widespread recognition that parents play a central role in mediating their children's experiences, this role received little attention in the literature on the effects of migration on children.

The present study attempts to contribute to the existing literature by exploring a range of Soviet immigrants' parental attitudes and perceptions of their children's problems in Israel, as well as providing an understanding of the causes for parental stress and tension, related to immigration. This is important since such parental attitudes could ultimately affect children's adjustment.

METHOD

Sample

The sample consists of 210 Soviet Jewish families with at least one school-age child. At the time the study was conducted, these families had been residing in Israel between 6 and 42 months, with a mean of 28.6 months. Fathers' mean age was 39.3 and mothers' was 37. The marriages were a first marriage for the vast majority of spouses, with their having lived together for about 15 years. The number of children in the family ranged from 1 to 3, with a mean of 1.6 (SD = .57). The children's mean age was 11.6. In most of the participating families, both spouses indicated they were Jewish; in 14.5% of the families, one of the spouses indicated he or she was not Jewish. Most respondents (74.8% of the males and 72.9% of the females) had a minimum of 14 years education. All male respondents and the majority of females worked outside the home before emigration. Most of the families originated from large cities from three countries in the former USSR: Russia, 31%; the Ukraine, 32.4%; and Byelorussia (White Russia), 16%. A typical family profile consisted of a highly educated, relatively young couple with 1 or 2 children, at least one of school age, representing an average urban Soviet Jewish family. Similar characteristics emerged in other studies of Soviet Jewish families who immigrated to the United States (Aronowitz, 1992; Chiswick, 1993; Simon & Brooks, 1983-1984).

Instruments and Procedure

This study was conducted in the North of Israel, where more than one third of the new immigrants settled during the most recent wave of immigration. A general questionnaire was designed to explore the variables related to adjustment. It dealt with family relations, intergenerational and childrearing problems, the decision making process and preparation for emigration, satisfaction with life in Israel and children's education, and the use of social support services, which could ultimately affect adjustment in children. The questionnaires were administered to each spouse individually, by the interviewer, in the subjects' own homes. In addition, *parental stress* (PS) and *parental tension* (PT) were measured by two scales, one developed by Pearlin and Lieberman (1979) and the other by Pearlin and Schooler (1978). *Parental stress*, defined as a distressful emotional experience, is constructed of nine adjectives in the Parental Stress Scale including *frustrated, bothered, stressed,* and *emotional weakness*. For example, parents were asked, "How often do you feel frustrated?" and asked to rate their frustration on a 4-point Likert scale ranging from 1 (*often*) to 4 (*never*) to measure the frequency of each perceived emotion. The Parental Stress Scale is an additive scale, ranging from a score of 9 to 36; the higher the score, the more stress. Internal validity, as measured by the Cronbach alpha, was .89.

Parental tension is defined as continuing problems directly relating to parenting which may lead to threatening feelings. Subjects are asked to respond on a 4-point Likert scale, ranging from 1 (*never*) to 4 (*often*), to such questions as: "How often do you feel that your children: 'Treat you without respect,' 'Ignore your advice and guidance,' 'Do not apply themselves at school,' 'Do not use their time effectively,' " and so on (Pearlin & Liberman, 1979; Pearlin & Schooler, 1978; Sharlin, Katz, & Lavee, 1992).

Results

A major finding connected with parenting and childrearing was that 60% of the respondents consider it harder to be a parent and must deal with more childrearing problems in Israel than in the former USSR. The question may be raised as to why childrearing should be more difficult for Soviet immigrants in Israel? In trying to provide an answer, let us first begin with a brief description of the motives and preparations for emigration and the family's subsequent adjustment in Israel.

The Process of Immigration. Findings on the decision to emigrate to Israel show that among these families, only 62.4% of them made a joint, conscious decision involving all family members (see Table 13.1).

In 21.4% of the cases, however, the best explanation for emigrating was: "It just happened." Only 22.6% of the respondents admitted that they had any knowledge about life in Israel and even fewer—11.7%—had any information about the educational system. Not all parents prepared their children for a difficult transition period. Approximately 50% of the respondents tried to speak with their children about Israel and generate curiosity, and 26.2% discussed all stages of immigration with their children. Parents reported that children were too young and they did not consider them able to understand emigration problems. Parents were often afraid to tell their children about emigration plans, lest the children discuss these plans outside the family circle (Elshanskaya & Sharlin, 1993). This kind of secrecy was considered necessary in an atmosphere indicative of anti-Semitic undercurrents in Soviet society, leading parents to dread serious consequences to themselves and their family, should these plans become known. However, a better explanation supported by our data is that the majority of parents—69.8%—decided to emigrate for their children's sake (see Table 13.1) and perhaps considered this sufficient to ensure their children's happiness. Similarly, 36.4% of the parents answered that they were "more concerned with their own absorption but not the children's, because they had often heard it would be very good for them in Israel."

There are many adverse factors connected with immigration to Israel. People arriving from large Soviet cities often have to adjust to smaller Israeli towns, villages, and kibbutz environments. About 60% of our sample settled in Haifa, which has a population of under 250,000; the balance chose smaller Israeli towns. In addition, about 50% of our respondents reported they had to share living quarters with the older generation. This may be a contributing cause of tensions in the family. Furthermore, about 14% of the men and 28% of the women were unemployed at the time of the study. About 50% of those employed were working outside their profession. Professional women often had to settle for domestic jobs or remain at home with the children, both previously unacceptable alternatives. Thus, it is not surprising that only about one third of the respondents reported satisfaction with their life in Israel, whereas approximately 40% reported dissatisfaction, and the rest were undecided. Our study suggests that these adverse conditions lead to hardships in family life and childrearing. Many respondents pointed out increased tensions between spouses and in relationships with the older generation, as well as significant problems with children (see Table 13.2).

TABLE 13.1
Decision Making Process About Emigration to Israel as Perceived by Soviet Immigrants in Israel (N = 420 in Percentages)

	Right	It is Difficult to say	Wrong	Mistake	Total
Decision About Emigration					
To emigrate to Israel was a joint conscious decision of all family members	62.4	15.2	20.5	1.9	100
We emigrated mainly for our children's sake	69.8	17.9	10.5	1.9	100
The best description for our emigration and its reasons may be "It just happened"	21.4	15.5	56.7	6.4	100
Information					
We had true general information about Israel and different aspects of life in it	22.6	19.3	57.4	0.7	100
We had true information about the education system in Israel	11.7	19.8	68.1	0.5	100
Children Involvedness					
We discussed all stages of the emigration with our children	26.2	11.2	60.5	2.1	100
We tried to tell our child(ren) about Israel, to generate their curiosity	49.8	14.0	34.3	1.9	100
Readiness for Hardships					
We tried not to think about forthcoming hardships of the absorption	39.0	21.0	38.6	1.4	100
We consciously prepared ourselves for absorption hardships	59.8	22.1	17.6	0.5	100
We were more concerned about our own absorption but not the child(ren)'s, because we had often heard "It is very good for children in Israel"	36.4	22.1	39.8	1.7	100
We had true conceptions of what child rearing problems could appear in our family after immigration	23.6	27.6	45.7	3.1	100

TABLE 13.2
Increasing Tension and Problems in the Family as Perceived by Soviet Immigrants

Aspect	Right	Difficult to Say	Wrong	Mistake	Total
Immigration hardships increased tension between spouses	30.0	18.1	46.9	5.0	100
Immigration caused tension in relationship with the older generation	39.8	16.2	35.5	9.5	100
Immigration caused some child-rearing problems in the family	36.2	21.4	29.5	12.9	100

Childrearing problems. In an attempt to understand the variety of problems, we start by analyzing those problems related to parental concern. Among 420 respondents, about half of them answered the following open-ended question: "Please indicate some of the childrearing problems you are most concerned with." Because some respondents indicated more than one reason, we received about 300 replies. Discounting the usual normative childrearing problems (slightly more than one fifth of answers), such as teenage problems, "they don't want to read," "they don't help around the house," and so on, the majority of answers referred to other problems which appeared after immigration. It is possible to categorize some of the most problematic issues. More than one third of the concerns expressed by respondents dealt with education and schooling problems, considered of primary importance. Dissatisfaction with education in general is widespread and the range of complaints quite varied. One respondent indicated that "the method of study in Israel is different; it encourages a great deal of independent work, but our children are not familiar with this system and find it difficult to cope." Other responses included "unsatisfactory education" and "fewer demands and requirements at school (i.e., discipline) as compared to our normal expectations."

The next largest group of complaints—about 15%—dealt with parental feelings of guilt and ineffectiveness towards their children. Some typical answers were: "We cannot afford to pay for a better school [private school] to ensure a higher standard of education for our children"; "Our children now regard us as incompetent in many areas, as a result of our lowered social standing"; "We are conscious of our reduced social standing and the humiliation of not being able to afford the simple things we were used to, such as books, theater, cinema, and access to swimming pools."

About 10% of the answers dealt directly with children's absorption hardships, or with instances when children do not understand family problems brought on by immigration. These responses reflect the discrimination children experience at schools, as well as poor relationships with native-born peers. Parents also worry about cultural differences between themselves and their children. Answers ranged from full rejection of Israeli culture, for example, "I do not want my children brought up in the traditional Israeli culture"; and "I am worried my son will not get a valid European education," to pointing out the increasing cultural and generation gap. For example, "We did not have sufficient time to lay a solid cultural foundation before emigration and now it is no longer possible"; and "We and our children belong to different cultures, because we acquired knowledge from different sources." Parents expect children to maintain their Russian language along with Hebrew. Moreover, parents are not satisfied with the way their children spend their leisure time. They claim that the children do not want to read, spend too much time on computer games, and do not have suitable extracurricular activities.

Other subjects raised included security, nationality (for children whose mother is not Jewish), health care, drugs in the schools, teachers' strikes, and so on. We obtained a similar picture, illustrating the same parental concerns, from answers to the other open-ended question: "Have you asked for advice from teachers, consultants, psychologists, or other specialists on your child's behavior and other related problems, and if you have, please indicate the problems and the assistance you received." Almost one quarter of the parents (23%) actually sought some assistance and advice. In more than two thirds of these cases, the reasons were school problems and language difficulties, various forms of discrimination, or problems relating to native children. Parents were accustomed to appealing to teachers for assistance, so here too they tried to obtain advice about school-related issues. Only some parents turned to school psychologists and social workers for help in other areas, including children's health, developmental and psychological difficulties.

The intensity and extent to which childrearing problems were perceived are illustrated in Table 13.3. In response to the following question: "Read the following immigrant families' childrearing problems and mark down if 'many,' 'some,' 'few' [and so on] families you know have such problems." The responses ranged from *in many families* and *in some families* to *in very few families*, or *in none at all.* As evident in Table 13.3, school problems are perceived as widespread and painful. Relationships with other children were also perceived as very problematic. In about 75% of the cases (46.2% in

TABLE 13.3

Conflicts and Tension in Immigrant Families in Connection With Children and Child Rearing Problems as Perceived by Soviet Immigrants
(N = 420 in Percentages)

Problems	In Many Families	In Some Families	In Very Few families or Not at all	Mistake	Total
School					
Children don't want to go to school	46.2	32.6	19.5	1.7	100
Children don't do well at school	50.0	29.0	19.0	1.9	100
Lack of attention given at school to immigrants' children	59.3	21.9	11.2	7.6	100
Parents' inability (because of difficulties with Hebrew) to help with homework	74.8	14.5	5.0	5.7	100
Children's Relations With Peers					
Children have problems in their relationships with others	56.0	26.0	11.9	6.2	100

Parent-Child Relations After Immigration

Parents experience disorientation in child-rearing problems under new circumstances	48.6	30.0	15.0	6.4	100
Parents pay less attention to their children in comparison to the situation before immigration	46.2	28.6	19.3	6.0	100
Lack of parents' supervision	43.1	31.9	19.3	5.7	100
Increasing disagreements with spouses' parents on child rearing problems	35.2	38.1	20.5	6.2	100
Parents vent their frustration on to children	25.2	32.6	36.0	6.2	100
Children reproach parents for immigrating	8.1	22.9	62.4	6.7	100
Children are isolated from parents (they try to adjust to new conditions by themselves)	20.0	34.0	39.5	6.4	100
Children are ashamed of their parents (if they are not adjusted or have lost their social status)	15.0	31.7	46.0	7.4	100
Because the children spoke Hebrew sooner, they became the "parents" of the family	20.7	31.0	42.1	6.2	100

"many" families and 28.6% in "some" families) parents reported perceiving other parents as paying less attention to their children currently than before immigration. Parents experiencing disorientation in childrearing, under new circumstances, and a lack of parental supervision was also perceived.

There appear to be serious problems with the parents' poor adjustment to their new country. More than half of the respondents felt that, in many or in some families, parents vent their frustration on the children. About 45% of the respondents reported that they perceived many or some families with children who were ashamed of their parents. About half of the subjects perceived children as isolated and trying to adapt to new conditions by themselves, and about one third of the subjects perceived children as reproaching their parents for immigrating (see Table 13.3).

Parental Stress and Tension. The level of stress in parental functioning, as measured by the same scales which researchers at the Center for Research and Study of the Family used to investigate Israeli parents, is quite high, even higher than the level of stress reported by the most problematic Israeli families in that study, as shown in Table 13.4 (Sharlin et al., 1992).

The effect of various immigration-related factors on parental stress and tensions is presented in Table 13.5. A closer look at this table reveals the following:

Table 13.5 presents a number of factors found to be related to parental stress, such as low satisfaction with life in Israel and diminished social status of the parents, dissatisfaction with school and parenting under new conditions. Such factors as weak Jewish identity, absence of joint or conscious decision making about emigration and deteriorating family relations after immigration, are also related to higher parental stress.

There are no significant differences in parental tension between parents who made a conscious decision to emigrate and those who did not, nor are there significant differences between parents with a high or low degree of satisfaction with their life and social status (these categories were excluded from Table 13.6 because they were not significant). However, such factors as Jewish identity, changes in family relationships after immigration, and children's attending school with pleasure all affect how parents evaluate their children's behavior (see Table 13.6). The combined findings presented in Tables 13.5 and 13.6 suggest that PS and PT are influenced not only by actual childrearing problems but also by conditions such as satisfaction with life in Israel. Parental tension, on the other hand, is impacted the most by the presence of child and family problems.

No significant gender differences in PS and PT were found in the variables studied, except for occupational status (see Tables 13.7a and 13.7b). Parental stress among unemployed males is higher than among the employed. Females who do not work have significantly less PT than working females.

TABLE 13.4
Analysis of Variance (ANOVA) of Parental Stress (PS) of Three Types of Populations in Israeli
Society in Comparison to the Soviet Immigrants

| | Israeli Families | | | Soviet Immigrant Families |
	1	2	3	
Male				
N	111	76	169	196
PS (M)	14.2	16.5	21.2	22.5
SD	5.1	6.5	7.6	5.7
Female				
N	106	73	205	200
PS (M)	14.1	15.9	21.1	23.5
SD	4.8	5.6	7.3	5.7

Notes. 1 = Regular, well-to-do families (healthy and medium to high income)
   2 = Families at risk. includes families living in same block or housing as 3 but not
      known to the Department of Social Services
   3 = Families receiving help from the Department of Social Services
   $p < .01$ = Referring to all three Israeli groups

Discussion

In trying to explain the intensity and diversity of parenting problems faced by Soviet immigrant families, we find that parental stress and tension may be rooted in various factors, some of which may be universal for all immigrants, whereas others are specific to the Soviet Jews in Israel. These factors include the following:

1. Genuine immigration hardships and the absence of advance information and adequate preparation; and
2. The perception of an inferior Israeli educational system in the immigrants' minds, based on the high value traditionally placed on education by Soviet Jews, combined with significant differences between the Soviet and Israeli educational systems.

We found that the more thorough the family's preparation for immigration, and the higher the satisfaction with life in Israel, the lower the parental

TABLE 13.5
Effect of Selected Factors on PS (ANOVA)

Variables	N	PS (M)	SD	ANOVA		Scheffe Test		
				F	P	1-2	1-3	2-3
1 - Joint conscious decision to emigrate	255	22.1	5.6					
2 - Difficult to say	62	24.5	5.3	9.1	.0001	*	*	-
3 - No	85	24.6	5.7					
1 - High satisfaction with life in Israel	135	20.1	4.3					
2 - Medium satisfaction	112	22.6	5.6	41.9	.0000	*	*	*
3 - Low satisfaction	159	25.7	5.9					
1 - High satisfaction with social status	83	20.5	5.9					
2 - Medium satisfaction	75	21.8	5.1	15.2	.0000	-	*	*
3 - Low satisfaction	250	24.1	4.7					
1 - Strong Jewish identity	109	21.3	5.1					
2 - Medium Jewish identity	163	23.0	5.7	9.06	.0001	*	*	-
3 - Weak Jewish Identity	93	24.6	5.8					
1 - Immigration has not increased tension between spouses	194	20.9	5.1					
2 - Difficult to say	74	23.9	5.1	29.3	.0000	*	*	-
3 - Immigration Increased tension	124	25.5	5.8					
1 - Children go to school with pleasure	178	21.6	5.2					
2 - Not always	197	23.8	5.7	11.7	.0000	*	*	-
3 - No	26	26.2	6.5					
1 - It is easier to be a parent in Israel than in the USSR	44	21.0	5.2					
2 - The same	143	20.8	5.6	28.6	.0000	-	*	*
3 - More difficult	218	24.9	5.2					
1 - Immigration has not caused child-rearing problems in our family	122	19.7	4.8					
2 - Difficult to say	89	23.3	4.9	37.7	.0000	*	*	*
3 - Immigration caused child-rearing problems	150	25.3	5.7					

Note. * - $p < 0.05$.

TABLE 13.6
Effect of Selected Factors on PT (ANOVA)

Variables	N	PT (M)	SD	ANOVA		Scheffe Test		
				F	P	1-2	1-3	2-3
1 - Strong Jewish identity	111	21.1	4.5					
2 - Medium Jewish identity	162	22.8	4.7	5.9	.003	*	*	-
3 - Weak Jewish identity	94	23.3	5.2					
1 - Immigration has not increased tension between spouses	194	21.2	4.7					
2 - Difficult to say	76	23.1	4.7	9.1	.0001	*	*	-
3 - Immigration increased tension	125	23.5	5.2					
1 - Children go to school with pleasure	179	20.8	4.6					
2 - Not always	197	23.1	4.5	25.5	.0000	*	*	*
3 - No	2	27.2	6.4					
1 - It is easier to be a parent in Israel than in the USSR	44	22.0	5.9					
2 -The same	143	21.4	4.8	5.4	.0046	-	-	*
3 - More difficult	219	23.2	4.8					
1 - Immigration has not caused child-rearing problems in our family spouses	121	20.7	4.3					
2 - Difficult to say	89	22.6	4.6	11.1	.0000	*	*	-
3 - Immigration caused child-rearing problems	150	23.4	5.2					

Note. * - p < 0.05.

stress. Relationships in the family after immigration appear to increase both stress and tension with perceived deterioration in family relationships. One could argue that perceived poor parental adjustment in Israel, as well as dissatisfaction with life in Israel, weak Jewish identity and lack of preparation for emigration cause parental stress and may ultimately lead to poor child adjustment.

The different ways variables affect PS and PT relate to the definition of PS and PT. Parental stress is influenced by an entire spectrum of absorption difficulties, and not necessarily by children's problems alone. However, PT is expressed by the parents' perception of their children's behavior. It is

TABLE 13.7A
ANOVA of Parental Stress (PS) and Occupational Status

Occupational Status	N	PS	SD	F	p
Male					
Work	169	22.0	5.7	8.5	.004
Do not work	29	25.3	5.3		
Female					
Work	143	23.4	5.6	.02	.9
Do not work	60	23.5	6.0		

TABLE 13.7B
ANOVA of Parental Tension (PT) and Occupational Status

Occupational Status	N	PT	SD	F	p
Male					
Work	169	22.4	5.0	.04	.52
Do not work	30	23.0	5.0		
Female					
Work	145	23.2	4.7	10.	.0018
Do not work	59	20.8	5.1		

affected mainly by ongoing childrearing and family problems, such as children's relationships with peers, school performance, and deteriorating family relations.

Our findings show that the only marked statistical difference between male and female PS and PT is found in connection with occupational status. Parental stress in unemployed males is higher than among the employed. For females, the difference is in the opposite direction; that is, PT in unemployed females is lower than among those employed. This implies that professional employment is of vital importance to the males and that un-employment may be related to emotional stress in their roles as fathers. As for the mothers, the findings suggest that the more time they have to devote to their children, the less tension they experience in parent–child relations. Another specific factor appears to be the immigrants' Jewish identity. The stronger the Jewish identity, the lower the PS and PT.

With regard to the immigrants' complaints about the Israeli school system, it is suggested that further research should be undertaken, specifically because of the perceived high quality of education in the former Soviet Union. When asked to qualify a happy future for their children, Soviet parents always put education first (Titarenko, 1987, p. 126). Soviet parents have always paid close attention to their children's scholastic achievements, are used to helping with homework, and insist on a high quality academic education (Titarenko, 1987). This is particularly true for Soviet Jews, who generally aspire even more to a higher education than the average Soviet, as indicated by respondents in our study.

In addition, due to anti-Semitism, Jewish children had to excel at school in order to enter university. Soviet Jews, therefore, have high demands and expectations from the educational system, which perhaps relates to stress. It should be mentioned here that originally parents decided to emigrate for their children's sake, hoping to be able to provide them with a good education, including university studies. Parents felt frustrated as they faced a totally different school system, which, rightly or wrongly, they perceived as inferior to the Soviet system. All this is compounded by difficulties with the Hebrew language, for both children and parents. Poor economic conditions do not enable immigrants to live in the best of districts and, therefore, the schools they attend may not be of the highest standards in the country. Without recognizing some of the advantages of the Israeli educational system, and constantly comparing it to the Soviet system, parents focused only on the disadvantages, thus exacerbating negative parental attitudes and disappointment. As perceived by the parents, the Israeli educational system was inadequately prepared to absorb such a large number of immigrant children from a totally different system and unable to provide them with the kind of support that they and their parents had come to rely on in the old country. These attitudes may reflect certain realities and, thus, further research in this area is recommended.

In the face of these cultural conflicts in expectations, it may be that a network of liaisons between teachers and parents should be developed in order to facilitate better adjustment to a new educational system. The more satisfied the parents are with their new country and with their decision to emigrate, the less the PS and the more effective the adjustment of the children—in short, a more successful absorption process all around.

ACKNOWLEDGMENT

The authors wish to thank Dr. Solly Dreman for his invaluable remarks and contribution.

REFERENCES

Aronowitz, M. (1984). The social and emotional adjustment of immigrant children: A review of the literature. *International Migration Review, 18*(2), 237–257.

Aronowitz, M. (1992). Adjustment of immigrant children as a function of parental attitudes to change. *International Migration Review, 26*(1), 89–110.

Brodsky, B. (1988). Mental health attitudes and practices of Soviet Jewish immigrants. *Health and Social Work, 19*(1), 130–136.

Castex, G. (1992). Soviet refugee children: The dynamic of migration and school practice. *Social Work in Education, 14*(3), 141–151.

Chiswick, B. R. (1993). Soviet Jews in the United States: An analysis of their linguistic and economic adjustment. *International Migration Review, 27*(2), 260–285.

Elshanskaya, I., & Sharlin, S. A. (1993). *Parent–child relations before and after immigration to Israel from the former U.S.S.R.* Unpublished manuscript.

Pearlin, L., & Liberman, M. (1979). Social sources of emotional distress. *Research in Community and Mental Health, 1*, 217–248.

Pearlin, L., & Schooler, C. (1978). The structure of coping. *Journal of Health and Social Behavior, 19*(1), 2–21.

Sharlin, S. A., Katz, R., & Lavee, Y. (1992). *Family policy in Israel, final report* (Vol. 4). Haifa, Israel: University of Haifa, The Center for Research & Study of the Family.

Simon, R., & Brooks, M. (1983–1984). Soviet Jewish immigrants' adjustment in four U.S. cities. *Journal of Jewish Communal Service, 60*(1), 56–64.

Titarenko, V. (1987). *Semia i formirovanie lichnosti* [Family and child development]. Moscow: Isdatelstvo Misl. (Misl Publishing).

14

IMMIGRATION AS A CHALLENGE: IMPLICATIONS FOR INDIVIDUALS AND FAMILIES[1]

Solly Dreman
Eva Shinar
Ben Gurion University of the Negev

Since its founding, Israel has perceived itself as the homeland for all Jews. The Declaration of Independence (1949) states that by the Law of Return every Jew is entitled to settle in Israel and to become a citizen. Large waves of immigration were often prompted by intolerable distress in the countries of origins or the wish to fulfill the Zionist dream of *Aliya* or ascending to Israel. In this context, approximately 500,000 persons emigrated to Israel from 1989 to 1993 due to the social unrest existing in the Soviet Union in the post-*Perestroika* and -*Glastnost* era (Ginath & Maoz, 1993).

Immigration is widely recognized as a stressful event which increases psychological vulnerability (Berry, Kim, & Minde, 1987; Hertz, 1993; Selye, 1974; Weekes & Simple, 1978), change in cognitive style, language, emotional life, and personality (Knight & Kagan, 1977). Hertz (1993) recently noted that adolescent immigrants constitute an extremely high-risk population. A possible explanation is that in the process of identity formation there is a need to cope with profound physiological, psychological, and social transformations, in addition to the uprootedness precipitated by the immigration process (Erikson, 1956, 1960; Mirsky & Kaushinsky, 1989). Similarly, the adolescent immigrant's need for autonomy and separation–individuation are particularly conflicting, because his or her desire for change is accompanied by severe anxiety and dependence needs in the face of cultural transition (Mirsky &

---

[1]A modified version of this chapter appeared as: Dreman, S., & Shinar, E. (1996). "Aliya as a challenge": An innovative workshop for the sociocultural integration of immigrant students. *The Israeli Journal of Psychiatry and Related Sciences, 33*, 5–12.

Kaushinsky, 1989). This follows, because the immigrant's identity is threatened in the new culture, because it represents a rupture in the history of the individual related to a change of space, time, and relationships (Mirsky, 1990). There is a profound need to build a bridge linking the present identity with that of the past, which permits joining the new culture.

Among the immigrant newcomers are many students in late adolescence, ranging in age from 17 to 24. Helping them in the absorption process is the fact that they share a common heritage, Judaism, with their Israeli hosts and receive financial support from the government, including tuition fees, dormitory accommodations and a social/academic support network. In spite of these benefits, many experience academic and social difficulties, complaining of loneliness, alienation, and an inability to befriend Israeli students. As a result they frequently turn to university sponsored student counseling services for psychological help (Guttfreund & Mirsky, 1992).

Ginath and Maoz (1993) recently noted that very few intervention programs providing emotional support to immigrants have been established or evaluated. In a rare program (Guttfreund & Mirsky, 1992) designed to help immigrant students, homogeneous groups of either Spanish or French university students were led by facilitators who had a similar cultural background. These groups were conducted in the native language of the group involved. The authors concluded that cultural homogeneity and using the mother tongue appeared to be necessary conditions for the effectiveness of these two groups, as compared to a Russian and a Persian group in the same project in which Hebrew was used.

The intervention described here is unique in that it employed heterogeneous groups composed of both new immigrant (*Olim*) and native Israeli students (*Vatikim*). The basic assumption was that in order for a bridge to be created between the past and the present identity, an active encounter must occur between representatives of the respective cultures, encouraging both the process of mourning–separation and that of joining–individuation. The groups were conducted in Hebrew because language acquisition was considered central to acquisition of a sense of competence in the host culture. In contrast to previous interventive attempts (Guttfriend & Mirsky, 1992), our research employed assessment measures in the form of standardized questionnaires to assess changes in attitudes, affect, and behaviors.

METHOD

Goals

The workshop "Immigration as a Challenge" is meant to facilitate the sociocultural integration of new immigrant students. This chapter focuses on the early stages of the project in which the immigrant groups dealt with included only students from the former Soviet Union. In more recent years, however, immigrant students from Ethiopia were also incorporated into the project. The workshop is given as an academic course at Ben Gurion University in Israel with requirements including regular attendance, readings on transition, stress on immigration, and a final term paper integrating the readings and workshop experience.

The consensus amongst mental health professionals in Israel is that the students from the former Soviet Union tend to avoid participation in settings with a group-dynamic nature in which psychological probing is involved (Guttfriend & Mirsky, 1992). In addition, they prefer to mix with others from the former Soviet Union due to their inherent suspiciousness and guardedness toward "outsiders." It was also observed that these *Olim* do not persevere in a group setting when there is not a "pay-off" involved. Taking the above into account we constructed our groups using the following principles:

1. The course was advertised as discussing "different aspects of immigration," including how the process affects *Olim* (new immigrant) and *Vatikim* (native students). A psychological description was avoided in order to diminish resistance. Similarly, reactions such as euphoria, denial, depression, and concentration difficulties were described, and it was emphasized that these were normative reactions to the immigration process. The development of appropriate coping skills was also discussed in detail.

2. In contrast to prior groups, which concentrated on separation and consisted of homogeneous immigrant groups, our groups were heterogeneous, including *Olim* and *Vatikim*, in order to encourage the joining process of the *Olim*. Similarly, the workshop was conducted in Hebrew because language acquisition was considered to be integral to joining and to acquisition of competence and self-esteem in the host culture.

3. To increase motivation, academic grade-point credit was offered to students who fulfilled the course requirements.

4. Only *Olim* who had lived in Israel at least 2 year prior to the workshop were selected because it was felt that immigrants located at the earlier stages would be too anxious and disoriented to benefit.

Structure and Process

The workshop groups comprised, on the average, 26 participants—13 *Olim* and 13 *Vatikim*—and 2 facilitators, clinical psychologists, or social workers with training in groupwork. They were conducted in either a one-semester, 12-session or a two-semester, 24-session format. We describe here the activities of the two-semester workshop, because the first semester resembles the one-semester workshop, whereas the second semester reflects unique group processes and content.

Direct confrontation regarding immigration was avoided in the first semester in order to diminish resistance. This was accomplished by the workshop leaders' implementing structured exercises and simulations of a nondirective and projective nature in the initial stages of the workshop. These activities created an atmosphere of group cohesion, openness, and increased willingness to speak about the process of immigration and absorption in the second semester. In the second semester students directed the activities of the workshop by themselves, with groups of 4 to 5 students each conducting a workshop presentation concerning the immigration process. Some of the activities of the group in both semesters and their implications are discussed here.

First Semester. In the first meeting, *Olim* and *Vatikim* students were paired and asked to tell their partners something about themselves and then introduce the partner to the group. For many of the students this was the first time they had spoken with a member of the other group and stereotypes, such as that Israelis do not read or that the former Soviets speak poor Hebrew, were dissipated.

A few sessions were devoted to discussing normative transitions in the family life cycle such as marriage, the birth of the first child, adolescence, and the empty nest, as well as paranormative, less expected transitions, such as sudden death, divorce, and immigration. A theoretical model of transition in the family (Carter & McGoldrick, 1988) was presented by the group leaders, and students then discussed how their personal experiences related to this model. Considerable time was devoted to the subject of loss and transition-related stress such as that involved with immigration to a new country or the death friends or relatives.

In other meetings exercises of a projective, nonconfrontative nature such as planning a "landing on a strange planet" were performed in heterogeneous groups of 4 to 5 students. Such tasks permitted the discussion of "neutral" topics indirectly related to the problems of immigration. In this context students discussed such issues as who would set out to explore the planet first and who would guard the spaceship, the need to gradually become familiar with the inhabitants, as well as the uncertainty and stress involved in the process.

In subsequent meetings the working groups were asked to perform a psychodrama that was relevant to individuals 20 years of age and older. Such themes as cohabitation, pregnancy before marriage, and blind dates were portrayed in these skits. In one skit, a group portrayed a young unmarried couple who request their parents' consent to cohabitate in a student apartment. In the discussion that followed, it was noted that living together as a couple did not occur in the Soviet Union, because people did not have the means to buy or rent an apartment. In Israel, however, this phenomenon occurs more frequently among *Olim* because accommodations are more readily available. These skits helped to illustrate to the group participants that many of the subjects related to the 20-plus age group are universal subjects, not restricted to any particular cultural context.

The group leaders then presented a theoretical model (Spencer & Adams, 1990) of coping with the foregoing life transitions. This process was described as initially characterized by severe shock, with accompanying periods of euphoria and denial, followed by depression and diminished functioning, culminating in cognitive and emotional integration of the pre- and posttransitional realities. A female student from the former Soviet Union described the process in a final term paper as follows:

1. *Losing Focus*. "A short time after I came to Israel I felt completely lost. What shall I do? I don't know the language. This country is completely foreign to me! Where do I begin?"

2. *Minimizing the Impact*. "At this stage I felt that things actually weren't so bad. The shops are full of goods and one can purchase anything. I have been promised work, an apartment, a secure future and there is no reason to worry!"

3. *The Pit*. "The situation is very difficult here. There is no work. Even though there is an abundance of goods available, I can't afford them."

4. *Letting Go of the Past*. "I'm already here. There is no way of return. I must learn to survive. I must leave the past behind and try to cope with the present."

5 *Testing the Limits*. "My situation is not bad. I'm studying towards a master's degree. Now it's possible to think of new goals—I'm going to try being a teacher at a Hebrew language center."

6. *Searching for Meaning*.

7. *Integration of Vision*. This student felt she had not yet reached these levels and was still testing the limits.

The foregoing illustrates how the didactic part of the workshop helps workshop participants understand and cope more effectively with transition and change. Toward the end of the first semester group members were asked to discuss the process occurring in the workshop and to represent this in a drawing. In one group each student drew his own hand in a different color, with the hands meeting at the middle of the page. They explained that the drawing exemplifies the cohesiveness established between group members, as well as their attempts to maintain individuality. In the last meeting of the semester participants were asked to draw pictures representing childhood experiences and these were later grouped together in terms of common themes such as "the first day at school" or "summer holidays."

In a term paper at the end of the year one group summarized this experience as follows: "We discovered that the experiences from childhood were more or less common to all of us. However, while the Vatikim are still strongly attached to places and people from their childhood, it was apparent that for the Olim, childhood is perceived as part of a past which is impossible to retrieve in the present." These two sessions vividly illustrate how the emergence of group cohesiveness and commonalities contributes to the process of joining the host culture, while at the same time saliencing the loss experienced by the immigrant student in the process of emigration.

Second Semester. In this semester working groups of 3 to 4 students each made a class presentation of an immigration-related topic of their choice. Group cohesiveness attained earlier resulted in the formation of heterogeneous self-selected work groups of *Olim* and *Vatikim*. Illustrative of the subjects chosen were "military service in the Soviet Union versus Israel," "the Russian immigrant as perceived by the Israeli" and "media depiction of the Russian immigrant and the Israeli." Students met outside of the classroom to prepare their presentations which involved social games, video presentations, and riddles.

In the meeting "military service in the Soviet Union versus Israel" the Israelis were surprised to learn that the *Olim* demonstrated willingness to serve in the army and to defend their "homeland," Israel. The *Olim* identified strongly with the "Jewish State" and perceived the Israeli Defense Forces as the defender of the Jewish people, both in the Diaspora and Israel. This contrasted with the Israelis, who viewed the army as primarily serving the defense needs of the State of Israel. In the meeting "the Russian immigrant as perceived by the Israeli," students conducted video interviews of Israelis in two different urban settings, a market place and a shopping center. Whereas interviewees in the marketplace described the Russians in negative terms such as *swindlers*, *prostitutes*, and *thieves*, those at the shopping center described them as *intelligent*, *academicians*, and as a *positive contribution to the state*.

In the class discussion that followed, it was suggested that interviewees in the lower-class market place were engaged in direct competition with new immigrants for employment and other resources, resulting in more negative stereotypes towards them. Those in the shopping center, in contrast, were mainly middle class, their impressions being based more on hearsay and professed ideology than actual experience. In the class discussion it was suggested that intergroup contact in more positive, less competitive circumstances, might promote less malignant, more realistic attitudes towards *Olim*.

The student presentations were usually preceded by meetings outside the class setting in order to prepare, whereas the actual class presentations usually involved intense discussions and interest. One group described the process as follows in their final term paper:

> At this stage we were better acquainted with the group members. Thus activity in the small groups, including the involvement required to present a topic, contributed to more intimate acquaintances and cooperation. Similarly, we learned about a variety of subjects that characterize the different cultures such as military service, music, theater, the feelings of Vatikim and Olim towards Israel, Zionism, and related topics. The atmosphere in these meetings was pleasant and enjoyable, group cohesiveness was established, and a unique path was established for personal expression.

EVALUATION

Measures and Findings

Psychometric instruments, with known reliabilities and validities, were used to compare the group before and after workshop participation on dimensions of personal and interpersonal change. Matched control groups of Russian-speaking and native Israeli students who did not participate in the workshop were also administered these tests at equivalent time periods. Among the measures included were sense of coherence (Antonovsky, 1987), self-esteem (Rosenberg, 1979), social support (Dreman & Orr, 1985), state anxiety (Spielberger, Gorsuch, & Lushene, 1970), state anger (Spielberger, 1988), as well as attitudes towards the "typical Israeli student" and the "typical student from the former Soviet Union" (Bales, 1950). Some of the findings obtained were:

1. The *Olim* had higher state anxiety, lower self-esteem, and a lower sense of coherence than the *Vatikim* as expected in the initial stages of immigration (p's < .05).

2. Whereas male *Vatikim* had higher self-esteem than female *Vatikim*, female *Olim* had higher self-esteem than male *Olim* (interaction: Country of Origin × Gender, $p < .001$). This may be indicative of a more egalitarian society in the former Soviet Union, or alternatively, that the relative status of the male Olim diminishes in initial stages of the immigration process.

3. The group, as a whole, rated *Vatikim* more positively than *Olim* ($p < .02$). This is not surprising, because host culture members are usually rated more positively than immigrants.

4. *Olim* turned more to family for social support than to friends, whereas *Vatikim* turned more to friends than family (interaction: Country of Origin × Sources of Social Support, $p < .05$). *Vatikim* also reported more satisfaction from help received from friends than did the *Olim* ($p < .05$). This reflects the close family bonding that some researchers reported in the former Soviet family (Mirsky, 1990; Mirsky & Kaushinsky, 1989).

A supplement to the standardized test battery was the questionnaire constructed by the students towards the end of the workshop. Students worked in subgroups of 4 to 5 students and constructed questions related to the effectiveness of the workshop, and the attitudinal and behavioral changes that workshop participants had undergone. As opposed to the standardized measures cited earlier, the student questionnaire directly tapped the world of content of the students in terms of relevant dimensions of workshop effectiveness and change engendered. The disadvantage of the instrument is that it was only administered at the end of the workshop and no preworkshop measures were obtained. In the future the authors hope to remedy this by administering this questionnaire both before and after workshop participation. On the questionnaire statements listed below the following results were obtained:

1. "Following the workshop my attitudes towards the *Vatikim* are more positive"—*Olim* had a significantly higher level of agreement on a 5-point scale than did *Vatikim* ($p < .022$).
2. "Following the workshop my attitudes towards the *Olim* are more positive"—*Vatikim* had higher levels of agreement than *Olim*, although these findings did not reach statistical significance.
3. "Following the workshop I feel more Israeli"—Olim reported a larger degree of agreement than *Vatikim* ($p < .05$).
4. "Following my participation in the workshop I understood the culture of the former Soviet Union"—*Vatikim* indicated a higher level of agreement than *Olim* ($p < .011$).
5. Seven out of 11 *Olim* students tested indicated that they had made friends with *Vatikim*, whereas 7 out of the 12 *Vatikim* tested indicated that they had made friends with *Olim* during the workshop.

These findings suggest that attitudes, understanding and behavioral dispositions towards the "other" group improved after workshop participation.

The Family Adaptability and Cohesion Evaluation Scales (FACES III; Olson, Portner, & Lavee, 1985) was recently introduced in the workshop as a measure of the ability of families of the *Olim* and *Vatikim* to maintain closeness as well as to adapt to change. Although no significant differences between *Olim* and *Vatikim* were found for family cohesiveness, significant differences on adaptability ($p < .037$) were found, with *Olim* having higher levels than *Vatikim*. Olson's (1993) curvilinear model proposes that extreme levels of cohesion or adaptability may be maladaptive because they might be representative of pathological family functioning as represented in enmeshed families in the case of extreme cohesion or chaotic families in the case of extreme levels of adaptability. The migration process is often characterized by the usurping of traditional family roles and status, including role reversals in which children become "parentified," because they adapt more quickly to the host culture in the early stages of migration. This might be reflected in the more chaotic family structure obtained on FACES III in the families of *Olim*. Future research might investigate the relation between such measures of family process and actual adjustment parameters at different stages in the migration process.

DISCUSSION

The workshop "*Aliya* as a Challenge" is an interventive program, with a research component, which is designed to facilitate the sociocultural integration of immigrant students. The educational aspect aims to create better understanding and more positive social interaction between the host and immigrant cultures. The research aspect attempts to examine sociopsychological parameters of change amongst participants and to assess workshop effectiveness. Ostensibly, these goals might be perceived as being difficult to attain since the Soviet immigrant group has been portrayed as socially reserved, as well as being resistant to psychologically oriented research activities. However, the format of the present workshop helped to overcome these obstacles. Thus, in the area of social interaction activities requiring intergroup cooperation eventually led to increased group cohesiveness and better interpersonal relations between the *Olim* and *Vatikim*. Research participation was encouraged by making this component, including filling out of questionnaires, a necessary requirement for obtaining academic credit for workshop participation.

Unlike previous approaches that utilized homogeneous immigrant groups and that were conducted in the native language of the immigrants (Guttfreund & Mirsky, 1992), the present project implemented heterogeneous groups in which both new immigrants (*Olim*) as well as native Israeli (*Vatikim*) participated, with the language of the host culture, Hebrew, spoken. This strategy was adopted to provide an opportunity for *Olim* to join the host culture, a process that was perceived as important to identity development in these late adolescent immigrants. In this context, the heterogeneous peer group facilitated separation from the mother culture, while at the same time providing a role model for joining and attaining individuation in the new culture. This in turn, helped to bridge the discontinuities in space, time and relationships precipitated by the immigration process.

One other aspect of the group work was its non-confrontive, structured nature and its emphasis on normative transitional processes. This strategy diminished resistance, promoting learning and group cohesiveness which ultimately contributed to the group's effectiveness. Also contributing to the learning process was the fact that only *Olim* who had been in the country more than 2 years were selected. This was done because it was felt that students at earlier stages of immigration would be relatively anxious and disoriented and less able to integrate the workshop experience.

Another feature of the workshop was that the process of successful immigration was perceived as being reciprocal, with change expected in both the host and immigrant groups. The successful attainment of this goal was evidenced in the fact that change was evidenced in both groups as expressed in more positive attitudes and willingness to engage in social interaction with the other group.

A New Dimension

The recent "blood scandal" in Israel, in which the Ministry of Health secretly dumped all donated blood from Ethiopians for fear it contained the AIDS virus (see in this regard, Donnelley, 1996), provided a new dimension to the understanding of the immigration process in this country. Israel's 56,000 Ethiopians, or "Black Jews," who emigrated in two great waves from Africa— Operation Moses in 1984 and Operation Solomon in 1991—brought into the open the possibility of discrimination along color lines in what is thought to be one of the most liberal and democratic countries in the Western world. Many Ethiopians cite examples of racism in their daily lives, accusing White-skinned Israelis of moving away from them on buses or of Israeli-born *sabra* children uttering cries of *cushi masriah*, Hebrew for "stinking Black," at their new Ethiopian playmates. In addition, whereas for the most part urban Russian immigrants came with the intellectual, psychological and social tools to fare well in the host culture, the Ethiopians arrived as mostly rural uneducated farmers with limited means of navigating their way in the Western world. These factors contributed strongly to the relatively negative attitudes held by certain segments of Israeli society towards this ethnic group.

In our initial experiences of working with groups of new former Soviet students and Israeli *Vatikim*, the Soviet group often expressed very negative and racist attitudes towards these "Black, primitive and apelike immigrants," to quote one Soviet participant. In addition, the fact that the Ethiopians competed for scarce economic and other resources, such as scholarships in institutions of higher learning, also exacerbated such attitudes. These developments increased our resolve to include former Soviet and Ethiopian individuals in our groups, because it was felt that the inclusion of relatively elite and educated Ethiopian representatives in the noncompetitive and supportive atmosphere of the workshop would help break down some of the cultural stereotypes prevailing. amongst the former Soviets and native Israeli students. As a result, immigrant students from Ethiopia have been participating along with former Soviet and *Vatikim* students in the last two years of the project. While only a limited number of Ethiopian students have participated to date, the results have been very positive, with extensive attitude change and more positive social interaction taking place between the former Soviets, Ethiopians, and native Israeli students.

In summary, the educational and research facets of this project should contribute not only to the students involved, but also to educators, mental health personnel and institutions dealing with immigration in individuals and families. As for its application beyond the "ivory towers" of the university setting, students as "opinion leaders," may be able to lead similar groups in their own communities and thus help in breaking down the negative stereotypes and attitudes prevailing in their respective reference groups. Similarly, this program could be introduced in other institutes of higher learning in Israel and with minor modifications into the high school curriculum as well.

ACKNOWLEDGMENTS

We gratefully acknowledge the support of the Joint Distribution Committee, the Ministry of Absorption, and the Dreman Foundation in this project.

REFERENCES

Antonovsky, A. (1987). *Unravelling the mystery of health: How people manage stress and stay well.* San Francisco: Jossey-Bass

Bales, R. F. (1950). *Interaction process analysis: A method for the study of small groups.* Cambridge, MA: Addison-Wesley.

Berry, J. W., Kim, V., & Minde, T. (1987). Comparative studies of acculturative stress. *International Migration Review, 21,* 491–511.

Carter, B., & McGoldrick, M. (Eds.). (1988). *The changing family cycle: A framework for family therapy.* New York: Gardner Press.

Donnelley, J. (1996, February 1). Ethiopians, Israelis: United by religion, divided by Culture. *The Miami Herald.*

Dreman, S., & Orr, E. (1985). *Changes perceived by mothers in the social, familial and personal constellation after filing for divorce in the rabbinical court in Israel.* Unpublished manuscript, Ben Gurion University of Negev, Bandy Steiner Center for Single Parent Families.

Erikson, E. H. (1956). The problems of ego identity. *Journal of the American Psychoanalytic Association, 4*, 21–56.

Erikson, E. H. (1960). *Identity and uprootedness in our times: Uprooting and resettlement.* Geneva: World Federation for Mental Health,

Ginath, Y., & Maoz, B. (1993). Adjustment and distress among new immigrants to Israel. *Israel Journal of Psychiatry and Related Sciences*, 203–210.

Guttfreund, D. G., & Mirsky, J. (1992). Immigrant students in Israel: A cross cultural primary prevention program to facilitate their adaptation. *Cross-Cultural Psychology Bulletin, 26*, 3–8.

Hertz, D. G. (1993). Bio-psycho-social consequences of migration stress. *Israel Journal of Psychiatry and Related Sciences, 30*, 204–212.

Knight G. P., & Kagan S. (1977). Acculturation of prosocial competitive behaviors among second and third generation Mexican American children. *Journal of Cross-Cultural Psychology, 8*, 273–284.

Mirsky, J. (1990). Individuation through immigration to Israel: Psychotherapy with immigrant adolescents. *Journal of Contemporary Psychotherapy, 20*, 47–61.

Mirsky, J., & Kaushinsky, F. (1989). Migration and growth: Separation–individuation processes in immigrant students in Israel. *Adolescence, 95*, 725–740.

Olson, D. H. (1993). Circumplex model of marital and family systems: Assessing family functioning. In F. Walsh (Ed.), *Normal family processes* (2nd ed., pp. 7–37). New York: Haworth Press.

Olson, D. H., Portner, J., & Lavee, Y. (1985). *Family adaptability cohesion evaluation scales (FACES III).* St. Paul, MN: University of Minnesota, Family Social Science.

Rosenberg, M. (1979). *Conceiving the self.* New York: Basic Books.

Selye, H. A. (1974). *Stress without distress.* Philadelphia: Lippincott.

Spencer, S. A., & Adams, J. D. (1990). *Life changes: Growing through personal transitions.* San Luis Obispo, CA: Impact Publishers.

Spielberger, C. D., Gorsuch, R. L., & Lushene, R. (1970). *Manual for the State–Trait Anxiety Inventory: STAI.* Palo Alto, CA: Consulting Psychologists Press.

Spielberger, C. D. (1988). *Manual for the State-Trait Anger Expression Inventory (STAXI).* Odessa, FL: Psychological Assessment Resources.

Weekes, C., & Simple, A. (1978). Affective treatment of agoraphobia. *American Journal of Orthopsychiatry, 32*, 357–369.

FAMILY ASSESSMENT IN A SYSTEMS CONTEXT

FAMILY STRESS AND COPING: A MULTISYSTEM PERSPECTIVE

David H. Olson
University of Minnesota

Whereas family stress has been found to impact the emotional and physical health of individuals, a multisystem perspective on stress and coping focuses on four areas of life (individual, work, couple, and family). The *Multisystem Assessment of Stress and Health* (MASH) model builds a biopsychosocial model that is multidimensional and is designed to bridge research, theory, and practice. The model builds on the earlier family theory and research focusing on stress, coping and adaptation with individuals, couples and families. The model is multidimensional and utilizes a multisystem perspective including four areas of life: personal, work, couple, and family.

A comprehensive assessment tool has been developed and validated that builds on the MASH model which is called the *Coping and Stress Profile* (CSP). The CSP assesses stress, coping resources (cohesion, flexibility, communication and problem solving) and satisfaction for all four areas of life. Six scales were developed for each area of life, making a total of 24 scales. In addition, six personal coping resources were added along with assessment of psychological distress and physical symptoms. All the CSP scales have high reliability, content validity, and construct validity. The CSP is designed for research, individual assessment, and counseling and programs for people in a variety of settings (work, couples, families, religious groups).

Studies in the United States (Stewart, 1988; Tasci, 1995), Germany (Schneewind, Weiss, & Olson, 1994), and of Norwegian clergywomen (Piper, 1995) demonstrated that the CSP scales are reliable and valid across other cultures. These studies also demonstrated that the MASH model is valid and helps to clarify and expand our understanding of the interconnection of various aspects of life. Although stress can come from all aspects of life, coping resources from one area of life can also be used to help a person manage stress in other areas of life. For example, a supportive spouse can help a partner better deal with a stress at work.

The ultimate goal of the MASH model and the CSP is that they be used in research, theory building and in practical settings. As a counseling tool, the CSP is designed to help individuals and groups develop resources to more effectively manage stress. The CSP is currently being used for counseling and in helping work groups be more effective and productive.

A PERSONAL PERSPECTIVE ON INTERNATIONAL COLLABORATION

Before coming to Israel, I informed my elderly mother about the trip. She is currently 86 years old, is rather frail, and we just moved her to a nursing home. Her response was: "Why are you going to Israel now?" What she was really saying as she has become more dependent on her two children is: "Why are you, the eldest son, leaving me and going so far away to a dangerous country?" She was also thinking: "Why would they invite a Norwegian like you from Minnesota to talk about family stress in such a different culture?"

Her initial question caught me off guard and forced me to think more about her and also about why I was invited and what I could contribute to such a topic at an international conference. The more that I thought about it, however, the more I realized that my travel to Israel was perhaps no more strange and surprising than the fact that the Norwegians were actively involved in facilitating the peace agreement between Israel and the Palestinians. The latter event clearly demonstrated that we live in a global society and that international collaboration can be potentially valuable.

INTERNATIONAL PERSPECTIVE ON FAMILY STRESS

Family stress is something that families in all cultural groups have in common, although the cause of the stress and the ways of coping with the stress may greatly differ. Some of the commonalties about family stress across cultures will be briefly presented. In addition to seeking commonalties, it is also important to be open to important differences, which I hope will increase our appreciation of diversity and our opportunity to learn from these differences.

1. *Families from all cultures experience family stress.* Although the specific causes of family stress and the specific types of issues that are most stressful may vary by culture, all families seem to experience and understand the concept of family stress.

2. *All stressors either begin or end up in the family.* Whether the stressful issues come from outside the family system or are created inside the family system, most stressful issues end up affecting the entire family system.

3. *All families must find resources (internal or external) to help them better manage the stress in their lives.* Families from various cultures probably differ in the specific resources that they use to manage the stress in their family. However, resources are an important way in which families manage their stressful life issues.

4. *All families have some internal strengths that they use for managing stress in their family system.* Many studies of various ethnic groups have assumed a deficit model of family functioning, often based on a eurocentric model. Cross cultural studies of families have seldom sought to identify family strengths within a cultural group, but have tended to focus on the problems in families from different cultures. By building on a family strengths model, it is possible we will more clearly identify useful coping strategies across cultures.

5. *Families will tend to first use internal resources (inside the family system) before using external resources (outside the family system) to manage their family stress.* The definition of the family system used here is broad and it includes both the nuclear and extended family systems. It is probably more common in many cultures that the extended family system will play a more significant role as a resource for managing family stress than the nuclear family system.

6. *Families from various cultures will use a variety of different approaches or strategies to successfully manage their family stress.* Although some work has been done to understand successful coping strategies in various cultures, there appears to be little work focused on identifying the range and variety of coping resources used by different cultural groups. This type of information could greatly enhance our understanding of stress and coping across cultures. It is hoped that future collaborative studies across cultures will help to enhance our mutual understanding of stress and coping.

THE MASH MODEL

This chapter provides an overview of a theoretical model that combines elements of previous family and individual stress models into an integrated MASH model. The MASH model has three major components: stress, coping resources, and adaptation. These major three components are assessed at four system levels: the individual, couple, family, and work system. Measures of stress at each of the four levels focus on specific dynamic issues rather than on life events. Coping resources focuses on four generic relationship resources of problem solving, communication, cohesion, and flexibility. Adaptation focuses on physical health and psychological measures of adaptation and satisfaction at each of the four system levels.

The goals of the MASH model are to build upon and extend the previous work on family stress and to develop a multidimensional and biopsychosocial model. Assessment scales built on the MASH model are included in a self-report questionnaire called the Coping and Stress Profile (CSP). The CSP is a computerized assessment of the stress, coping, and adaptational dimensions at four system levels. The CSP can provide a comprehensive and practical assessment for the family professional for research and clinical assessment.

REVIEW OF FAMILY STRESS MODELS

Family stress researchers often focused on individuals and families in crises. Stress research in the social sciences resulted in extensive investigations of either the family or the individual. Reuben Hill's (1949, 1958) pioneering work on family stress grew out of his study of war separation and reunion. His ABCX model became the foundation on which much of the work on family stress has been built. Hill's theory had four components: A—the stressor event—which interacts with B—the family's crisis-meeting resources—which interacts with C—the definition the family makes of the event—producing X—the crisis. The resources (B) and family's definition of the event (C) come from within the family, whereas the event and the hardships associated with the event (A), comes from outside the family.

Building on Hill's ABCX model, McCubbin and Patterson (1983) developed the double ABCX model by adding postcrisis adaptation in families. In the double ABCX model, the C factor was expanded to include the family's perception of the original stressor event and the pileup of stressor and strains (the A factor). In addition, the concept of coping was added to the model and it included both cognitive and behavioral strategies.

A sense of coherence was added to the double ABCX model based on Antonovsky's work (1979) that focused on the family's ability to know when to take charge and when to trust in the power of others. Antonovsky (1987) developed the sense of coherence (SOC) model that emphasizes the personal feeling of confidence that is composed of three dimensions: comprehensibility, manageability, and meaningfulness. Comprehensibility assumes that life is structured, predictable, and explicable. Manageability assumes a person has the resources to meet the current demands. Meaningfulness provides the context that the challenges are worthy of investment. Antonovsky (1994) reported extensive research validating the sense of coherence scale and model.

In order to emphasize adaptation, the next step historically was the development of the family adjustment and adaptation response (FAAR) model by Patterson (1988, 1989). This model integrated both the Hill's ABCX model and the double ABCX model. This provided a greater focus on additional life stressors and strains which affect the family's adaptation.

Boss (1988) helped to expand the ABCX model to make it more systemic by adding several new concepts. Boss introduced the concept of *boundary ambiguity*, which focuses on whether a person is defined as being in or out of the family system. Presence or absence is considered on both the physical and psychological dimensions. A major premise is that families are most highly stressed when their losses are ambiguous.

Boss (1988) also clarified the difference between coping as a family resource and coping as a process. Boss provided a variety of reasons why the concept of *managing stress* is more useful than the concept of *coping with stress* as an outcome of dealing with stress. The family's coping resources are, therefore, considered strengths of the individuals and family members, but having these strengths does not mean that the family will use them.

Burr and Klein (1994) provided an exciting addition to the field of family stress by providing a more systemic model of family stress compared to the ABCX model, which is more linear and deterministic. They focused on nine salient dimensions of family life (i.e., cohesion, marital satisfaction, communication, daily routines, contention, family development, leadership, family rituals, and emotional climate) and interviewed 46 families that experienced one of the following six stressors (bankruptcy, troubled teens, displaced homemaker, handicapped child, muscular dystropic child, and infertility). They assessed how the family's response to the stressor impacted the family system functioning (roller coaster, increased, no change, mixed, decreased). Their descriptive analysis demonstrated the diversity of resources the families used and also the varied impact on their functioning over time.

Burr and Klein (1994) also provided an excellent summary evaluation of the coping strategies that were found in past studies to be the most useful for families. They identified seven general strategies that contain a total of 20 more specific coping strategies. Their review demonstrated the salience of these coping strategies for a range of family stressors. Table 15.1 provides a summary of the coping strategies summarized by Burr and Klein (1994) and the major coping strategies integrated into the CSP. This analysis clearly demonstrates the comprehensive nature of the CSP as it attempts to include a diverse variety of the most salient coping strategies.

TABLE 15.1
Coping Resources summarized by Burr and Klein and Coping Resources in the Coping & Stress
Profile

General Resources	Specific Resources	Resources in CSP
Cognitive	Gain knowledge	**Problem Solving--** (At Four System Levels)
	Reframe Situation	**Mastery**
Emotional	Express Feelings	**Communication--** (At Four System Levels)
	Resolve Negative Feelings Be Sensitive to Other's Emotional Needs	
Relationships	Increase Cohesion	**Cohesion (Closeness)--** (At Four System Levels)
	Increase Adaptability	**Adaptability (Flexibility)--** (At Four System Levels)
Community	Seek Help and Support	**Social Support**
Spiritual	Involved in Religious Activities and Faith	**Spiritual Beliefs**
Individual Development	Develop Autonomy and Independence	**Self-Esteem**

Note. Based on analysis and table designed by Burr and Klein (1994, p. 133). They developed the first two columns.

COGNITIVE APPRAISAL MODEL
OF STRESS AND COPING

Lazarus and Folkman (1984) developed a model of stress and coping based on individual cognitive psychology. It is included here because of its parallels to the double ABCX model and because of the unique contributions Lazarus made to reconceptualizing stressor events and proposing a multilevel model of coping and adaptation.

Lazarus (1980) regarded *stress* as "a complex rubric, like emotion, motivation, or cognition rather than a simple variable" (p. 175). Influenced by neobehaviorist doctrines, Lazarus conceptualized appraisal and coping as processes mediating between antecedent variables and outcomes, with appraisal processes and coping responses determining the long-term adaptational outcomes.

In their conceptual model, Lazarus and Folkman (1984) described how the person and environmental interact in a way to produce a range of appraisals that regard the encounter as irrelevant, benign, or stressful (similar to Hill's

C factor). If the encounter is appraised as stressful, the person engages various coping responses. In the process of appraisal, the variables of values and commitments the person has are integrated with environmental conditions that are faced, producing a variety of responses. Thus, appraisal affects the coping process, which in turn has an impact on the immediate outcome of the encounter and the long-term adaptational outcomes.

Lazarus and Folkman (1984) emphasized that in such a multivariate, multiprocess system model, no single variable in and of itself accounts for stress. Stress, therefore, occurs when the demands exceed the person's resources and the person perceives the demands as important. Lazarus and Folkman (1984) argued that research in stress, coping, and adaptation should be multilevel and interdisciplinary.

Hobfoll (1988, 1989) developed a model of stress called conservation of resources (COR) the central tenet of which is that individuals and systems strive to maximize resource gain and minimize resource loss. Four types of resources are object resources (home), condition resources (good marriage), personal resources (self-esteem, mastery), and energy resources (money). Individuals and families can gain new resources to offset loss of resources.

Hobfoll and Spielberger (1992) completed an excellent overview of the family stress models and stress research. They identified the commonalties and differences among family stress theorists and demonstrated the important resources across all models. Many of the ideas in the COR model are similar to other family theorists discussion of resources. For example, Boss (1992) maintained resources are derived from all aspects of life: psychological, economic, sociological, and physical.

MASH MODEL: A BIOPSYCHOSOCIAL APPROACH

The MASH model has three major components: stress, coping, and adaptation. Each of these components has four levels or systems of analysis: the individual, couple, family, and work systems. Each of the four systems contains stressors and strains, coping behaviors and coping resources, and adaptation. The coping resources and system types are mediating variables between stress and adaptation. The MASH model focuses on stress at four levels, coping resources at the four levels and adaptation at the four levels. Each of the resources interact to produce a level of adaptation at the individual, couple, family, or work level.

The MASH model builds on the previous work on individual and family stress and coping models that focus on stress, coping, and adaptation. Whereas most stress and coping models have focused on one system level (individual, work, family), the MASH model integrates the four system levels. This integration across system levels enables one to capture the interconnection and interplay of the dimensions within and across system levels.

The MASH model is an attempt to develop a biopsychosocial model by providing a more integrative and ecosystemic approach to the relationships between stress, coping, system variables, and adaptation at four different system levels. The model can provide a *within-systems analysis* that would examine, for example, aspects of couple stress, the variety of couple coping behaviors and styles, and the degree of couple satisfaction (adaptation). This could be done separately for any of the four levels—individual, couple, family, or work levels. The model can also provide a *between-systems analysis* that would examine stress across the four levels, resources at all four levels that might mediate the stress, and the final adaptation at one or all four levels (see Fig. 15.1).

The need to include more than one system to the diagnosis and treatment of physical illness was raised by Dym (1987) in which cybernetic concepts were applied. More recently, the clinical application of the biopsychosocial approach and its advantages was clearly presented by McDaniel, Campbell, and Seaburn (1989). A unified biopsychosocial field is assumed to supersede previous designations of illness as being merely "physical" or "psychological." Illness can be located in the ongoing interaction of biochemical, psychological, and social experience. Dym argues that designating an illness as "physical" is an arbitrary punctuation of the larger field. Assuming a biopsychosocial model would move beyond such limitations and allow for diagnosis and treatment in a more holistic framework.

A cybernetic model presupposes both stable patterns and regular patterns of adjustment or change that are known as recursive cycles. Such

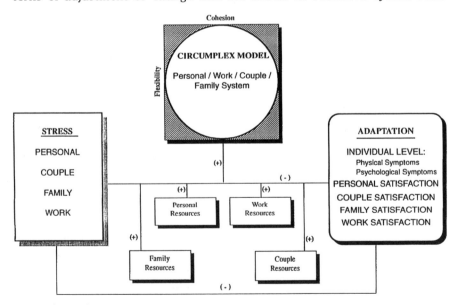

FIG. 15.1. The multisystem assessment of stress and health (MASH) model.

recursive cycles can describe the relationship among various system levels: the biological, psychological, and interpersonal levels. These three system levels coevolve in continuous recursive cycles. This recursive cycle then becomes the basic level of analysis or diagnosis. Such an analysis would allow one to see that processes in one level trigger processes in another level and are triggered by processes at another system level.

Dym's proposal of a biopsychosocial model, Lazarus and Folkman's (1984) proposal of an interdisciplinary model for studying stress and the MASH model are attempts to move beyond previous linear models. It is assumed that multisystem cybernetic models will prove more heuristic in future theory and research on the family and health behavior.

Stress, coping, and adaptation need to be placed not only in a larger, multileveled context but approached cybernetically as well. The search for specific etiologies is seen as arbitrary. Unresolved stress can contribute to the onset of many emotional and physical illnesses. Yet there are many who lead stressful lives, smoke, drink, eat poorly, and still do not contract these diseases. Dym argued that it is often unproductive to search for causes or the onset of some specific illnesses. A cause can look like an effect and an effect can look like a cause. Traditional notions of *cause* and *effect* have reciprocal relationships. They coevolve during the biopsychosocial course of illness and can be tracked in their recursive cycles.

Review of Stress Assessment

The MASH model includes the component of stress at the individual, couple, family and work levels. *Stress* is defined as a state in which individuals are challenged by situations so that it overtakes the personal and collective (work, couple, family) resources and threatens the well-being of the person. At the individual level, *stress* is conceptualized as life strains or "daily hassles." Strains are used as issues for the assessment of stress at the couple, family, and work levels. New scales have been developed for each assessment of stress at these four levels.

Even though major life events are the standard for much stress research, research by Lazarus (1980) shows that minor life strains, or daily hassles are better predictors of subsequent psychological symptoms. Previously, the magnitude of life-event predictions of dysfunction in various retrospective and prospective studies has typically been low. An area of inquiry that was emphasized by Lazarus and Folkman (1984) was the study of everyday events or minor stressful life incidents or "daily hassles." Kanner, Coyne, Schaefer, and Lazarus (1981) conducted a study of 100 middle-aged adults over 9 months using measures that assessed daily hassles and uplifts, major life events, and psychological symptoms. Hassles were found to be better predictors of both concurrent and subsequent psychological symptoms than scores of traditional major life events.

The results of a rigorous study (Monroe, 1983) were consistent with Kanner's work. Monroe found evidence that the daily hassles concept was significant in understanding stress and illness. It was found that daily hassles are a significant predictor of prospectively assessed psychological symptoms even when initial symptom levels were controlled. Daily hassles were better predictors of subsequent psychological symptoms than major life events.

The use of *strains* to assess couple, family, and work stress grew out of the work of Pearlin and Schooler (1978) who studied everyday role strains. These role strains related to social roles of people in their daily lives, as they go about fulfilling their personal, family, and occupational roles. Pearlin, Menaghan, and Lieberman (1981) concluded that events or transitions to new roles affect people by altering the enduring and everyday circumstances of their lives. The event does not act directly on one's inner life, producing psychological disturbances. Instead, events are channeled through the persistent problems of ongoing role strains. This is not to say that non-normative events, such as a job disruption, do not make a difference. Such occupational losses were often found to accompany enduring role problems. These events can also create problems in family relations and financial affairs, but they are often because of role changes.

Review of Personal Coping Resources

Self-esteem and *mastery* serve as fundamental personal resources that play a major role in the coping process as they influence the appraisal within the individual. Hobfoll and Lieberman (1987) found that self-esteem is a very important stress-resistant factor in individual stress research. Pearlin and Schooler (1978) in their pioneering stress research hypothesized and found that internal coping resources are important aspects of successful coping with stress: (a) self-esteem—how positively one feels toward oneself; (b) self-denigration—how much one holds negative attitudes toward oneself; and (c) mastery—how much one feels in control over his or her life versus how much one feels ruled by fate. Wheaton (1985) proposed a similar set of concepts called *flexibility* and *fatalism*. These resources often affect the illness outcomes by indirectly influencing aspects of coping activity and are seen as variables in the coping process. This is done by affecting the definition or appraisal one makes of the stressful situation and then determining what will be done to cope with the stress once it is appraised as threatening.

Another well-researched resource important to both individuals and families is *social support*. Social support was found to mediate the effects on a person's physical health (Cooke et al., 1986). Parkerson, Broadhead, and Tse (1995) developed the Duke Social Support and Stress Scale, which was designed to assess these dimensions in the patients. They found that family stress scores were the highest predictors of more severe illness, more hospitalizations, and more cost than were social stresses or any of the support variables (Parkerson et al., 1995).

Review of Relationship Coping Resources

In a major review of family stress theory and research by Hobfoll and Spielberger (1992), they concluded that a few family resources have been identified as especially important in helping people cope with stress. The variables that they indicated were: (a) flexibility or adaptability versus rigidity; (b) cohesion versus separateness; (c) communication versus privacy; (d) boundary ambiguity versus boundary clarity; and (e) order and mastery versus chaos and helplessness. The first three of these characteristics are the major dimensions of the circumplex model of marital and family systems (Olson, 1993).

The MASH model is primarily built upon the circumplex model of marital and family systems developed by Olson, Russell, and Sprenkle (1989). The circumplex model has been widely used in couple and family research on healthy and dysfunctional families (Olson, 1993). The model was formulated when Olson and his colleagues synthesized a number of concepts in the fields of family theory and family research into three dimensions of family cohesion, family flexibility, and family communication.

Using the current self-report assessment of family cohesion and family flexibility by Olson, Portner, and Lavee (1985), these three dimensions are hypothesized to function in a linear manner so that higher levels of cohesion and flexibility are seen as more functional for dealing with stress (Olson, Stewart, & Wilson, 1991). Using the linear assessment model, it is hypothesized that: Balanced systems that are higher in cohesion, flexibility and communication will have higher levels of well-being than systems low (unbalanced) on these dimensions (see Fig. 15.2).

Previous research has primarily focused on the use of the circumplex model in assessing couple and family systems (Olson, 1993). The system dynamics are based on the circumplex model and include all four system levels. In this more comprehensive multisystem MASH model, cohesion, flexibility and communication are also assessed within work system and individual system (personal style) levels. The work level focuses on the work group, department, or whatever type of work group that is most relevant to a person.

Relationship resources in the MASH model, at the individual level, include a measure of emotional expression. How one communicates with others and the link between unexpressed emotions and adverse health outcomes was well documented in the literature on psychosomatic medicine (Campbell, 1985). Therefore, the inclusion of an assessment of emotional expression was deemed an important link in the overall model.

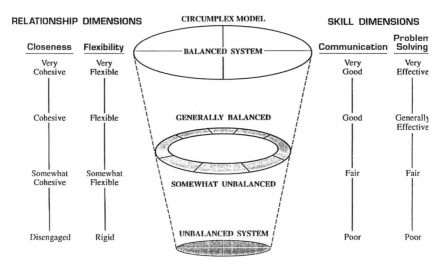

FIG. 15.2. Linear assessment of coping resources.

In summary, a linear relationship is hypothesized to operate with cohesion, flexibility, and communication at all four system levels and overall adaptation (satisfaction). This is because the self-report research scales are based on FACES III, which is a linear measure.

Review of Adaptation: From Pathogenic to Salutogenic Models

In early stress research on the family by Hill (1949) the outcome was the degree of crisis in the family system following a stressor event. It referred to the degree to which the family system became disrupted and incapacitated and could not restore its stability. However, such disruptions are neither always unwelcome nor do they always result in negative consequences for the family. Sometimes the family might even welcome the changes and see them as opportunities to restructure itself in a more positive manner. This is congruent with systems theorists (Bertalanffy, 1986) who suggest that living systems tend to evolve toward greater complexity.

Lazarus and Folkman (1984) considers adaptation on a continuum. In their interdisciplinary, multilevel model, they described physical, psychological, and social health outcomes. These levels are related to three major long-term adaptational outcomes: (a) somatic health and the physiological changes generated by stressful encounters; (b) morale and the negative or positive affect a person may have both during and after stressful encounters; and (c) social functioning, or a range of effectiveness with which demands from stressful encounters are managed.

McCubbin and Patterson (1983) suggested that a continuum from bonadaptation to maladaptation might be a more useful concept to describe the postcrisis adjustment of the family. Bonadaptation is when a demand–capability balance is achieved between the individual and family and between the family and community. Family integrity is either maintained or strengthened, family independence is maintained, and family members can further grow and develop. Maladaptation, on the other hand, is characterized by imbalances in family functioning, deterioration in family integrity, decline in family independence, and deterioration in the personal health and well-being of the family unit.

The MASH model attempts to incorporate adaptation into a continuum by providing a measure of physical health and mental health at the individual level and separate measures of satisfaction at the individual, couple, family, and work system levels. By doing so, one can examine the presence or range of stress-related physical symptoms as well as the extent of depression and anxiety that might exist at the physiological and psychological level within the individual. On the psychosocial level, the degree of personal, couple, family, or work satisfaction are also assessed.

The value of shifting from pathogenic models—which have psychopathology or illness as an outcome—to salutogenic models which have wellness as an outcome has been suggested by Antonovsky (1987) as an important distinction for the field of stress research. He argued that we cannot assume that stressors are intrinsically bad. Although some indeed might be, there are others that might be neutral, others that might even be salutary for the individual, and yet others that might have both negative and positive outcomes for the individual.

The same shift to a salutogenic model has been done with family models like the double ABCX model. Lavee, McCubbin, and Olson (1986) found that family strains were positively associated with a more positive appraisal of the stressful situation. When marital adjustment was held constant, as family strain increased, so did the sense of coherence (the general orientation that things will work out well) in the family. The experience of overcoming their difficulties may have a salutary effect on families by bolstering their sense of competence and confidence.

What is needed in stress research, according to Antonvosky, are more studies of families that do well and even prosper in the face of stress. Instead of studying the symptoms of disease, we might learn much by studying the symptoms of wellness. All of us are constantly being bombarded by stressors. If this is so, the following question needs to be asked: How is it that some individuals (or families) respond better to stress than others?

The heart of Antonovsky's salutogenic model involves the study of successful coping or behavioral immunology. He argued that instead of studying what keeps people from getting sick, we might ask ourselves what facilitates a person becoming healthier? He suggests that coping variables need to be abstracted one step higher in order to find "generalized resistance resources" that will help researchers and scholars better understand how the individual copes successfully to reinforce health. By assessing not only individual resources, but also social support and family system resources, the multisystem MASH model attempts to lay the groundwork for such an approach.

CSP: ASSESSMENT OF THE MASH MODEL

Constructs within the MASH model are measured by a number of self-report instruments included in the CSP by Olson, Stewart, and Wilson (1991). These assessments are based on the previous research of the authors and other researchers in the stress and health fields. For an overview of assessment scales used in the CSP, see Table 15.3. All 34 scales have rather good internal consistency reliability (alpha) averaging .83 with a range of .71 to .96 (see Table 15.2).

Study Validating MASH Model

A study by Stewart (1988) investigated 440 adults using the initial version of the CSP in order to test the utility of the MASH model. More specifically, the study was designed to assess what resources at each of the four system levels were most characteristics of those who coped well with stress versus those who were under high levels of stress and high levels of physical or psychological symptoms. The 440 adults completed the CSP at a family medical practice clinic, from several courses on stress management, and an accidental sample of church members from a variety of denominations.

One hypothesis was that *personal satisfaction correlates negatively with physical symptoms and psychological distress*. The findings were statistically significant with personal satisfaction being correlated negatively ($r = -.63$) with psychological distress and negatively ($r = -.36$) with physical symptoms (see Fig. 15.3). As expected, psychological distress and physical symptoms were positively correlated ($r = .52$). All three of these assessments were based on self-reports, which could have affected the results.

In order to test the significance of various resources for coping with stress at the individual, couple, family, and work levels, five separate multiple regression analyses were done with satisfaction as the outcome for each level. Multiple regression was also done predicting overall satisfaction with life, which was based on a summary standardized score of personal, couple, family, and work satisfaction. A measure of overall stress was obtained by summing the stress at the four system levels. The overall measure

TABLE 15.2
Coping & Stress Profile (CSP): Scales

Issues	Personal	Work	Couple	Family
Stress	Personal Stress Psychological Distress Physical Symptoms	Work Stress	Couple Stress	Family Stress
Relationship Coping Resources	Closeness Style Flexibility Style Communication Style Problem Solving Style	Work Problem Solving Work Communication Work Closeness Work Flexibility	Couple Problem Solving Couple Communication Couple Closeness Couple Flexibility	Family Problem Solving Family Communication Family Closeness Family Flexibility
Personal Coping Resources	Self-esteem Mastery Spiritual Beliefs Exercise Nutrition Social support			
Satisfaction	Personal Satisfaction	Work Satisfaction	Couple Satisfaction Social Desirability	Family Satisfaction

273

TABLE 15.3
Coping & Stress Profile (CPS): Scales and Reliability

	Scales	Source	Items	Reliability
Stress				
Personal:	Personal Stress	Olson & Stewart, 1989	50	.93
	Physical Symptoms	Olson & Stewart, 1989	20	.83
	Psychological Distress	Viet & Ware, 1983	10	.93
Work:	Work Stress	Fournier, 1981	28	.89
Couple:	Couple Stress	Olson & Stewart, 1989	20	.87
Family:	Family Stress	Olson & Stewart, 1989	20	.85
Coping Resources				
Relationship Coping Resources				
Individual:	Closeness Style	Olson & Stewart, 1989	10	.76
	Flexibility Style	Olson & Stewart, 1989	10	.73
	Communication Style	Olson & Stewart, 1989	10	.79
	Problem Solving Style	Olson & Stewart, 1989	7	.79
Work:	Work Closeness	Olson & Stewart, 1989-WACES	10	.85
	Work Flexibility	Olson & Stewart, 1989-WACES	10	.87
	Work Communication	Olson & Stewart, 1989	10	.88
	Work Problem Solving	Olson & Stewart, 1989	6	.82
Couple:	Couple Closeness	Olson & Stewart, 1989-MACES	10	.78
	Couple flexibility	Olson & Stewart, 1989-MACES	10	.82
	Couple Communication	Olson et al., 1986	10	.85
	Couple Problem Solving	Olson & Stewart, 1989	10	.85
Family:	Family Closeness	Olson & Stewart, 1989-FACES	10	.81
	Family Flexibility	Olson & Stewart, 1989-FACES	10	.75
	Family Communication	Barnes & Olson, 1982	10	.79
	Family Problem Solving	Olson & Stewart, 1989	10	.83
Personal Coping Resources:				
	Self-esteem	Rosenbert, 1965, 1988	10	.87
	Mastery	Pearlin & Schooler, 1978, 1981	7	.77
	Spiritual Beliefs	Olson & Stewart, 1989	10	.92
	Exercise	Olson & Stewart, 1989	5	.74
	Nutrition	Olson & Stewart, 1989	10	.72
	Social Support	Olson & Stewart, 1989	10	.71
	Alcohol Use (-)	Selzer, 1971-MAST	10	.84
Satisfaction				
Personal:	Personal Satisfaction	Viet & Ware, 1983	10	.96
Work:	Work Satisfaction	Olson & Stewart, 1989	10	.88
Couple:	Couple Satisfaction	Olson et al., 1986	10	.91
	Social Desirability	Olson, 1986 (Rev. Edmonds '67)	5	.83
Family:	Family Satisfaction	Olson & Stewart, 1989	10	.91

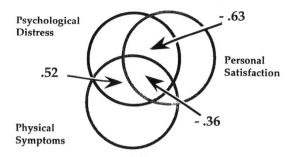

FIG. 15.3. Interconnection of health and satisfaction.

of satisfaction was inversely related to the measure of physical symptoms and psychological distress (see Fig. 15.4).

The results of these five analyses strongly support the value of a multi-system level model since they demonstrate that resources at all four levels were important in distinguishing people who managed stress well from those who were not managing stress well. Also, the fifth analysis demonstrates that they can use resources from all other aspects of their life to cope with their overall life stressors (see Fig. 15.4).

If the MASH model and CSP assessment only focused at one of the levels (i.e., individual, couple, family, or work) it would not have given a realistic or comprehensive picture of all the resources that people actually have in their life. Although these findings are intuitively obvious, this study clearly demonstrates the value of a multisystem model.

German Study Validates CSP

The entire CSP was translated into German by Klaus Schneewind and Joachim Weiss (1995) at the Institute for Psychology at the University of Munich. They had 171 Germans adults complete the CSP, and they completed a variety of analyses. The means scores and alpha reliability on the CSP were very similar to the results of studies in the United States. The alpha reliability of the scales with U.S. data averaged .83, which is similar to the German results of .79. They concluded that, "In the German study, these high alpha reliabilities were all in all replicated with the exception of the measures of 'closeness style,' 'eating habits' and 'social support' " (p. 18).

An interesting finding from the German data was the intercorrelation of stress from the four areas of life. Figure 15.5 illustrates the significant correlations between the personal stress and work stress ($r = .42$), between personal stress and couple stress ($r = .47$), between personal stress and family stress ($r = .65$) and between couple stress and family stress ($r = .47$). This data clearly demonstrates the value of the multisystem perspective and the interplay between the various areas of life.

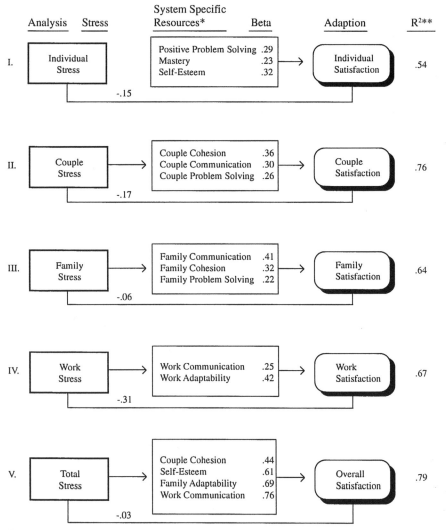

* Variables in each of the five regression analysis are listed in the order they appeared in the analysis. Stress was entered after the resources in the step wise regression.
**R² Amount of total variance accounted for in each analysis.

FIG. 15.4. Five analyses identifying resources significant for coping with stress.

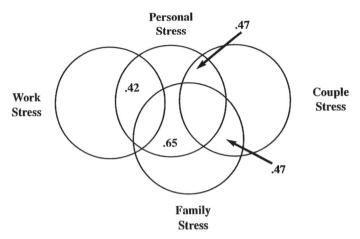

FIG. 15.5. Interrelationship of stress in the four systems (correlations).

Coping and Stress Profile (CSP): Self-Scoring Version

The Coping and Stress Profile Questionnaire is divided into four separate content area sections: individual, couple, family, and work. A person would complete one or more of the relevant profiles. Everyone would complete the background information and the individual profile, which contains 16 scales and takes about 20 to 30 minutes to complete. Each of the couple, family, and work profiles take about 10 to 15 minutes to complete.

The self-scoring CSP is available. It focuses on stress, coping resources, and levels of adaptation (satisfaction) for each of the four areas. A CSP Summary Profile can be created that demonstrates the person's stress levels, coping resources, and satisfaction at the individual, couple, family, and work areas (see Fig. 15.6).

This CSP Summary Profile in Fig. 15.6 clearly illustrates the value of a multisystem perspective. This profile demonstrates the relationship between stress, coping and satisfaction at the four separate levels as well as the interplay of the four levels of life. For this person, the *couple system* has the lowest stress level, the highest level of resources and the highest satisfaction level. Conversely, *the work system* has the highest stress, the lowest level of resources and the lowest satisfaction. A similar but less extreme pattern to the work system is the *family system*. The *personal system* is the most moderate with higher levels of communication and flexibility.

Clinical Use of the Coping & Stress Profile

For mental health and health professionals, the MASH model and the CSP offers a comprehensive assessment of patients that present with stress-related physical symptoms as well as emotional symptoms of distress. This

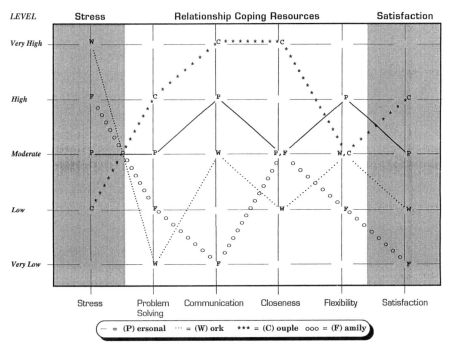

FIG. 15.6. Coping and stress profile—Profile summary.

type of assessment could help facilitate professionals using a biopsychoso-cial approach rather than being fixated on somatic complaints as described by McDaniel et al. (1989).

The MASH model provides a more complete picture of the patient's situation than assessments that focuses only on personal or family stress. Obviously, even the most comprehensive self-report assessments cannot or should not stand alone. However, when used in conjunction with a personal interview, a more fruitful conversation can take place about sources of stress and how a patient is managing to cope or not cope with these situations.

Even though no assessment instrument can be as comprehensive as we might want them to be, they can serve as starting points for conversation. Psychological and psychosocial assessments can be misused if they are seen as specifying the "truth" about a person. However, if an assessment is considered as a snapshot of some phenomena about the person at a given point in time, then one can avoid using them in a reductionistic manner. The value of the CSP is to identify stressful issues, coping resources, and levels of adaptation (satisfaction) in four important aspects of an individual's life. Hopefully, this will facilitate a more meaningful dialogue between health professionals and clients and ultimately provide more efficient and cost effective treatment.

REFERENCES

Antonovsky, A. (1979). *Health, stress and coping*. San Francisco: Jossey-Bass.

Antonovsky, A. (1987). *Unraveling the mystery of health*. San Francisco: Jossey-Bass.

Antonovsky, A. (1994). The structure and properties of the sense of coherence scale. In McCubbin, H. I., Thompson, E. A., Thompson, A. I., & J. E. Fromer (Eds.), *Sense of coherence and resiliency: Stress, coping and health* (pp. 21–40). Madison: University of Wisconsin Press.

Antonovsky, A., & Sourani, T. (1988) Family sense of coherence and family adaptation. *Journal of Marriage and the Family, 50*, 79–92.

Barnes, H., & Olson, D. H. (1986). Parent–adolescent communication. In D. H. Olson & H. I. McCubbin (Eds.), *Family inventories* (pp. 29–44). St. Paul, MN: University of Minnesota, Family Social Science.

Bertalanffy, von, L. (1986). *General systems theory*. New York: Braziller.

Boss, P. (1988). *Family stress management*. Thousand Oaks, CA: Sage Publications.

Boss, P. (1992). Primacy of perception in family stress theory and measurement. *Journal of Family Psychology, 6*(2), 113–119.

Burr, W. E., & Klein, S. R. (1994). *Reexamining family stress*. Thousand Oaks, CA: Sage Publications.

Campbell, T. L. (1985). *Family's impact on health*. Washington, DC: National Institute of Mental Health.

Cooke, B. D., Rossman, M. M., McCubbin, H. I., & Patterson, J. M. (1986). *Measuring social support: Application to parenthood*. Unpublished manuscript. University of Minnesota, St. Paul.

Dym, B. (1987). The cybernetics of physical illness. *Family Process, 1*, 35–48.

Fournier, D. G. (1981). *PROFILES: Personal reflections on family life and employment stressors*. Stillwater, OK: Oklahoma State University.

Hill, R. (1949). *Families under stress*. Connecticut: Greenwood Press.

Hill, R. (1958). Generic features of families under stress. *Social Casework, 39*, 139–150.

Hobfoll, S. E. (1988). *The ecology of stress*. Washington, DC: Hemisphere Press.

Hobfoll, S.E. (1989). Conservation of resources. A new attempt at conceptualizing stress. *American Psychologist, 44*, 513–523.

Hobfoll, S. E., & Leiberman, Y. (1987). Personality and social resources in immediate and continued stress resistance among women. *Journal of Personality and Social Psychology, 52*, 18–26.

Hobfoll, S. E., & Spielberger, C. D. (1992). Family stress: Integrating theory and measurement. *Journal of Family Psychology, 6*(2), 99–112.

Kanner, A. D., Coyne, J. C., Schaefer, C., & Lazarus, R. S. (1981). Comparison of two modes of stress measurement: Daily hassles and uplifts versus major life events. *Journal of Behavioral Medicine, 4*, 1–39.

Lavee, Y., McCubbin, H. I., & Olson, D. H. (1986). The effect of stressful life events and transitions on family functioning and well-being. *Journal of Marriage and Family, 49*, 857–873.

Lazarus, R. S. (1980). The stress and coping paradigm. In D. Eisdorfer, D. Dohen, & A. Kleinman (Eds.), *Conceptual models for psychopathology* (pp. 173–209). New York: Spectrum.

Lazarus, R. S., & Folkman, S. (1984). *Stress, Appraisal, and Coping*. New York: Springer Publishing.

McCubbin, H. I., & Patterson, J. M. (1983). The family stress process: The double ABCX model of adjustment and adaptation. In H. I. McCubbin, M. B. Sussman, & J. M. Patterson (Eds.), *Social stress and the family: Advances and developments in family stress theory and research* (pp. 7–37). New York: Haworth Press.

McCubbin, H. I., & Patterson, J. M. (1983). Family stress and adaptation to crises: A double ABCX model of family behavior. In D. Olson & B. Miller (Eds.), *Family studies review yearbook* (pp. 123–147). Beverly Hills, CA: Sage Publications.

McCubbin, H. I., Thompson, E. A., Thompson, A. I., & Fromer, J. E. (1994). *Sense of coherence and resiliency: Stress, coping and health*. Madison, WI: University of Wisconsin.

McDaniel, S. H., Campbell, T., & Seaburn, D. (1989). Somatic fixation in patients and physicians: A iopsychosocial approach. *Family Systems Medicine, 7,* 5–16.

Monroe, S. M. (1983). Major and minor life events as predictors of psychological distress: further issues and findings. *Journal of Behavioral Medicine, 6,* 189–205.

Olson, D. H. (1988). Family types, family stress and family satisfaction: A developmental perspective. In C. Falicoi, (Ed.), *Family Transitions: Continuity and Change Over the Family Life Cycle* (pp. 16–43) New York: Guilford Press.

Olson, D. H. (1993). Circumplex model of marital and family systems: Assessing family functioning. In F. Walsh (Ed.), *Normal family processes* (2nd ed., pp. 104–137) New York: Guilford Press.

Olson, D. H., Fournier, D. G., & Druckman, J. M. (1989). *Counselor's manual for PREPARE/ENRICH,* (Rev. ed.). Minneapolis, MN: PREPARE/ENRICH.

Olson, D. H., McCubbin, H. I., Barnes, H., Larsen, A., Muxen, M., & Wilson, M. (1989). *Families: What makes them work,* (Rev. ed.), Newbury Park, CA: Sage Publications.

Olson, D. H., Portner, J., & Lavee, Y. (1985). *Family adaptability and cohesion evaluation scales (FACES III).* St. Paul, MN: University of Minnesota, Family Social Science.

Olson, D. H., Russell, C., & Sprenkle, D. H. (Eds.). (1989). *Circumplex Model: Systemic Assessment and Treatment of Families.* New York: Haworth Publishers.

Olson, D. H., & Stewart, K. L. (1989). *Health and Stress Profile* (HSP). Minneapolis, MN: Life Innovations.

Olson, D. H., Stewart, K. L., & Wilson, L. R. (1991). *Coping & Stress Profile (CSP).* Minneapolis, MN: Life Innovations.

Parkerson, G. R., Broadhead, E., & Tse, C. J. (1995). Perceived faily stress as a predictor of health-related outcomes. *Archives of Family Medicine, 23,* 357–360.

Patterson, J. M. (1988). Families experiencing stress: The family adjustment and adaptation response model (FAAR). *Family System Medicine, 6*(2), 202–237.

Patterson, J. M. (1989). A family stress model: The family adjustment and adaptation response (FAAR). In C. Ramsey (Ed.) *The science of family medicine* (pp. 95–118). New York: Guilford.

Pearlin, L. I., Menaghan, E. B., Lieberman, M. A., & Mullan, J. T. (1981) The stress process. *Journal of Health and Social Behavior, 221,* 337–356.

Pearlin, L. I., & Schooler, C. (1978). The structure of coping. *Journal of Health and Social Behavior, 19,* 2–21.

Piper, J. (1995). *Work stress in Lutheran clergy women in the U.S. and Norway.* Unpublished doctoral dissertation, University of Minnesota, St. Paul.

Rosenberg, M. (1965). *Society and adolescent self-image.* Princeton, NJ: Princeton University Press.

Schneewind, K. A., Weiss, J., & Olson, D. H. (1995). *Coping & stress profile: A German and American comparison.* Unpublished manuscript. University of Munich and University of Minnesota, St. Paul.

Selzer, M. L. (1985). Michigan Alcohol Screening Test (MAST). La Jolla, CA: Largo.

Stewart, K. L. (1988). *Stress and adaptation: A multisystem model of individual, couple, family, and work systems. Dissertation Abstracts International, 49,* 8A, (Univeristy Microfilms No. 88-23570)

Tasci, D. L. (1995). *Family ghosts in the corporate setting: Comparison of family of origin and work system using the Coping and Stress Profile.* Unpublished doctoral dissertation, University of Colorado.

Viet, C. T. & Ware, J. E. (1983). The structure of psychological distress and well-being in general populations. *Journal of Consulting and Clinical Psychology, 51,* 730–742.

Wheaton, B. (1985). A comparison of the moderating effects of personal coping resources and the impact of exposure to stress in two groups. *Journal of Community Psychology, 10,* 312–325.

CONCLUSIONS

16

IS THE FAMILY VIABLE?
SOME THOUGHTS AND IMPLICATIONS
FOR THE THIRD MILLENNIUM

Solly Dreman
Ben Gurion University of the Negev

LESSONS OF THE 21st CENTURY

This volume describes some of the trends characterizing the family of the 20th century as well as draws implications for the next millennium. This century has been characterized by an increasingly technological and global transnational society, transcending the boundaries of the traditional nuclear family and demanding increasing instrumental and emotional investment in the work sphere. Relatedly, changing gender roles, decreased marriage and fertility rates, increased divorce rates, ambiguity in parental roles, "high-tech" reproductive methods, family violence, and other evolving phenomena have resulted in a breakdown in the traditional family infrastructure which served as a basis for the education, nurturance, and identity of its members. Individualism, autonomy, and the pursuit of career-related status may usurp traditional family values such as community, belonging, and family-related status as society "progresses" along the inevitable pathways of increasing modernization.

A grain of optimism and hope, which counters the gloomy perspective portrayed by the family pessimists, is offered by the contributors to this volume. Instead of viewing the family as outdated, the optimists perceive the family as providing the stability, belonging, and sense of community neces-sary to a society characterized by flux, alienation, and individualism. The prevailing theme seems to be that a sense of family roots and belonging may complement rather than undermine a person's search for autonomy by diminishing the existential anxiety precipitated by a changing and sometimes incomprehensible world. Most family theorists and therapists know that "paradoxically" family stability promotes flexibility in the face of change, that family and communal belonging promote healthy autonomy, whereas interpersonal nurturance and connectedness contribute to individuality and individual achievement (Carter & McGoldrick, 1988; Olson, 1993). The work and domestic realms are complementary rather than antagonistic spheres of influence (see Steyn, chapter 5, and Edgar, chapter 9) and can cross-fertilize and contribute to more optimal performance in each domain.

In line with a systems perspective, this volume suggests we look at the dynamic interaction at the interface of the different facets of family living—individual, couple, family, extended family, work, community, and culture—when assessing, educating, or planning educational, intervention and treatment programs for families (see Olson, chapter 15). Dumon (chapter 11) and Goldscheider (chapter 4) point out, in this respect, that the changing demography and lifestyles of individuals can affect the family at several levels. At the interface of the individual with family roles, increased longevity has resulted in couple relations of longer duration, which often outlive parenting roles and hence require more nurturing relations between spouses. In addition, the increased life span may require less hierarchical relations between older children and their aging parents. Considering the interface of the family with society, social planning and concomitant government support of family care for the aged may be necessary to promote optimal conditions for aging individuals and their care-taker families.

Changing individual and family demography has also caused the rarefaction of children and of fathering as pointed out by Golini and Silvestrini (chapter 12). Hence, there are fewer children and more only children in families, with all the psychosocial implications that this phenomenon involves. Fathering has also become rarefied and the importance of the fathering role diminished due to increasing divorce rates, decreasing marriage rates and unwed motherhood. These changes require increasing psychological and perhaps social remedies which will contribute to the psychological development of such children, as well as protecting the rights and positive contributions to childrearing of contemporary fathers.

As for younger adults, the increasing influx of single-person domestic units due to such developments as the increasing autonomy of youth, late marriages, and increasing divorce rates and other related phenomena may require housing subsidies and other government provided benefits that promote positive functioning in these populations. Similarly, the family of divorce may require societal provisions that enable them to reorganize both in the domestic and work realms. Stricter legislation to ensure child support, guaranteed visitation rights for the noncustodial parent, work benefits and concessions, adequate child care and good mental health facilities are some of the measures which can contribute to better functioning of these family units.

Earlier versions of family systems theory often stressed the effects of interpersonal behavior patterns, neglecting the role that individual physical or mental illness or other developmental disorders can play in reaping havoc with family life. Hence just as families influence the socialization and development of individuals, individuals also influence the life course of their families. Teichman (chapter 3) looked at this interface and addressed the issues of individual depression in the marital context. Her findings suggest that besides examining the individual and interpersonal facets of family life described above, we must also consider biological dimensions in assessing and treating families. Just as marital relations affects spousal depression, spousal depression can affect the marital relation. Whereas treatment remedies in this study were directed at recurring interpersonal behaviors, such as the spousal hostility, that maintained the depression, individual interventions such as psychopharmacological treatment also contributed to resolving the depressive illness as well as the couple difficulties. This finding argues against earlier notions of family therapy that view psychopathology as residing solely in the interpersonal context and not in the realm of intrapsychic dynamics (Haley, 1977) and supports more contemporary systems theories that pay attention to biological, psychological, and social components of individual development in their interaction with the interpersonal domain.

Extended family may play an important role in increasingly industrialized societies. This follows, because extended family provides a basic unit of social and economic solidarity as was pointed out by Lomnitz (chapter 7) in her discussion of Latin American societies. The extended family provides a sense of trust, belonging and stability which help to ameliorate some of the alienation, isolation, and uncertainty brought on by increasing modernization and social change. In contrast, Weiner (chapter 6) noted that there has been some attrition in the traditional family unit in America because of these developments. However, like Lomnitz she stressed the need for a strong interpersonal support base, which allows for difference and diversity, although not necessarily in the form of the traditional nuclear family.

The interface between society, families, and individuals is relevant when we consider such phenomena as family violence, sexual harassment, and gender discrimination in the work place. Birns and Birns (chapter 8), for example, pointed out that society must empower battered women and their children by providing adequate legal provisions, child care and health care facilities that overcome the abuses of male entitlement. Of course, this will also necessitate a major change in those societal values and attitudes which have promoted distorted values in a contemporary society which frequently pays only "lip service" to notions of gender equality.

In a world of increasing transnationalism and increased mobility, immigration, accompanied by multiple situational transitions and changes in the life space, must be addressed. In the present volume Sharlin and Elshanskaya (chapter 13) discussed how transition-based attitude change can lead to stress and tension in parents, perhaps ultimately affecting both their own and their children's adjustment. Dreman (chapter 1) suggested that reciprocal exposure between the host and the new immigrant, under favorable circumstances, can produce positive attitude change, a more positive emotional climate, and even result in positive behavioral dispositions between the native student and the newcomer. Besides immigration, there are also other situational contingencies, characteristic of contemporary living, that should be addressed in order to promote positive family functioning and health in the next millennium. For example, early retirement, increased leisure time, and unemployment may all increase as society becomes increasingly technocratic and relies on machines and computers more than on human resources. Social scientists, planners, and policy makers would be well advised to carry out research and think of social policy which would deal with such changes in the work–leisure–domestic balance, so that families, the workforce, and society at large continue to be productive and experience satisfaction in different life spheres.

In summary, whereas contemporary society is definitely experiencing the "slings and arrows" of societal transition, with profound changes occurring in the nuclear family, attention to "the family in context" can contribute greatly to modern family life. This is important because the survival of the family appears to be integral to the modernization and advancement of society in the next millennium. It should be noted that the phenomena discussed above like aging, single-adult households, divorce, unmarried motherhood, female employment, and family violence were once considered to be signs of individual or family weakness, deviation, or pathology. In contrast, this volume suggests that for the most part these are normative developments in a changing family life cycle and in the case of family violence a reflection of behaviors reinforced by ingrained social attitudes.

CHANGES IN FAMILY FUNCTIONS: THEIR IMPLICATIONS FOR MILLENNIAS TO COME: THEORY, RESEARCH, AND INTERVENTION

Increasingly, researchers, educators, social policy makers, and clinicians are becoming aware of the importance of family systems and an ecological approach to research, intervention, and treatment. This volume suggests that the family would be well served if family life is perceived in a dynamic systems context and that the interface of different levels of family life—individual, family, work, community, society, and culture—be considered. A recent scan of the social science literature from 1990 to 1995 by the editor of this volume revealed a wide range and diversity of family issues, both theoretical and applied, that are being addressed in the framework of such a systems approach. Some of these recent findings and observations are discussed below.

Looking at the normative spectrum of family life, it is important to consider cultural differences in investigating individual and family development. Prevailing cultural beliefs, values, and attitudes, or what has been referred to as the *macrosystem* (Bronfenbrenner, 1979, 1986), may not only affect adjustment, but they could also affect the assessment and treatment of psychopathology. For example, if minority group behavior differs from the prevailing cultural norms, these behaviors may be unjustly judged as deviant or even pathological, often resulting in self-fulfilling prophecies that eventually result in maladaptive behavior. A recent review of the development of children of minority status from birth to 5 years proposed five major sources of influence on the developmental outcome of these infants: cultural beliefs and caregiving practices, health status and health care practices, family structure and characteristics, and socioeconomic factors and biological factors (Garcia-Coll, 1990). It was noted that differences exist between minority and Anglo families in their developmental goals and interactions during infancy. These factors act synergistically to place these infants in alternative, not necessarily deviant, developmental pathways. This study illustrates the need to consider cultural differences in developmental routes when assessment and intervention are undertaken, since prevailing cultural norms may bias judgments of both deviancy and normalcy.

In the area of work versus domestic roles, it was pointed out by Steyn and Edgar (chapter 5) that the work and family spheres could complement each other, promoting good adjustment in both realms. It is important, however, to view this issue through the prisms of the dynamic context of the family life cycle as well as individual differences among family members. A recent theoretical and research review on the subject of commitment to work and family does this by examining the relationship of work and family to the life course, gender, age, social origin, and race (Bielby, 1992). This approach allows both the researcher and practitioner to investigate optimal work–family balances throughout the life course and to be cognizant of individual differences in such balance as well. Such a perspective permits a more sophisticated understanding of the interplay of the work and domestic realms on family life.

Changing family roles, catalyzed by increased female employment and the feminist movement, are also part of the fabric of contemporary family life. How do men and women juggle work, family, and social obligations given the change in the intergender balance of the domestic versus the work arena? Whereas more androgynous roles are expected from both men and women in order to promote healthy family and work relationships, manifest behaviors often reflect more "lip service" to gender equality than actual role change and accommodation to changing realities (Hochschild, 1989). Therapists themselves are often guilty of adopting traditional and patriarchal attitudes with regard to goals of self-realization, including those of career achievement in women. In response to calls from feminist scholars to address potential biases against women in theories of family therapy, Knudson (1994) summarized findings from studies of female development and formulated an expanded model of Murray Bowen's (1978) family systems theory. A review and critique of the constructs of differentiation and emotional fusion, underpinning Bowen's theory, were presented and an expanded model for diagnosis and treatment, designed to alleviate some of these gender biases, was outlined. In the normative context, it is also important that employers, educators and social policy makers be more active in changing gender-based discriminative attitudes and work policies in contemporary society.

The notion of empowering women outlined by Birns and Birns in their chapter (chapter 8) on violence against women and children is also being addressed with greater frequency. Schonberg (1992), for example, pointed out that although the responsibility for the protection of children against sexual abuse falls mainly on women, society does not provide them with the tools they need to do the job properly, even though there has been some improvement since the late 1970s. A review of the recent literature points to the importance of such empowerment, so that both women and children will be protected. Concepts, actions, and interventions that might move society toward empowerment of women are also discussed.

Another phenomenon which is rapidly becoming normative is the separation between marriage and parenthood. A recent study (Seltzer, 1994) reviewing the effects of marital instability on children's welfare focused on how children's economic, emotional, and social needs are often not met when parents separate. The authors' findings show that the consequences of changes in marriage and childrearing differ by gender. For women, marriage and parenthood are distinct institutions—women's providing for their children needs whether or not they are married to their children's fathers. For men, however, marriage defines responsibilities to children, and fathers typically disengage from their biological children when they divorce. When they remarry they may acquire new children whom they help to support at the expense of their biological children. Although the author speaks mainly of the family of divorce it is clear that the implications also hold true for children who are born outside the context of a marital relationship. Family policy makers and legislators must address these social inequities as we approach the 21st century.

The influence of high-tech reproductive techniques in families is a recent development that also requires more applied research and intervention. A literature review (Colpin, 1994) of the issues involved in having a child by artificial reproduction are discussed. This review identifies the impact of the infertility problem, discussing such issues as the medical context, the artificial character of the conception, the intervention of other persons (doctor and donor), the vulnerability of such pregnancies, as well as their significance for parents and children. Also explored is the matter of secrecy versus more open communication regarding this type of conception. The need for research focusing specifically on the emotional development of children conceived through artificial reproductive technologies is proposed. It is concluded that couples considering artificial reproduction should receive holistic counseling that includes a focus on their expectations for the conceived child.

At the other end of the developmental spectrum, aging is being increasingly investigated by family researchers as life expectancies and the relative proportion of elderly citizens increase in contemporary society. Abuse of the elderly is a societal ill that has to be addressed seriously. Greene (1991) suggested that practitioners need to be aware of the family dynamics that may lead to this form of family violence. She discussed issues related to working with older adults and their families in protective service situations dealing specifically with abuse and neglect of the elderly. In addition, a systems-based model is provided for practitioners to use when assessing and intervening in such families.

Family care and other support systems are important options for the elderly in addition to institutional care. A Canadian study (McDaniel & McKinnon, 1993) examined the interrelationships among such ties and elderly health status. It was found that ties with family and friends are frequently maintained. On the average, Canadian elders are healthy well into old age with health status found to be related to informal support systems. However, whereas older men rely largely on their spouses, women diversify their emotional supports, although both elderly men and women are often without any form of support system. These finding suggests that men may need more encouragement and help in seeking out support systems. In addition, elderly people, regardless of gender, may be in need of professional or volunteer assistance for the provision of social support.

Dellman-Jenkins, Hofer, and Chebra (1992) reviewed the recent literature on caregiving to identify viable ways to educate families to care for elderly relatives in the home. An important contribution of this study was that the demands and stresses currently associated with providing home care were discussed, followed by an overview of support services designed to enhance families' home-caregiving capacities. Although home care for the elderly is often advocated, a recent review of the literature suggested that family care of frail elders is not necessarily superior to institutional care when costs, relationships, and quality are considered (Strawbridge & Wallhagen, 1992). It is argued that home care will not reduce long-term care costs, family relationships are not the main source of elderly psychological support, and family members do not necessarily want to care for one another. Adopting a systems perspective, family care may have negative consequences when it impedes income and employment equality for caretaking women and increases the guilt feelings of family members-at-large. It is concluded that there is a need to increase the quality of institutional care for the elderly as a viable alternative for family care for those elderly citizens who have no families or for whom family care is inappropriate.

In the realm of mental and physical illness, recent family studies suggest ways in which a systems perspective can be employed in trying to understand and promote better family coping and adjustment. A recent review of the family burden of mental illness (FMB) found that the most common individual variables associated with FMB were aversive patient behavior, adverse effects of the illness, and poor patient role performance (Maurin, 1990). As for interpersonal variables, the most significant mediators included social support, as well as family coping skills. Although this research looks at mental illness and its interaction with personal and interpersonal variables, Maurin noted that most of the research in the area lacked a theoretical framework and employed cross-sectional designs that did not provide a dynamic picture of the interplay between the many variables involved in family coping and adjustment with the illness. Future studies should employ longitudinal designs, including multiple measures, which permit the investigation of systemic individual and family influences over time and capture the dynamic nature of family coping and adjustment in the face of mental disorder.

As for physical illness, the increasing incidence and prevalence of AIDS, in both Western and developing countries has profound implications for individuals, families and society at large. Bor, Miller, and Goldman (1993), in reviewing studies describing the impact of HIV, made special reference to the definitions of *families, same-sex relationships*, and the *African family*. Topics addressed include family roles and structure, communication and disclosure, stress and coping, isolation, social support, social stigma, and the impact of bereavement. Such a multisystem approach to the study of the impact of AIDS on individuals and families is consistent with the approach adopted throughout this volume (see for example Olson, chapter 15) in considering family assessment and treatment. In line with this view, these authors anticipate a change in the focus of psychosocial research as the focus of treatment shifts from the individual to the family.

Including the family in treatment considerations is also being adopted in studying and treating illness in such diverse areas as cancer (Sales, Schulz, & Biegel, 1992), children with disabilities (Hanline, 1991), chronic illness (Patterson, 1994; Wood, 1994), traumatic brain injury (DePompei & Williams, 1994), child obesity (Kinston, Miller, & Loader, 1990), substance abuse (Friedemann & Musgrove, 1994; Mackensen & Cottone, 1992), and mental retardation

(Shulman, Margalit, Gadish, & Stuchiner, 1990). In this context, Fleck (1994) recently presented a schema by which family functioning before and during an illness event can be assessed. This schema is based on a five-pronged systems analysis that estimates the qualities of leadership, boundary management, affectivity, communication, as well as task and goal performance throughout the life cycle. This is a dynamic assessment, based on assessing what families must accomplish at various stages of the life cycle to promote good development and functioning. Genograms, taking account of at least three generations, highlight the clinically relevant relationships and conditions as they relate to health and illness.

As for intervention and treatment, considerable attention has been devoted to the treatment of disturbed families and families in crisis by the family therapy movement and other schools of family intervention. In addition to focus on applied aspects, considerable attention has been devoted to the theoretical aspects of family life and a number of different schools have arisen, each of which has a different approach to family intervention and treatment. In recent years there have been attempts to bridge the interface between these different schools of intervention and other therapeutic approaches in order to develop more integrative treatment modalities that link individual cognitions, emotions, and behavioral dynamics with structural aspects of family life. Rigazio-DiGilio (1994), for example, argued that the mental health counselor, working within an ecosystem context, needs a cogent theory of human and systemic development to guide assessment and treatment. Developmental counseling and systemic cognitive–developmental therapy represent integrative models that unify individual, family and network treatment within a coconstructive developmental framework.

As for situational contingencies and their effects on the family, a recent review of the literature (Hanks & Liprie, 1993) traced migration trends in South Africa in Botswana, Lesotho and Swaziland from the early 1900s to the 1980s to determine the effects of migration on the family system. While migration was a necessary element for a strong economy in South Africa, the emphasis was not on the migrant as a family member, but as a means for economic growth. This approach resulted in considerable family disruption. A study conducted in Central America (Leslie, 1993) looked at migration in the context of the civil wars and political unrest in El Salvador, Nicaragua, and Guatamela which led many families to leave their native countries for the United States. The demographics of these immigrants, their reasons for leaving their native countries, the realities of their new lives and the kinds of issues that migration raises for them and their families is described via a literature review. It is concluded that migrant families are highly stressed, often have limited resources for coping with the demanding circumstances they face and rarely receive the kind of systematic support they need from their host country. They appear willing to accept such hardships, however, in exchange for the promise of safety and a better life.

It should be pointed out that the process and consequences of migration are not universal and much depends upon the specific characteristics and interaction between the host society and the migrant. In Israel, for example, Jews automatically are allowed to become Israeli citizens by the Law of Return, which encourages people of the Jewish faith who live in the Diaspora to settle there. As a result, there is a considerable concern and responsibility expressed for the immigrant family both by government agencies and society at large. This manifests itself on the official level through the provision of government sponsored economic benefits such as subsidized housing, help in securing employment, as well as in informal attempts by veteran Israelis to create social bonds with these newcomers. Hence, the common bond of Judaism serves as a link between the host culture and the new immigrant, facilitating their absorption and integration into the societal mainstream.

As for recent theoretical and clinical attempts to deal with the problem, Hertz (1994) recently attempted to present the characteristics of adjustment of migrant families exposed to intense environmental stressors (separation, migration, and acculturation). In introducing the concept of crisis in the understanding of the acculturation process of migrant families, the necessity of accepting the developmental approach in dealing with the stress of migration is emphasized. No migration can be carried out without emotional and often physical stress and traumata which expose the migrant or immigrant family to somewhat predictable but frequently unexpected additional stress factors. Some normative reactions to this stressful constellation are described before the migrant reaches the state of emotional and social stability following migration. To support the theoretical considerations, the course of positive family adjustment is described in detail. In addition, adjustment differences in traditional versus westernized families, as well as other factors like the effects of earlier experienced traumatic stressors, as well as aging, on migration are described. Hertz suggests that the process of acculturation will be better understood when approached with such a multidetermined biopsychosocial perspective. By laying out a set of normative guidelines for migration, the author provided a tool for both the researcher and clinician in understanding normative reactions as opposed to pathology arising due to the stress of the immigration process.

In summary, migration, coping and adjustment are complex, multi-determined processes influenced by a myriad of cognitive, motivational, and situational influences. To illustrate, I remember when I was a young man, more than three decades ago, I migrated from Canada. I still remember my initial feeling of belonging, excitement, and enthusiasm on making *Aliya* (ascent) to the land of my brethren, learning Hebrew, and "returning" to the homeland, Israel. This initial enthusiasm and sense of belonging, though waxing and waning due to personal and situational circumstances over the years, has prevailed to this day in spite of the numerous difficulties I have experienced in immigrating. These have included repeated acts of war and terrorism, in which I have taken an active part in as a soldier and officer in the Israeli Defense Forces, as well as a standard of living and lifestyle which are infinitely more trying than would have been the case if I had remained in the peaceful and relatively ensured environs of my country of birth, Canada.

In summary, whereas the workplace and society at large have become increasingly diverse and complex, this volume suggests that family life is still a vibrant and integral dimension to contemporary societal development. Viewing and understanding the family in a multidimensional, contextual, and dynamic systems framework will permit family researchers, educators, practitioners, social planners, and policy makers to increase the quality of family life and well-being in the next millennium.

REFERENCES

Bielby, D. D. (1992). Commitment to work and family. *Annual Review of Sociology, 18,* 281–302.

Bowen, M. (1978). *Family therapy in clinical practice.* New York: Jason Aronson.

Bor, R., Miller, R., & Goldman, E., (1993). HIV/AIDS and the family: A review of research in the first decade. *Journal of Family Therapy, 15,* 187–204.

Bronfenbrenner, U. (1979). *The ecology of human development.* Cambridge, MA: Harvard University Press.

Bronfenbrenner, U. (1986). Ecology of the family as a context for human development: Research perspectives. *Developmental Psychology, 22,* 723–742.

Carter, B., & McGoldrick, M. (1988). *Changing family life cycle: A framework for family therapy* (2nd ed.). New York: Gardner Press.

Colpin, H. (1994). Parents and children of reproductive technology: Chances and risks for their well-being. *Community Alternatives, 6,* 49–71.

Dellman-Jenkins, M., Hofer, K., & Chebra, J. (1992). Eldercare in the 1990's: Challenges and supports for educating families. *Educational Gerontology, 18,* 775–784.

DePompei, R., & Williams, R. (1994).Working with families after TBI: A family-centered approach. *Topics in Language Disorders, 15,* 68–81.

Fleck, S. (1994). The family in health and disease. *New Trends in Experimental and Clinical Psychiatry, 10,* 41–51.

Friedemann, M. L., & Musgrove, J. A. (1994). Perceptions of inner city substance abusers about their families. *Archives of Psychiatric Nursing, 8,* 115–123.

Garcia-Coll, C. T. (1990). Developmental outcome of minority infants: A process-oriented look into our beginnings. *Child Development, 61,* 270–289.

Greene, R. R. (1991). Clinical interventions with older adults in need of protection: A family systems perspective. *Journal of Family Psychotherapy, 2,* 1–15.

Haley, J. (1977). *Problem-solving therapy.* San Francisco: Jossey-Bass.

Hanks, D. E., & Liprie, M. L. (1993). South African migration and the effects on the family. *Marriage and Family Review, 19,* 175–192.

Hanline, M. F. (1991). Transitions and critical events in the family life cycle. Implications for providing support to families of children with disabilities. *Psychology in the Schools, 28,* 53–59.

Hertz, D. G. (1994). Family function in a changing environment. In D. G. Hertz (Ed.), *Family issues: An interdisciplinary view on family stresses and their consequences* (pp. 67–94). Jerusalem: Gefen.

Hochschild, A. (1989). *Second shift: Working parents and the revolution at home.* New York: Viking.

Kinston, W., Miller, L., & Loader, P. (1990). Revealing sex differences in childhood obesity by using a family systems approach. *Family Systems Medicine, 8,* 371–386.

Knudson, M. (1994). The female voice: Applications to Bowen's family systems theory. *Journal of Marital and Family Therapy, 20,* 35–46.

Leslie, L. A. (1993). Families fleeing war. The case of central Americans. *Marriage and Family Review, 19,* 193–205.

Mackensen, G., & Cottone, R. (1992). Family structural issues and chemical dependency: A review of the literature from 1985 to 1992. *American Journal of Family Therapy, 20,* 227–241.

Maurin, J. T. (1990). Burden of mental illness in the family: A critical review. *Psychiatric Nursing, 4,* 99–107.

McDaniel, S. A., & McKinnon, A. L. (1993). Gender differences in informal support and coping among elders. *Journal of Women and Aging, 5,* 79–98.

Olson, D. H. (1993). Circumplex model of marital and family systems: Assessing family functioning. In F. Walsh (Ed.), *Normal family processes* (2nd ed., pp. 104–137). New York: Guilford Press.

Patterson, J. M. (1994). The impact of chronic illness on families: A family systems perspective. *Annals of Behavioral Medicine, 16,* 131–142.

Rigazio-DiGilio, S. A. (1994). A co-constructive-developmental approach to ecosystemic treatment. *Journal of Mental Health Counseling, 16,* 43–74.

Sales, E., Schulz, R., & Biegel, D. (1992). Predictors of strain in the families of cancer patients: A review of the literature. *Journal of Psychosocial Oncology, 10,* 1–26.

Schonberg, I. J. (1962). The distortion of the role of mother in child sexual abuse. *Journal of Child Sexual Abuse, 1,* 47–61.

Seltzer, J. A. (1994). Consequences of marital dissolution for children. *Annual Review of Sociology, 20,* 235–266.

Shulman, S., Margalit, M., Gadish, O., & Stuchiner, N. (1990). The family system of moderately mentally retarded children. *Journal of Mental Deficiency Research, 34,* 341–350.

Strawbridge, W., & Wallhagen, M. I. (1992). Is all in the family always best? *Journal of Aging Studies, 6,* 81–92.

Wood, B. L. (1994). A biobehavioral family model of chronic illness in children. *Journal of Family Therapy, 16,* 53–72.

Author Index

A

Adams, D., 133, 136, 144
Adams, J. D., 249, 256
Adler, A., 215, 224
Ainsworth-Smith, I., 187, 200
Alexander, K. L., 33, 45
Alland, D., 133, 144
Alwin, D. F., 174, 179
Anderson, E., 132, 145
Anivar, R., 135, 135, 145
Antonovsky, A., 262, 263, 271, 279
Arbitell, M., 132, 144
Ariès, P., 201, 224
Aronowitz, M., 229, 230, 231, 244
Arthur, J., 53, 56, 68, 69
Aubey, R. T., 120, 124

B

Balbo, L., 219, 224
Bales, S. F., 251, 255
Bandura, A., 52, 53, 68
Bar-El, Z., 52, 58, 70
Barnes, H., 274, 279
Barnes, J. A., 118, 124
Baumrind, D., 34, 45
Beach, S. R. H., 49, 51, 67, 68, 70
Beck, A. T., 49, 52, 53, 54, 59, 60, 68
Belmont, L., 217, 224
Belsky, J., 19, 27, 45
Bengtson, V. L., 91, 99
Bennett, L. W., 133, 145
Berkson, I. B., 105, 112
Bernard, J., 169, 179
Bernstein, B., 174, 179
Berry, J. W., 245, 255
Bertalanffy, von, L., 52, 68, 270, 279
Biegel, D., 290, 294

Bielby, D. D., 287, 293
Bien, W., 182, 199
Biglan, A., 53, 56, 68, 69
Bird, G. W., 92, 99
Birns, B., 131, 133, 141, 144
Blair, S. L., 90, 99
Bloom, B. R., 133, 144
Blum, A., 183, 200
Bor, R., 290, 293
Boss, P., 263, 265, 279
Bosworth, W., 133, 144
Boulding, E., 164,
Bowen, M., 4, 12, 288, 293
Bowker, L. H., 132, 144
Bowlby, J., 216, 218, 224
Bradshaw, I., 105, 112
Broadhead, E., 268, 269, 280
Brodsky, B., 229, 244
Brody, G. H., 17, 45
Bronfenbrenner, U., 4, 12, 287, 293
Brooks, M., 231, 244
Browne, A., 130, 131, 132, 135, 144
Bruynooghe, R., 187, 199
Bullock, L., 132, 139, 145
Bumpass, L. L., 210, 224
Burr, W. E., 263, 264, 279
Buss, A. H., 65, 68

C

Cain, R. L., 57, 70
Caldwell, J., 174, 179
Campbell, T. L., 266, 269, 278, 279, 280
Caplan, G., 20, 45
Carlson, R., 105, 112
Carter, B., 248, 255, 284, 293
Carver, K. P., 89, 99
Cascardi, M., 131, 135, 136, 143, 144

295

SUBJECT INDEX